LOW-RISK INVESTING

Also by Gordon Pape

INVESTMENT ADVICE
Building Wealth

FICTION
(with Tony Aspler)
Chain Reaction
The Scorpion Sanction
The Music Wars

NON-FICTION
(with Donna Gabeline, Dane Lanken)
Montreal at the Crossroads

From Pop — to one of his better investments —

June 1989

LOW-RISK INVESTING

By Gordon Pape

Prentice-Hall Canada, Inc., Scarborough, Ontario

Canadian Cataloguing in Publication Data

Pape, Gordon, 1937-
    Low-risk investing

Includes index.
ISBN 0-13-541293-5

1. Investments. I. Title.

HG4527.P36 1989   332.6'78   C88-095364-9

Portions of Chapter One originally appeared in *Moneywise* magazine.
Portions of Chapter Twelve originally appeared in *The Moneyletter*.

Prentice-Hall Inc., Englewood Cliffs, *New Jersey*
Prentice-Hall International, Inc., *London*
Prentice-Hall of Australia, Pty., *Sydney*
Prentice-Hall of India Pvt., Ltd., *New Delhi*
Prentice-Hall of Japan, Inc., *Tokyo*
Prentice-Hall of Southeast Asia (Pte.) Ltd., *Singapore*
Editora Prentice-Hall do Brasil Ltda., *Rio de Janeiro*
Prentice-Hall Hispanoamericana, S.A., *Mexico*

Editor: Sharyn Rosart
Design: David Montle
Manufacturing Buyer: Luca Di Nicola
Composition: Jay Tee Graphics Ltd.
Cover Photo: Paul Lawrence (courtesy of the Toronto Stock Exchange)
ISBN: 0-13-541293-5

Printed and bound in Canada by WEBCOM

1 2 3 4 5 W   92 91 90 89 88

To Tony Aspler

Who gave me a push when it was needed most.

TABLE OF CONTENTS

Stop Feeling Inadequate

Chance generally favours the prudent.
— Joseph Joubert

YOU'VE PROBABLY SEEN Johnny Carson doing his Carnac routine on "The Tonight Show."

You know, the one where he puts on his swami outfit, holds an envelope to his forehead, and divines the answer to the sealed question inside.

Before we get to the serious stuff, how about trying it yourself, just for fun. You don't have to rush out and rent a swami suit. Just pretend you're holding the envelope to your forehead.

I'll even cheat a bit and give you the answer: Sex and Money. Now, what's the question?

Take your time.

Give up? Okay, here it is:

What two things give people the most pleasure and the most misery?

If they were to conduct a Gallup Poll on the things that make people feel most inadequate, I have no doubt these would top the list.

Since I'm not a sex therapist, I'm afraid I can't be of any help on that score.

But money — well, that's a different matter.

Financial impotence is usually caused by a combination of lack of knowledge and failure of resolve.

This book is designed to help cure both problems. By the time you've finished, you'll have all the information you need to embark on a successful, low-risk investing program. And that knowledge will help you develop the self-discipline and determination you need to implement your personal investment plan.

Before we go any further, let me make a couple of points.

First, this book is not about basic money management. You won't find much about budgeting, savings advice, credit cards, bank accounts, borrowing, or the like. If you feel you need help in those areas, I suggest you obtain a copy of my book *Building Wealth*; it contains all the information you'll require.

This book is about investing — specifically, low-risk investing. It's intended for people who have funds available for an investment program (or expect to have money soon) and the interest and desire to manage their own plans.

These investment funds may be in one of two forms: tax sheltered or non-tax sheltered.

For most people, tax sheltered funds are held within a Registered Retirement Savings Plan (RRSP). In fact, improving the return on your RRSP money should be your number one investment priority.

Non-tax sheltered investments should be made only *after* you've completed the basic steps to financial independence, which I outlined in *Building Wealth*: purchasing a home, paying down your mortgage, and eliminating any consumer debt. If you haven't achieved these goals, then you should do so before you consider a non-tax sheltered investment portfolio.

The advice in this book won't make you a millionaire overnight, although you have every reason to expect to achieve that goal in time. My main purpose is to explain techniques that investors can use to earn above-average returns, keep tax bills to a minimum, and protect capital against financial disaster.

It's very easy to lose money. People do it every day. Just holding on to what you have is tough enough. To actually make it grow at an above-average rate — better than you'll get from Canada Savings Bonds, for example — well, that's an accomplishment of which anyone can be proud.

By the time you've completed this book, you should be able to invest your money so as to realize a return at least two percentage points higher than what you would get from a five-year GIC.

That means if five-year GICs are paying 11% today, you should be able to realize an average return of at least 13% over the next five years on your money — with very low risk.

Perhaps that objective seems modest to you. The fact is, however, that when you achieve it, you'll be in an elite group. Very few people consistently manage to obtain that kind of return on their money.

Don't underestimate that extra 2% a year — it can add up to a great deal of money in the long run. If you invest $3,000 a year in a tax sheltered environment over 25 years at 11% compounded annually, you'll have securities worth $343,239 at the end of that time. If you achieve a 13% return, you'll have $466,859 — a difference of more than $123,000. So those two percentage points really do add up.

In addition, your investment portfolio will be solid and safe. That's what low-risk investing is all about.

Let me stress one point: we're talking about low-risk investing here, not no-risk investing. One of the chapter titles in *Building Wealth* is "There's No Such Thing as Riskless". Never forget that. Even an investment that looks absolutely rock-solid can fall apart under adverse economic or political circumstances.

In early 1988 I attended an international investment conference in Fort Lauderdale, Florida. Many of the delegates were shocked when one of America's top investment advisors outlined a depression scenario that might put such a strain on U.S. government finances that Washington would be forced to declare a moratorium on interest payments on bonds and Treasury bills. The odds are heavily against such draconian action, of course. But the point is that even such supposedly risk-free securities as American Treasury bonds could conceivably be hit if conditions were bad enough. I'll deal with this whole subject in more detail in a later chapter, but for now just keep in mind that any investment you make will carry *some* element of risk. The objective of this book is to keep it as low and as manageable as possible.

Who exactly is a low-risk investor? You qualify if:

Your primary concern is safety. Let's not beat around the bush on this point: this is a book for conservative investors who are interested in better-than-average returns with minimum risk. If you're looking for a get-rich-quick manual, this isn't the right book for you. There are plenty of those around, if that's what you want. A word of caution, though: remember that big gains only result from big risks. If you really want to roll the dice, be sure you can afford the losses if things don't work out.

You are patient. Low-risk investors are content to build their fortunes gradually. They prefer reasonable rates of return over a long period of time to big swings in their financial position from one month to the next.

You like to sleep well. Low-risk investors don't like worrying about what their money is doing. There are enough other problems in life to be concerned about; they'd just as soon not add their investment portfolios to that list.

If this sounds like you, then read on. If it doesn't, then you can recover your investment in this book by giving it to a friend or relative as a birthday gift.

The advice that follows is based largely on experience, not theory. I'm an active investor, with a family securities portfolio worth almost half a million dollars. Yet just a decade ago my wife and I had less than $35,000 in personal investments. In the years since, I've had many successes — and some notable failures. Each one has taught me something valuable.

One of the main lessons I've learned is that almost anyone with the interest, the willingness to commit some time, and the patience can become a successful investor. Contrary to the myth, you don't have to be a financial wizard to achieve respectable results. With common sense and dedication, you can do very nicely.

Not convinced? Let me tell you my own story.

It starts at the lowest point in my life. It was the summer of 1982, and my world was falling apart.

We were in the midst of a recession so deep that many people seriously believed it was the beginning of the 1930s all over again. Interest rates were at ridiculously high levels. Once-profitable companies were reporting huge losses. The stock markets were at rock bottom. People were being laid off by the thousands — not just unskilled workers, but even senior managers.

The middle class, which had known nothing but non-stop prosperity since the end of the Second World War, was suddenly discovering what the term "hard times" meant.

I was one of them.

At the time, I was publisher of *Today* magazine, the newspaper supplement that was the successor to the old *Canadian* and *Weekend* magazines. *Today* represented a last-ditch effort by Canada's three major newspaper publishing groups — Torstar, Southam and Thomson — to salvage the national supplement concept.

We'd been making progress, cutting the deficit from almost $9 million annually in the late 1970s, but the magazine was still losing close to $5 million each year.

When the recession almost wiped out Southam and Torstar profits, they decided to pull the plug.

I received the news in June. By October, after overseeing the winding-down process, I was on the street.

Like so many other senior executives who lost their jobs during that time, I was shocked, hurt and fearful. I'd been with the Southam organization and *The Montreal Gazette*, which it acquired while I was there, for 22 years, my entire career. I'd begun as a lowly police reporter and worked my way up to president and publisher of a magazine with a $20 million annual budget. I'd never thought of myself as anything but a company man — but the company had abandoned me.

I had no idea what I would do. I was 46 years old, the sole breadwinner in the family. I had a wife, three teenaged children, a home with a $50,000 mortgage, and virtually no cash reserves (anything we'd saved along the way had gone into RRSPs or towards paying down the mortgage principal). Given the state of the job market at the time, my prospects for finding another position were bleak.

But I did have two things going for me. One was a reasonable settlement. The other was years of experience as a reporter in Canada and abroad for *The Gazette* and Southam News Services.

As it turned out, they came together to open up a career I never would have envisaged.

Once the initial shock of being jobless was over, I sat down with my wife and took stock. We discussed starting a full-scale job search, but the streets were full of out-of-work executives. I knew it would be a long, discouraging effort. There had to be an alternative.

At that point my wife reminded me of a boast I'd made during my days as a reporter: "Just give me a typewriter and I can make a living anywhere." Prove it, she said, in effect. I decided to give it a try. I might not make a lot of money, but I could probably earn enough for us to live on.

That decided, the number one priority became the management of the money I'd received as a settlement. It was not something I was particularly sanguine about.

Many business people are notoriously incompetent when it comes to handling their own financial affairs. I think it's because they devote so much time and energy to the pursuit of their careers that there's none left for anything else.

Certainly, I was that way. My investing record to that point was dismal. You're supposed to buy stocks low and sell high, right? I bought high and sold low. I had no clear investing philosophy, no objectives beyond making money, and no reason for choosing one particular security over another beyond the fact that my broker said it might be a good idea.

My broker liked Northern and Central warrants so I bought 150 of them at $10 each just before the 1973-74 stock market dive. I lost half my investment. I purchased Pamour Porcupine Mines for $26.50 and sold for $13. I put money in CCL Limited at $7.50 and sold out at $4.80. I don't have to go on; you get the picture.

Not every investment lost money, of course. There were a few winners in the bunch. But it was all hit and miss, with the losers far outnumbering the gainers.

I tried giving some money to an investment counsellor to manage for me. Things didn't get any better; my failure to provide any clear guidance and direction resulted in the loss of about a third of my funds before I pulled my money out.

About the only thing I did right was to buy a house. But even at that, I sold my first one, in Ottawa, in 1972 for a very modest profit. Two years later I could have doubled my return.

Not exactly a track record to be proud of. No wonder I wasn't confident about managing my severance payment.

So I did what a lot of people in my situation were doing: I sought professional advice. I went to one of the top financial planning firms in the country for assistance.

The first thing they recommended was to invest some funds in the GICs of a couple of trust companies that were paying exceptionally good rates. Their names may be familiar: Seaway and Greymac. A couple of months later, both were closed down by the Ontario Government in the great apartment flip scandal. If the federal Parliament hadn't hurriedly passed legislation retroactively raising the deposit insurance limit from $20,000 to $60,000, I'd have been out of pocket over $10,000.

Needless to say, I wasn't thrilled with the advice the high-priced pros had given me. I figured there had to be a better way.

That's when my reporter's instincts came to the fore. There was good information on money management out there. It was simply a matter of finding and using it.

My main concern at this time was taxes. A big chunk of my badly needed severance was heading straight for the maw of Revenue Canada unless I did something. So I started to research tax shelters.

I quickly found there wasn't much to research. Most of the material on tax shelters was either out-of-date, unintelligible to a lay person, misinformed, or promotional. I found little that was helpful.

Talk to your accountant or lawyer for advice, newspaper articles said. I did. They had no suggestions.

So I started digging. I got prospectuses on every tax shelter going. There were plenty of them around. MURBs (Multiple Unit Residential Buildings) were being flogged by everyone. There were still some Canadian movies available, although the industry was in the doldrums following a rash of money-losing ventures in the 1970s. Hotel and nursing home limited partnerships were popular. Yacht shelters were catching on. And there were the exotics, like race horse partnerships and jojoba bean farms in Arizona.

I waded through these documents, not understanding half of what I was reading. I became a bore at dinner parties by asking anyone with a financial background for definitions and explanations — although I took any advice they gave with a grain of salt, remembering what had happened with my financial planners.

Finally, things began to clarify. Being conservative by nature, and doubly so given my financial circumstances at the time, I wanted a tax shelter with relatively low risk. That may seem like a contradiction in terms — after all, tax shelters are by definition supposed to be high-risk ventures. But everything is relative. In this particular shelter, three major forest companies were putting funds into the project and two of the big chartered banks were prepared to advance millions of dollars in debt financing. I figured I was in pretty good company.

The shelter, Western Pulp Limited Partnership, was set up to modernize two tired British Columbia pulp mills, at Port Alice and Squamish. I liked the concept — my money would be going into a job-creating venture in an industry I could relate to, having been brought up in the pulp and paper town of Trois-Rivières, Quebec. I had learned by this time that the forestry industry is highly cyclical. Since it was going through a down phase during that period, I figured there had to be better days ahead.

I bought 12 units at $1,000 each. I was going to invest more, but a friend in the brokerage business counselled me to pull back. I wish I'd followed my own instincts.

Now, this was in the pre-Tory period, when tax shelter rules were much more generous than they are today. By the time all my allowable write-offs and investment tax credits had been claimed, the after-tax cost of those units was only $51 each! So instead of $12,000, the 12 units really only cost me $612.

That was in late 1983. In early 1988, with forest industry profits soaring, a takeover bid was made for the units held by the limited partners. The price: $825 per unit. I sold at a profit of over 1,500%, based on my true after-tax cost! Talk about confidence-builders! Of course, I never dreamed at the time I made the investment that Western Pulp would turn out so well. Yet I had felt the chance of a decent return was good.

Nevertheless, tax shelters, good as they might be, were a temporary expedient. I knew I needed to develop longer-term, low-risk investing strategies. It didn't come easily — there was (and is) a lot of trial and error involved. There were some good profits in the process, but there were losses too. I made mistakes, but I tried to learn from them. No one gets it right all the time, so don't let one or two bad investments spook you.

Gradually I came to realize that there are two simple keys to investing success: common sense and awareness.

The common sense involves sticking to investments you understand, not getting in over your head, and not being greedy. (There's an old investing cliché that's worth remembering: "Bulls make money and bears make money, but pigs never do.")

The awareness involves knowing what's happening in the world around you — and using that information to your own profit.

Let me give you an example. In the summer of 1984, there was a temporary upward spike in interest rates. It seemed clear to many people at the time that it was unsustainable — the economy couldn't tolerate rates at those levels for very long.

I'd been studying bonds — an investment form I'd never really understood before. That interest rate hike looked like a buying opportunity to me.

I instructed one of my brokers to buy Government of Canada stripped bonds, maturing between 1991 and 1994, with a face value of $70,000. They cost me just under $26,000, producing a yield of 13.6%.

Now, bonds have been a disaster zone for many investors over the past 25 years. Rising interest rates and periods of high inflation have eroded bond values. Many people therefore think of bonds as very risky — and stripped bonds, which can be quite volatile, as even more so.

I don't look at bonds that way. In fact, I see them as one of the key elements in any low-risk portfolio, as I'll explain in more detail later.

In this particular case, I felt my risk was very low. The bonds were Government of Canada — as solid as you'll find. Interest rates had to come down — the economy was too fragile to allow them to continue at such high levels for very long.

If I was wrong, what could happen? I'd be stuck with collecting 13.6% on my money until the bonds matured in the early 1990s. There are worse fates.

It all worked out as I had expected. Rates fell back, and the value of the strips rose accordingly.

In 1987, I sold about a third of my holdings. My profit on that part of the transaction was 73%. That worked out to an average annual return over the three years of better than 20% — all because I'd been paying attention to what was happening around me and had acted on that knowledge.

In the meantime, the writing career that I'd turned back to in desperation in 1982 was going well. I discovered my interest in money was shared by many other people. Much of what I learned not only helped me in my own investing but was material for articles and columns for a number of publications. I also returned to another old love, radio, doing regular financial commentaries for the CBC.

My understanding of money and investing was given a further boost when I joined Hume Publishing in 1984 and spent the better part of a year overseeing a major revision of the company's flagship *Successful Investing and Money Management* course. I left Hume in 1986 to return to my own business but retained my association with the company as a member of the Advisory Board and a Contributing Editor to *The Money-Letter*.

By the mid-eighties, all the research and experimenting was starting to pay off in a big way. The stock market was booming, and I made some nice profits from it. I even took a speculative flyer occasionally. But I continued to adopt a low-risk approach to my total portfolio.

As a result, Black Monday — October 19, 1987 — caused me little personal concern. I sat in front of the TV set periodically during the day, watching the Financial News Network and listening as one stock market expert after another squirmed and moaned. I wasn't completely out of the market, and the equities I was holding fell just like all the others. But I came through the crash unscathed because the profits I made on my bonds when interest rates dropped just about offset the losses on my stocks.

That's what a low-risk portfolio can do for you.

Incidentally, our family net worth increased by 36% during the year of the Crash. Not bad for a conservative approach.

What it all boils down to is that if I can do it, so can you. I started with no special knowledge, training or aptitude — just need, desire and personal commitment.

From that meagre base, I was able to construct a safe, solid program for building a personal fortune.

There is nothing terribly remarkable about it, no magic formula. Just common sense, basic money knowledge, self-discipline, and patience.

By early 1988 my annual income was well into six figures. Our family net worth — the value of our total assets less any liabilities — was rapidly approaching $1 million. We had a steadily growing portfolio of low-risk investments. And we were virtually debt-free.

Not rich by today's standards, perhaps, but not bad considering where we had been less than six years before. So it can be done. Read on and find out how.

Low-Risk,
Not
No-Risk

Let the fear of a danger be a spur to prevent it.
— Francis Quarles

I RECENTLY CONDUCTED a seminar on money and investing for a group of supervisors and middle managers of a large company.

Before I began, I had a series of questions.

First, I asked how many in the room were prepared to accept a high degree of risk in their investing.

A few hands went up.

A medium amount of risk?

A lot more hands.

No risk at all?

About half the hands in the room. And many of them were attached to the arms of people under 40.

I just shook my head in amazement. I know we Canadians are ultra-conservative when it comes to money, but this was ridiculous.

I spent the next half hour telling these people the facts of life: there is simply no such thing as risk-free investing. I made the point in Chapter One and I emphasize it again here because people don't seem to want to believe it. Perhaps it's a psychological block, brought on by the need for security. Whatever the cause, if you're one of those people who actually believes there are riskless investments out there, you'd better think again. They don't exist. Period.

Many people associate investing risks with such chancy ventures as commodities trading, currency speculation, penny stocks and the like.

The reality is that even such mundane vehicles as Canada Savings Bonds and Guaranteed Investment Certificates carry a certain degree of risk.

"Risk and uncertainty are an integral feature of financial institutions," said Grant Reuber, deputy chairman of the Bank of Montreal, in a presentation to the Conference Board of Canada a few years ago. If that's true for such huge mega-corporations as our chartered banks, it's certainly true for individual investors.

Let me give you an idea of some of the different types of risks you'll encounter when you set forth into the investment world. I'm not trying to scare you off, far from it. But you should be aware of the possible pitfalls when you're deciding on the best places to put your money.

INFLATION RISK

Let's suppose you're in the middle tax bracket. That means that you're being taxed at a rate of at least 40% on your interest income, depending on which province you live in. You've got $10,000 put aside and you want to put the money somewhere safe. A small trust company is offering 11% interest on a five-year GIC, paid annually. That's a better rate than the banks are paying and it represents $1,100 income each year, rock-firm. And, of course, the investment is protected by deposit insurance. The Canada Deposit Insurance Corporation, an agency of the federal government, will ride to your rescue if anything should happen to the trust company. It looks safe and solid. If anything is risk-free, this is it, right?

Well, not really.

Let's suppose the inflation rate when you invest your money is running at around 4-1/2%. Over the five-year period, it increases modestly, at a rate of half a percent per year. How much money, in real dollars adjusted for inflation, will you actually earn over the five years?

Take a look at the table below. It may shock you.

End of Year	Gross Income	Tax Payable (40%)	After-tax Income	Inflation Rate	Real Return (Inflation Adjusted)
1	$1,100	$440	$660	4.5%	$630.30
2	1,100	440	660	5.0%	598.79
3	1,100	440	660	5.5%	565.86
4	1,100	440	660	6.0%	531.91
5	1,100	440	660	6.5%	497.34

As you can see, by the time the GIC matures, your $10,000 investment isn't even generating a 5% after-tax return in terms of real buying power. So your income stream hasn't kept up with inflation.

Even worse, the $10,000 you'll get back from the trust company when the GIC matures will have a purchasing power of only slightly more than $7,500. Your safely invested capital has dropped in real value by almost 25% during that time. And this was during a period of only modest increases in the inflation rate, not the runaway, double-digit variety we experienced in the 1970s.

If someone told you in advance that the investment you were about to make would drop 25% in value and would produce after-tax returns that wouldn't even keep pace with inflation, would you go ahead anyway? Not likely. Yet GICs are one of the most popular forms of investment among Canadians, most of whom regard them as risk-free. As you can see, they're not.

This isn't to say you should never invest in a GIC. But it's a good investment only in certain situations, which I'll discuss later in this book.

The truth is that inflation is a major risk with any fixed-income investment. The longer the term of the investment, the greater that risk becomes. At an annual inflation rate of 5%, a $50,000 investment will be worth only about $30,000 in terms of real purchasing power after 10 years.

You protect yourself against Inflation Risk by having part of your portfolio in investments that will appreciate in value during inflationary times: stocks, precious metals and real estate are the three used most often. These are often regarded as higher-risk investments, as you'll see in a moment. But not to include them in your investment mix because of that can expose you to an unacceptable level of Inflation Risk.

TAX RISK

The hypothetical investment I just outlined contains another of the basic risks of which all investors must be aware: Tax Risk. I assumed for purposes of the example that you were in the middle tax bracket.

But suppose you were in the top bracket, with a taxable income over $55,000. Your marginal rate is now at least 45%, which means your after-tax return on a $10,000 GIC, before inflation is taken into account, is down to $605. The whole deal looks even worse.

Then consider this: your return on the GIC is locked in for five years. But your tax rate isn't fixed. It could well rise during that time, either because you move into a higher bracket (if you aren't in the top bracket now) or because the federal and/or provincial governments decide to increase their rates.

Let's take another look at the $10,000 GIC, this time factoring in some modest tax increases over the five-year period. This time we'll assume you're in the top bracket and that you're hit with tax hikes of one percentage point each year.

End of Year	Gross Income	Tax Payable	After-tax Income	Inflation Rate	Real Return
1	$1,100	$495	$605	4.5%	$577.78
2	1,100	506	594	5.0%	538.91
3	1,100	517	583	5.5%	499.84
4	1,100	528	572	6.0%	460.98
5	1,100	539	561	6.5%	422.73

Not a pretty picture, is it? In terms of the buying power of the dollar in Year 1, your after-tax, inflation-adjusted return on the GIC in Year 5 is down to a meagre $422.73. That's a long way from the $1,100 annually you were calculating on when you made the investment.

In this case, we've seen how Inflation Risk and Tax Risk combine to drive down the return on a Guaranteed Investment Certificate. Tax Risk can take other forms as well.

When Conservative Finance Minister Michael Wilson announced the final version of his tax reform package in December 1987, he made clear to investors just how serious Tax Risk can be. His new proposals changed all the rules of the investing game — to the detriment of people who had acted in good faith in making their decisions. Even the most carefully planned portfolios were hard hit.

Five examples:

■ The taxable portion of capital gains was increased. As a result, investments that were profitable on the basis of the old rules became much less so.

■ The promised $500,000 lifetime capital gains exemption was reduced to $100,000. Tax plans made on the understanding that the original limit would be maintained (and, after all, it was the same minister who had announced it just two years earlier) were blown out of the water.

■ Tax rates on dividends were jacked up.

■ The rules governing the deductibility of interest on money borrowed for investing purposes were radically altered. As a result, complex investment programs had to be entirely revamped.

■ Many tax shelters were either wiped out or so emasculated as to make them unattractive.

I said on a CBC radio broadcast after the tax reform plan was unveiled that it amounted to a tremendous disincentive to Canadian investors. I still believe that.

This isn't the place for a long tirade on the perfidious behaviour of governments. Just keep in mind that they can't be trusted. An investment that may look terrific today can turn rotten tomorrow because of changes to the tax laws.

You won't read about Tax Risk in the conventional textbooks on investing. But it's very real, and you'd be short-sighted not to take it into account. Any time the return on your investment is significantly influenced by tax breaks, be wary. The government can yank the rug when you least expect it.

Unfortunately, there's not a lot you can do to protect yourself against

Tax Risk. That's because the rules of the game can be changed at any moment on the strength of a politician's whim. The best you can do is structure your investment portfolio to take maximum advantage of the tax regime as it exists right now — and be flexible enough to make changes whenever you have to.

INTEREST RATE RISK

Let's go back once again to that $10,000 GIC which was paying 11%. We've already seen how Inflation Risk and Tax Risk can erode your real return. As if that isn't enough, there's still Interest Rate Risk to worry about.

For our previous examples, we assumed a gradual rise in inflation of half a percent per year. That's not the whole story, however.

If the inflation rate rises, it is probable that interest rates will also rise. So by the time your GIC is into its third year, five-year rates could well be in the 12% to 12-1/2% range. That's a lot better than your GIC is paying. But you're stuck — you're locked in for another two and a half years. You've just encountered one version of Interest Rate Risk.

In this situation, most people will simply wait until the GIC matures and then look for a better rate of return elsewhere. Of course, by then interest rates may have declined again, so the opportunity for a higher return has disappeared.

At least you can cash in a GIC for its face value at maturity. If you were holding conventional bonds, traded on the bond market, you'd find that a rise in interest rates produces a drop in the value of your securities. You won't even be able to get your principal back if you want to sell. You could wait until the bonds mature, of course. But that may not be for 15 or 20 years.

Interest Rate Risk comes into play with every type of fixed-income investment. The best way to minimize it is to hold some securities that are easily convertible into cash, such as Canada Savings Bonds and Treasury bills. If interest rates begin to move up, you can quickly switch your money into other investments that will maximize your short-term returns while keeping you flexible enough to make longer-range commitments when appropriate.

STOCK MARKET RISK

On October 19, 1987, the Dow Jones Industrial Index dropped more than 500 points. It was the biggest one-day drop in history and it triggered a world-wide financial crisis that savaged share prices on every major market, closed the Hong Kong Stock Exchange for four days and came within a hair's-breadth of shutting down the New York market entirely.

With visions of 1929 and the Great Depression dancing in their heads, investors panicked. They sold off their stocks at any price in their frenzy to get out. Automated computer trading programs added to the chaos by triggering pre-programmed sell orders when a stock dropped to a certain level.

A major stock market decline had been in the cards for several months. Many investment advisors had been issuing warnings, pointing out that the five-year bull market that began in August 1982 couldn't continue forever.

Yet many investors ignored those warnings, trying to wring out still more profit from their stocks. When Black Monday hit, mass hysteria took over.

As it turned out, governments around the world acted promptly to lower interest rates and pump money into the system in an effort to restore confidence. It worked; the stock markets subsequently rallied and those who had held on through the turmoil or who had added to their holdings when prices were low were handsomely rewarded.

But there was no way of knowing that on the morning of October 20. To many investors, it looked like the world was coming to an end.

Stock Market Risk is a constant fact of life for equity investors. And, like most other forms of risk, it is unpredictable. Until Black Monday, it had become an article of faith that there would never be another crash like that of 1929. There were too many safeguards built into the system, and we'd all become much more sophisticated.

Uh-huh. Remember: take nothing for granted when it comes to investing. Anything is possible.

If you're in equities, Stock Market Risk is something you must live with. You have no choice. Although you cannot eliminate it, you can *minimize* the risk in two ways: by holding quality stocks and by having a time horizon that's long enough to enable you to ride out any temporary setbacks. More on that point in a later chapter.

LIQUIDITY RISK

When investors bought preferred shares in Dome Petroleum several years ago, it looked like a pretty good deal. They were getting a stake in a leading Canadian-owned oil company, a high-profile player with extensive holdings in western Canada. And they were assured a good annual dividend of $1.94 per share, a return of about 7-1/2% to 8% on their money, depending on the purchase price of the stock.

Then hard times hit. The price of oil, which everyone had expected would go up forever, collapsed. Dome, which had borrowed heavily to finance its ambitious exploration and development program, found it had overextended itself. As losses mounted, the company was forced to suspend dividend payments on its preferred shares.

Investors who had been counting on that income suddenly found themselves cut off. They had come face to face with the reality of Liquidity Risk: the possibility that the issuer of the security you buy will not be able to meet its financial obligations.

It can happen with any type of investment: bonds, common stocks, GICs, term deposits, Treasury bills, you name it. And it doesn't happen only to individuals; the world's banks experienced their own version of Liquidity Risk when Brazil suspended interest payments on its international debt in 1987.

That's the most serious form of Liquidity Risk: governments defaulting on their securities. And it happens more frequently than you might think. Everyone has heard about worthless bonds issued by the Czarist regime in Russia and the Nationalist Government of Chiang Kai-Shek in China that were subsequently repudiated by the Communist governments that replaced them. But the relevance of those events is often lost on today's investors.

Well, the lessons of history should be remembered. As I said in the last chapter, I've heard some of America's leading investment advisors warn that even the U.S. government might default on its bond and Treasury bill interest payments in a severe economic crisis. So take nothing for granted.

The best way to minimize Liquidity Risk is to carefully check the solvency of the issuer before buying any security. There are services that rate various types of securities, such as bonds and preferred shares, in this way. A bond with an AAA rating is as solid a bet as you'll find;

one with a B rating should raise questions in your mind. A preferred share with a P-1 rating will be reasonably safe; one that's rated P-4 is dubious. Ask your broker for this type of information before going ahead with any such investment.

Incidentally, the holders of those Dome preferred shares who had originally paid in the $25 range for them ended up getting back only $6.93 when Amoco took over the bankrupt company. They not only lost out on their dividend payments, they also lost a big chunk of their original investment.

ECONOMIC RISK

The dramatic decline in oil prices affected not only Dome, but all the petroleum companies, both in Canada and abroad. Most survived, of course, but the value of their stocks took a beating. Economic forces over which investors had no control and which they had not foreseen resulted in big losses.

That's Economic Risk. It can occur in a variety of forms: a jump in the inflation rate that causes bond prices to drop, a bumper harvest that knocks down grain prices, a slowdown in consumer spending that leads to a drop in car and house sales — all of these have negative implications for investors.

Economic Risk can come in the form of mega-events. Or it can involve a specific industry. If you happened to have money in grain elevators, you were exposed to major losses when the drought of 1988 reduced wheat harvests in western Canada.

The only way to mitigate this risk is to maintain a high degree of awareness as to what's going on in Canada and the world — and how it may affect your investments. I'll discuss this in more depth in Chapters Four and Five.

SALES RISK

I have a copy of the first edition of a book titled *V*, by the novelist Thomas Pynchon. One day I read in a magazine that it was worth over $300.

Terrific, I thought. I'm not a collector of first editions. I didn't particularly care for the book. It was just gathering dust on a shelf. Why not convert it to cash?

Fine idea. But trying to find a buyer who would pay $300 for it was impossible. I visited several rare book stores along Toronto's Queen St. West. The best offer I got was $100. I still have the damn book!

That's Sales Risk. You may have an asset that's worth a lot of money, but it's no good unless someone is prepared to pay your price for it. If you can't sell it for what it's supposedly worth, you've got a problem.

It's a risk that crops up more often than you might expect. I have a friend who made quite a bit of money on paper in a real estate tax shelter. The problem is that he wants to take his money out — but there are difficulties with the management contract of this particular condo and until they're resolved he can't sell.

Sales Risk is reduced by ensuring that anything you invest in has a strong and ready market of potential buyers. If it doesn't, be cautious.

POLITICAL RISK

Finally, there's the risk that the politicians will somehow undermine your investment. A change in the tax rules is only one example of Political Risk. Another example is the ill-conceived National Energy Policy produced by the Trudeau Government. The NEP is still blamed by Westerners for exacerbating the depression in the oil market, adding to the already severe losses of petroleum companies and their investors. The policies of post-war Labour governments in Britain have been cited as a prime factor in the near-collapse of the private sector in that country, again at a high cost to investors. Expensive social programs financed on the backs of corporations cut profits and reduce stock values — almost every western country has examples.

Investors view politicians as the wild card in their calculations. Everything about an investment can look fine — and then government can find a way to mess it up. That's why it's important to keep tuned in to what's going on in Ottawa and other capitals.

It's hard to protect yourself against Political Risk because it can be so mercurial. Keep in mind that newly elected governments are potentially the most volatile. That's because they usually feel a commitment to fulfill at least some of their campaign promises — no matter how dumb those may have been.

So at election time, pay attention to what the parties are saying. If certain policies are potentially injurious to some of your investments, consider selling.

By now you're probably asking yourself, why bother to invest at all? With all the risks you have to take, you're probably better off burying the money in the backyard.

Well, it's not quite that bad. You can still make money by investing, despite the risks involved. The important thing is to recognize from the outset that there *are* risks — and to determine your investment decisions accordingly.

This is where something called the *risk/return ratio* comes into play. Simply put, it means that the greater the risk you're taking, the higher the potential return on your investment should be.

That's why commodities futures — high risk — offer a much greater potential reward than Canada Savings Bonds — low risk.

The generally accepted ascending ladder of risk/return investments looks like this, with low-risk, low-return investments at the bottom:

High Risk

Commodity Futures

Currencies

Options and Warrants

Gold and Precious Metals

Common Stocks

Preferred Stocks

Bonds

Mutual Funds

Guaranteed Investment Certificates

Canada Savings Bonds

Treasury Bills

Deposit Accounts

Low Risk

Take a close look at the order, but don't interpret it too literally. In the real world, it's too simplistic. I can show you mutual funds that are at least as risky as some commodity futures, but which offer a potentially lower payoff. There are some bonds that are more risky than common stocks, even though the potential return is not as high.

So the table is a guideline, nothing more. You'll find plenty of exceptions before you finish this book.

But, you say, by definition surely you should expect low-risk investing to offer smaller profits but greater security than higher-risk investing.

And, in fact, that will generally be true. The low-risk investor has to reconcile himself or herself to the fact that annual returns will be relatively modest compared to those achieved by the successful high rollers.

But notice I used the adjective "successful". Low-risk investors can also take consolation from the fact that they'll end up much farther ahead than the unsuccessful high rollers — who will sooner or later lose their capital and end up selling pencils on street corners.

Furthermore, there are ways for low-risk investors to improve their returns, and the purpose of this book is to help you identify and understand them. Everything doesn't have to be in CSBs!

When calculating the risk you are prepared to take, there are a number of key factors that will affect every investment decision you make. These are:

Your age. The younger you are, the more risk you can build into your investment portfolio. That's because you have many years to recoup your losses. If you invested a bundle in the stock market on Friday, October 16, 1987, you can be reasonably confident you'll eventually recover all your losses — if you haven't already done so — as long as you put your money in solid companies.

But if you're getting on in years, you don't have the luxury of time working for you. I was on the "Radio Noon" hotline show in Toronto on the Wednesday after the market crash, and a number of older people called in. Some of them were very emotional. I remember one woman in particular who told host David Shatsky and me that she was in her seventies. Her broker had advised her to keep all her assets in the stock market — everything! She had purchased blue-chip stocks, but of course they took a beating like everything else on Black Monday. She didn't know what to do — sell at a loss, hang on, jump off a cliff. She was extremely distraught.

Unfortunately, there wasn't a great deal I could say beyond some general advice to diversify her portfolio by selling some of her stocks into market rallies. The fact was that through bad advice she had ended up in a very high-risk situation. Had she been 30 years younger, I would have classified her risk as moderate. No one should have *all* their assets in the stock market — but if she had been in her forties, at least her blue-chip stocks would have had many years to recover.

Your family situation. The greater your family obligations, the less risk you can afford to assume. If you have dependants — young children, aged parents, or a disabled spouse — you must be far more cautious in your investing approach than if you're single and carefree.

Plain common sense should make that point clear. But even people with heavy family responsibilities are sometimes tempted to take higher than normal risks in the hope of a big payoff that will ease their ongoing family financial burden. It's not a great idea.

Security. Every investing portfolio should have security as its central theme. By this, I mean that preservation of capital is of paramount importance. If you lose that, you have nothing to invest with and it will take years to recover.

How much security you require depends on you and your objectives. But as a low-risk investor, I recommend that you structure your portfolio at the outset so that 75% of your money is not exposed to major risk. That way, the chances of a wipe-out are small, unless there's an international economic collapse. Use the other 25% to add more growth to your portfolio, through somewhat higher-risk investments. I'll suggest some ways to do this in subsequent chapters.

Income needs. If you are counting on your investments to generate income, you'll want to concentrate your portfolio in securities that pay a predictable return at specified intervals. We'll look at some of those later.

Growth. A high-growth portfolio will be constructed quite differently from one that emphasizes income. Usually, it will involve a higher degree of risk — although there are ways of mitigating this, as we'll see.

Diversification. Any solid investment portfolio must be diversified — not just in terms of the number of securities held, but also in the type of assets. If the woman who phoned "Radio Noon" after Black Monday had held a diversified investment portfolio, a large proportion of her assets would have been in bonds and cash — and she would have been feeling a lot more comfortable about her future.

Risk tolerance. For most investors, a high-risk strategy is unacceptable. They don't like the emotional rollercoaster involved in chancing everything to win big. A low-risk approach, with better-than-average growth potential, is much more attuned to their psychological make-up.

Those are the main points to keep in mind as you begin to put together your own investment plan. Each factor is relevant; don't lose sight of any of them. The trick is to create a proper balance among them to meet your specific needs. We'll explore ways of doing that as we go.

The Madness of Crowds

Men go mad in herds, while they only recover their senses slowly, and one by one.
— Charles Mackay

THERE'S A WONDERFUL BOOK that was written in the middle of the 19th century by the Englishman who penned that quote, Charles Mackay. It's titled *Memoirs of Extraordinary Popular Delusions and the Madness of Crowds*, but don't let that mouthful scare you off. The stories it contains about mass psychology and its impact on normally rational human beings are fascinating and highly readable. And they provide some valuable lessons for every aspiring investor.

Let me tell you one of his stories here. I'm sure the relevance will be immediately obvious to you.

In the early 17th century, tulip bulbs were brought to western Europe for the first time from Constantinople. Now that may not sound like such a momentous event. But the Europeans, especially the Dutch and the English, went mad over the flower. Mackay couldn't figure out why: "It has neither the beauty nor the perfume of the rose," he wrote. But that didn't matter; Tulipomania, as Mackay calls it, took over.

Holland was hardest hit by the tulip craze. By 1634, "the rage among the Dutch to possess them was so great that the ordinary industry of the country was neglected, and the population, even to its lowest dregs, embarked in the tulip trade".

You can sense the disbelief in Mackay's words when he writes of a single tulip bulb of the Viceroy species being exchanged for "two lasts of wheat, four lasts of rye, four fat oxen, eight fat swine, twelve fat sheep, two hogsheads of wine, four tuns of beer, two tuns of butter, one thousand lbs. of cheese, a complete bed, a suit of clothes and a silver drinking cup". All that for one bulb!

He goes on to describe how the speculation in tulips became such a passion that everyone from nobles to chimney sweeps got caught up in it.

"Many individuals grew suddenly rich . . . . Everyone imagined that the passion for tulips would last for ever . . . . People of all grades converted their property into cash and invested it in flowers."

Of course, it all came crashing down. The demand for bulbs began to decline. The wealthy of the world did not beat a path to Holland's door offering ever-higher bids for the flower. When the prices started to fall, panic set in. People who had spent their personal fortunes on bulbs began trying to unload them for whatever they could get.

"Hundreds who, a few months previously, had begun to doubt that there was such a thing as poverty in the land suddenly found themselves the possessors of a few bulbs, which nobody would buy, even though they offered them at one-quarter of the sums they paid for them . . . . Many who, for a brief season, had emerged from their humbler walks of life, were cast back into their original obscurity. Substantial merchants were reduced almost to beggary, and many a representative of a noble line saw the fortunes of his house ruined beyond redemption."

Mackay didn't say so, but one is left wondering whether the reason the Netherlands are so famous for their tulips today is because the people of the 17th century, with no market for their bulbs, ended up planting them themselves.

In any event, the whole incident is a sad commentary on human greed and folly. But, of course, that was the 17th century. People weren't as sophisticated then. That sort of thing couldn't happen today. Could it?

Let me tell you another story.

This happened in one of the world's great kingdoms, a very rich land. So rich, in fact, that at one time, the people in this realm had used gold as their medium of exchange. The country prospered, its economy was sound and stable, and all was well.

Then a king ascended to the throne who thought it was a bad idea for his subjects to own gold. So he decreed such ownership to be illegal and ordered that all the gold be collected and stored in the underground labyrinth of a great castle. In exchange, his subjects were given paper bills, which they were told were of equal value to the gold they had surrendered. The king made a firm commitment never to print more paper money than he had gold to support it. The system seemed to work, so life went on much as before under the king and his successors.

After some years, an especially foolish king emerged. He wanted to spend more money on weapons and travel and other goodies. When his treasurer told him the funds were not available and that taxes could not be raised any higher, he hit upon an ingenious solution. He ordered his treasurer to abandon the gold standard his predecessor had set up. The value of paper money would no longer be tied to gold. That meant he could print more paper money to finance his spending proclivities. He told his people the paper money continued to be strong. But as more and more of it flooded the country and the prices of flour and milk increased, his subjects became cynical, then restless, and finally rebellious.

When the king heard that an uprising was planned against him, he panicked. He rescinded the law making it illegal to own gold and announced that the gold from his underground vaults would be sold back to the public.

At the news that gold would once again be the coin of the realm, people rushed to trade their paper notes for the metal. But since there wasn't nearly enough gold to exchange for all the bills, the price of a gold wafer began to rise. Speculators moved in, acquiring all the gold they could and reselling it to the public at ever more outrageous prices. Like the Dutch and their tulip bulbs, the population began to sell everything they owned to acquire more gold.

At the height of the madness, buyers were standing in line for hours in rain and snow, just for the chance to acquire the precious metal at almost 25 times the price it had been worth before the frenzy began.

Naturally, the fever eventually came to an end. Within a few months, the value of gold had fallen to half what it was at the peak. Those who had sold everything to buy at the height of the market were ruined. The king, in the meantime, had been overthrown after his courtiers found he had been involved in theft, conspiracy and other duplicities.

I've told the story as a fable, and things didn't really happen quite this way. But if you detected certain parallels to what happened to gold in the United States in recent years, you're bang on the mark. It was Richard Nixon who, in the early 1970s, took the U.S. off the gold standard and made it legal again for American citizens to hold the metal.

The speculative furor that his actions touched off culminated in early 1980 when the gold price hit US $850 an ounce. That's when people were lining up for hours to buy. Of course, like the tulip craze, the gold mania eventually ended. Those who got in during its final days were badly burned; the price has never approached the $800 mark since. As this is written, in the autumn of 1988, it is languishing in the $400 to $420 range and even the most optimistic goldbugs aren't calling for more than $500 an ounce in the foreseeable future.

The Gold Craze isn't the only recent manifestation of Tulipomania. In 1982, stock markets around the world began a run which was to become one of the greatest money-making opportunities of this century. For five years, with hardly a pause for breath, this bull market stampeded on. By late 1986, everyone was caught up in the frenzy. People who had never dreamed of putting money in stocks got into the market. Financial institutions and stockbrokers increased their profits by loaning investors money to buy still more stocks and equity mutual funds. The stock markets became front-page news as the closely watched Dow-Jones Industrial Index continued to move up, past 2400, past 2500, past 2600. Highly respected forecasters called for 3700 on the Dow before the run would end. Magazine articles speculated on how long the bull market of the century would last.

Many investors who entered the market for the first time during this period began to believe prices could go nowhere but up. Everything they put their money into seemed to double in value overnight.

Predictably, things began to get out of hand. Not content with ordinary stocks, the investment community began developing increasingly sophisticated ways to make (or lose) money. Invested money was no longer being used to build new industries — the original intent of the stock market. Speculation took over, to the point where *Business Week* magazine ran a cover story proclaiming that America had become "The Casino Society".

Of course, you know what happened. Five years to the month after it began, in August 1987, the bull market came to an end. Any lingering doubts were dispelled in the crash of October 19, now known as Black Monday.

And, again, it was the latecomers to the party who got burned the worst. The smart investors had taken their profits and retired to the sidelines months before. The big losses were suffered by those who bought stocks in mid-summer, when the Dow was in the 2700 range. By the time Black Monday was over, it was below 1800 and the latecomers had learned that stocks do, indeed, go down.

I could give you other examples: the housing mania in several Canadian cities in 1981, for instance, that ended with a sharp fall-off in real estate prices.

The point is that Tulipomania still occurs. It takes different forms, but its characteristics remain unchanged: unrealistic values for a particular commodity, frenzied speculation that entices ever larger numbers of people, all culminating in an eventual collapse.

I said at the outset of this chapter that there are numerous lessons in Mackay's book for investors. Let me run through them, for the record:

Lesson One: Never believe that prices will always go up. Economic history shows us repeatedly that when prices reach unrealistic levels sooner or later they collapse. Yet many people I know simply cannot accept that fundamental truth. I'm constantly told: "I know the price is too high but I have to buy now because it's never going to be any cheaper". Believe me: if the price doesn't accurately reflect the intrinsic value of the investment you're making, it *will* become cheaper. It's simply a matter of time. A true low-risk investor will have the patience to wait.

Remember: the biggest single risk you can ever take as an investor is to put your money into something that's already been bid up dramatically in price with the idea of selling it later to someone else at a profit.

Lesson Two: Never get caught up in a speculative frenzy. This is an obvious corollary of Lesson One. And it sounds so easy — after all, now that you know about Tulipomania, you wouldn't dream of allowing the same thing to happen to you, right?

Despite your resolution, the time will come when you're sorely tempted; when the world has gone crazy over hummingbird tongues or antique harpsichords and you think there's no way you can lose.

Well, you *can* lose. So when the temptation hits, reread this chapter before you do anything. Or, better still, buy a copy of Charles Mackay's book (it's still in print) and read it. If his many tales of the follies of crowd madness don't convince you, nothing will.

Lesson Three: don't sell other assets to the exclusive benefit of a single investment. Think about the Dutch who sold their homes and lands to buy tulip bulbs. When the tulip market went south, they had nothing — not even what they had started with. They had gambled it all on a single investment and lost. It's a simple lesson in the value of diversification. Don't put all your bulbs in one basket!

Lesson Four: Never borrow to finance a speculation. Who was worse off than the Dutch who sold their houses and property to buy tulip bulbs? Those who borrowed still more money to acquire bulbs they couldn't afford. They not only ended up without a roof over their heads, they were also into the money merchants for a fortune.

Lesson Five: If you own something the world suddenly wants, sell it at a handsome profit and retire. You never know where the frenzy is going to strike next. Without any rhyme or reason, people may be suddenly willing to pay ridiculous prices for your lakefront cottage, or the oil painting you bought from a street artist, or even your insect collection. If a genuine mania begins to develop around something you own, take advantage of it. Wait until everyone you know seems to be in on the action and the price has been bid so high you can't believe it. Then sell. I guarantee you'll eventually be able to buy it back at a fraction of the price you receive.

These are fundamental maxims which every low-risk investor should bear in mind. The speculative frenzies that develop periodically are times of great danger. It is very easy to lose the profits of years of patient enterprise in the space of a few months. Don't be drawn into them, except as a seller. Other activity is at your peril.

Different Times, Different Strategies

We all know that life is full of surprises and that some of these are unpleasant.

— Grant Reuber,
Deputy Chairman,
Bank of Montreal

L ET'S DO A LITTLE time travelling. Through the magic of the printed page, you've been suddenly transported back to 1895. Now you're setting out to find some low-risk investments for yourself.

A lawyer you've met comes to visit you (remember, the telephone has been invented but it's not yet in general use). Some business contacts have approached him, looking to raise equity financing for an expansion program.

He explains the deal to you. The company has been in business for over 100 years. It has no long-term debt. The managers are solid businessmen, prudent, conservative, efficient. Profits have been steadily improving; last year sales were up 25% and net income by 30%. The product they manufacture is one that everyone requires — and they produce a wide range of styles and models to suit all needs. They're looking for no more than 100 investors to provide the capital required to build an additional factory to meet the growing demand for their product. The share position they're offering is priced very attractively because there's a bad recession right now. Expected dividend payments during the first year will be about 5% — very handsome by 1895 standards.

It sounds great — just the sort of deal you'd been looking for. You're just about to sign the contract of sale the lawyer has thoughtfully brought along, when it occurs to you to ask one more question.

DIFFERENT TIMES, DIFFERENT STRATEGIES

Exactly what business is this company in?

"Why, carriage making," the lawyer says proudly. "As solid and stable a business as you'll find anywhere."

As you close your chequebook, making a mental note as you do to check out a guy named Ford in some garage near Detroit, you reflect on the benefit of hindsight. If you hadn't known what was going to happen over the next 100 years, the lawyer's deal would have looked pretty good to you. He certainly won't have any problem finding those 100 investors.

They're the ones who'll discover the unpleasant surprises awaiting carriage builders within a few years.

Meantime, you'll be zipping back to the end of the 20th century, hopefully a bit wiser about the traps into which even the most wary investors can fall.

If you are going to succeed as a low-risk investor, you must never forget that nothing is forever. There is no such thing as a lifetime investment strategy. Business conditions change, consumer needs change, industries change, economic power blocs change, market conditions change, inflation rates change, governments change, tax laws change. In these conditions, there are times when the most risky thing you can do is nothing. Inertia can breed disaster. Or, as Francis Bacon put it: "He that will not apply new remedies must expect new evils."

Think about it. Would you have invested your money in the major companies of Germany and Japan in the late 1940s and early 1950s? The economies of those countries were in ruins, their cities were shattered hulks, their people were defeated and demoralized, and they were occupied by foreign powers. Not exactly a climate to encourage new investment and industrial growth. But you know what happened. Both countries experienced an economic miracle in the decades following the war. Anyone with the foresight to invest in firms such as Volkswagen, Nissan or Sony would have made a fortune many times over. And the signs were there for anyone who looked closely enough; by the mid-1950s it was clear both nations were on the way back to industrial strength. Investments made then would have paid off handsomely.

There are literally thousands of places you can put your money at any given time. How do you know which combine your objective of low risk with the greatest future potential?

It's not easy, of course. If it were, everyone would be a millionaire. But there are certain guidelines that can help you narrow down your range of selections.

Recently I attended an investment conference at which a prominent speaker referred to the future as "a spectrum of probabilities". No one can know exactly what will happen — unless future generations actually do discover how to travel through time. Nevertheless, based on the evidence around us today, it's possible to say that some probabilities on the spectrum are more likely to occur than others.

That's what you have to work out: based on the information available to you, what major trends are most likely to develop over the next decade and how can you benefit from them?

Not all investments will do equally well at all times. Some thrive in one type of economic climate and wilt in another.

In the early 1970s, for example, the best investment advisors were encouraging people to put their money into gold, real estate, oil stocks, fine art, and precious stones. Why? Because inflation was starting to take hold as the dominant economic force in the world. The 1950s and early 1960s had been relatively stable periods, with strong economic growth and low inflation. But events such as the Vietnam war and the OPEC cartel oil price increases changed all that. The cost of living rate began moving up dramatically until by the late 1970s it was in double-digit territory in Canada and even higher in some other countries, such as Italy and Britain.

Investors who had held such low-risk investments as long-term government bonds and blue-chip utility stocks in the fifties and sixties did all right for themselves. However, if they had maintained the same investment stance during the inflationary 1970s, they would have taken a terrible beating. Rising interest rates would have played havoc with the value of their long-term bonds. The utility stocks, which are also highly interest-sensitive (because of the heavy debt load arising from capital expenditures on plant and equipment) also suffered losses. What had been low-risk investments in one situation became not only high-risk but simply bad investments in another.

On the other hand, gold and gold shares, usually ranked among the higher-risk investments, were among the safest places to hold funds during this time. Once the U.S. made it legal for its citizens to hold gold in 1971 and ended the fixed rate of $35 U.S. per ounce of gold, the price soared, eventually peaking at $852 in 1980, as we've seen. Even without growing inflation, the value of gold-based investments would have climbed. But the release of the gold price combined with soaring prices for oil and other major commodities created an explosive mix. In those circumstances, investments in gold bullion or high-grade gold producers like Campbell Red Lake weren't a speculation. For those who got in early, they were virtually a sure thing. For those who came late to the party it was another matter, of course, as we saw in the last chapter.

What about interest rate investments, you may ask. In an inflationary period, interest rates move up. Why aren't bonds, mortgages and GICs good investments in these circumstances?

The answer is because rates *are* moving up. As they do, the value of any fixed-income investments you hold will decline. That's because new bonds or mortgages will pay their owners a higher rate of return than the ones you purchased a year ago. Who'd want to pay you $1,000 for a bond yielding 12% when they could purchase a brand new bond yielding 14% for the same price? If you want to sell yours, it will have to be at a discount. And the longer it has to go until maturity, the deeper that discount will be.

There's another point to consider as well. Although interest-based securities may be paying what appears to be a healthy rate of return, inflation and taxes will probably gobble up most of it. It's the combination of Inflation Risk and Tax Risk that we saw in Chapter Two coming home to roost. Hume Publishing did an analysis of real after-tax rates of return on fixed-income investments during the 1970-82 period, which it published in its first-rate *Successful Investing and Money Management* course. It shows that during that time, a person in a 40% tax bracket who invested in one-year Guaranteed Investment Certificates had an annual real after-tax return of -2%. That's right, you would have *lost* 2% each year after inflation and the tax department got through with you. That's something to think about when you're looking at supposedly "safe" investments.

Of course, timing becomes a major factor here. If you invest in interest-rate-based securities just as the inflation cycle reaches its peak, you can make a great deal of money. People who bought long-term government bonds in 1981, when returns of 16% and 17% were available, did extremely well when interest rates started to drop a few months later.

What about stocks? Surely the stock market is a good place to be in an inflationary period, right?

Not necessarily. It depends on which stocks you're in. You have to pick and choose pretty carefully. Stocks of oil and gold producers did just fine in the 1970s. If you had the foresight to put your money into Japanese stocks or a Japan-based mutual fund, you would have cleaned up. But the performance of the stock market as a whole was pretty mediocre during that time, especially in the early part of the '70s when the first OPEC oil shock spooked everyone and there was speculation that the industrialized world as we knew it was coming unstuck. The 1973-74 period was particularly bad for investors.

Looking at the market as a whole, the Hume study shows that investors in Canadian common stocks lost an average of .8% a year during the 1970-82 period, once the effect of inflation and a 40% tax rate is taken into account. Those who held U.S. stocks did even worse, losing 2.3% annually.

So how do you make money in inflationary times? What are the true low-risk investments in those circumstances?

Almost anything that has genuine intrinsic value. That's why gold and real estate flourish during such times. Stocks in resource-based companies will generally benefit from rising prices for their goods — mining firms, petroleum companies, forest products. High-quality collectibles — everything from rare stamps to antique silver — will increase in value during an inflationary spiral. In other times, most of these investments would be considered high-risk or even speculative. But inflation creates its own investment dynamic. No low-risk investor can afford to ignore it.

Remember, though, timing is critical. Don't wait until inflation has just about run its course before making your move. The key is to identify the trend *early* and take advantage of it while prices are still low. How do you do that? Watch for signs that inflationary tendencies are beginning to take hold in the economy: wage settlements higher than the current cost of living rate, full employment or close to it, strains on industrial capacity, and rising commodity prices are all tip-offs. Pay special attention to what governments are saying and even closer attention to what they're doing. Increased government spending and larger deficits to finance wars (e.g., Vietnam) or social services could be a signal that trouble is on the way.

If you see tell-tale signs appearing, position yourself to take advantage of them. Don't commit all your funds immediately, in case you've misread the tea leaves. Instead, gradually start acquiring the types of investments you know will do well if inflation really takes hold. As you see the pattern intensify, switch more of your funds.

Remember, however, the cycle will eventually run its course. As big profits emerge, take them. Don't allow yourself to become too greedy; you run the risk of being left holding the bag when the inflation house of cards collapses. Gold and oil have not been particularly good places to put your money in the 1980s.

What about other circumstances? In 1982 a different economic scenario emerged, one which was tagged with the label *disinflation*. During this period, inflation still remained a factor, but the rate slowed down. For smart low-risk investors, it signalled a fundamental change in approach.

The "safe" investments were no longer real estate and precious metals. They were the more traditional fixed-income securities: bonds, mortgages, GICs — the very ones you should have been shunning throughout the 1970s.

Why the change? Because with inflationary expectations dampened, investments like gold no longer held the same degree of appeal. Even more important, with interest rates in decline, high-yielding bonds became increasingly valuable. Some of the most impressive capital gains of the mid-1980s were made in plain, dull Government of Canada bonds that had been bought at the right time. For instance, when inflation and interest rates were peaking in the early 1980s, the Government of Canada issued bonds paying 15-1/2% interest and maturing in the year 2002. You could have purchased those bonds at the time at close to par ($1,000 per bond). If you'd decided to sell them in mid-1988, you would have received around $1,350 each. That's a 35% capital gain, on top of the 15-1/2% interest you collected each year. Not a bad return on a conservative investment with supposedly little profit potential.

So the number one priority for a low-risk investor in a disinflationary period should be interest-bearing securities — especially those with capital gains potential. These include bonds, fixed-income mutual funds, mortgages, and mortgage funds.

Canada Savings Bonds and GICs acquired early in the disinflation period, when rates are just starting to move down, will pay a good return. But the disadvantage of CSBs is that the interest rate is guaranteed only for the first year. After that, all bond issues up to 1987 had a minimum guarantee, but it rarely came into play, and it's now been dropped. Also, CSBs, like GICs, have no capital gains potential. There's no public market for them, so their value does not increase as rates decline. In the case of CSBs, you can at least cash them in at any time. GICs lock you in until the maturity date.

The disinflation of the 1980s also made the stock market attractive for the low-risk investor. The aftermath of the 1981-82 recession brought lower interest rates, increasing corporate profits, healthy consumer spending and a generally positive attitude about the future. All that was good for stocks, which enjoyed a five-year bull market from 1982 to 1987.

Yet the stocks that did best were, for the most part, not the safe ones that had performed well during the inflation of the 1970s. Rather, the leaders were found among well-established companies with solid earnings records: firms like auto makers, chartered banks, communications firms, transportation companies, consumer goods producers and the same utilities that had done so poorly during the previous decade. A successful stock market strategy in the 1980s was quite different from the one used in the 1970s. The true low-risk investments had changed.

The danger of disinflation, however, is that it can degenerate into deflation. And if that happens, the low-risk strategy changes yet again.

As this book is written, that hasn't occurred. But I've heard more than a few dire predictions of the doom and gloom that awaits us just around the corner as we turn into the 1990s. If there's a general fall in commodity prices, an increase in the already distressingly high number of bank failures in North America, a prolonged drought over several years and a major international debt default, watch out. Deflation may be on the way.

The last real deflation we experienced in North America was during the 1930s. It was an experience those who lived through it don't want to repeat and those who didn't want to avoid. Prices collapsed: anyone who hadn't switched gears from the 1920s and still had their assets in stocks or real estate or commodities was wiped out. The New York stock market lost 90% of its value between 1929 and 1932. Prime real estate was being given away.

But a deflationary scenario, like all the others, offers an opportunity for wealth — and at relatively low risk. The key is in the assets you hold. If your money is mainly in cash and high-yielding bonds going into the downturn, you'll do fine. You can wait until the rock-bottom prices materialize in real estate and on the stock market and buy value cheap. After that, it's only a matter of time until the cycle changes again and your investments pay off.

It all sounds simple. It isn't. Adjusting investment strategies requires, first and foremost, a high degree of flexibility on your part. You *must* be prepared to dump investments that have performed well for you over the years when the time comes. If you can't bring yourself to do that, you'll end up with a portfolio that's gone from low risk to high risk without a single security being bought or sold. All that's changed is the economic condition.

Next to a high degree of flexibility, a good sense of timing is important. That won't come overnight; you'll need to fine-tune your antennae to what's happening around you and how those events relate to the investment climate. Remember, you're not trying to predict every little twist and turn in the economy; all you're attempting is to identify major changes in direction early enough in the cycle to adopt the appropriate low-risk investment strategy. Those changes don't occur often, perhaps only once in a decade. And when they do, they stay in place for a number of years, offering plenty of opportunity for you to take advantage of the new climate. Just remember to take your profits and leave the party before the cycle changes again and you're left twisting in the wind. Better to depart a year too early than a month too late.

Watching the World

The only fence against the world is a thorough knowledge of it.
— John Locke

I T USED TO BE that events in the Far East or Africa or South America had virtually no impact on the success or failure of the ordinary person's investments. But all that has changed. Anyone who ignores developments in other parts of the world today does so at his or her peril. A hike in West German interest rates, a decline in the value of the yen, a meeting of OPEC, new U.S. trade deficit figures, a suspension of debt service payments by Brazil — any of these can have a significant effect on the performance of your investments.

That's why a low-risk investor today has to watch the world. Not doing so could mean missing a critical sell signal or an important buying opportunity.

Watching the world means different things to different people. I once listened in fascination to Dr. Iben Browning, an engrossing speaker who bases his investment strategies on such natural phenomena as sunspots and volcanic eruptions. His thesis — and I hope I got it right because it is quite complex — is that the debris emitted during periods of severe volcanic activity screens out sunlight, thereby lowering world temperatures. This in turn leads to drought, dust storms and crop failures, which are the harbingers of economic downturn.

When I last heard him speak, in the summer of 1986, he predicted these natural cycles would lead us into a terrible depression in the 1989-93 period. We're about to learn whether he was right.

40

I find this sort of world watching intriguing, but I don't pretend to understand it, or to know whether such predictions are worth anything. As a result, I concentrate on more concrete events, where I can see a clear cause and effect relationship on my own investing decisions.

Let me give you an example.

The June 1988 Economic Summit in Toronto was one of the grandest international set pieces ever staged in this country. The federal government built a special backdrop for it — a magical creation of rocks, ponds, greenery and tents in the heart of the city, erected on what had previously been a vast, ugly and very expensive parking lot across from the Metropolitan Toronto Convention Centre. The cast was loaded with stars: Ronald Reagan in his Summit swan song, revelling in the adulation of his fellow participants and the media; Margaret Thatcher, the woman who out-machos men, as his leading lady; the dour François Mitterand of France, cast as the villain because of his staunch opposition to any cuts in agricultural subsidies; and a strong supporting cast consisting of the leaders of Japan, West Germany, Italy, and the Common Market. Plus there was Anik, the beaver who divided his time between a parking lot pond and the bathtub of a luxury hotel suite. And, of course, there was Brian Mulroney, basking in all the reflected glory.

The press of the world descended on Toronto by the thousands to cover this event. Even the most trivial incident, such as the Italian premier's daughter's shopping trip, received breathless attention.

Don't get me wrong. As a former reporter, I understand media hype as well as anyone. If people want to read about it, it's news — regardless of how mundane it is. But there is an element in the press coverage of these events that has always disturbed me.

Collectively, the members of the North American media have tended to view themselves as the watchdogs of the public interest. This leads to a kind of worldly cynicism which is most in evidence at events such as Economic Summits. There is a tendency not to accept anything that is said at face value, to look for hidden motives or self-interest in every utterance.

In this context, every communiqué or press conference remark is perceived to be designed to achieve one of two things. It is intended either to enhance the image of the leader among his or her own constituents (hence the desperate battle waged by Brian Mulroney's people to have the final communiqué "strongly welcome" the Canada-U.S. trade pact as opposed to simply "welcome" it), or to manipulate and push world markets and events in a certain desired direction.

As a result, the media tend to discount the value of almost every statement to emerge from these conferences, dismissing them as rhetoric or posturing. This attitude has a rub-off effect on the casual TV viewer or newspaper reader.

If this media influence causes you to ignore the pronouncements from these meetings, it can cost you dearly. Because very often, buried in the statements or communiqués, are some nuggets of information that will help you make better investment decisions.

Let's look at the final communiqué of this particular Economic Summit for some examples.

The first thing that hit me was the very strong statement the leaders made on the subject of inflation. They clearly identified it as economic Enemy Number One and stated that "the eradication of inflation and of inflationary expectations is fundamental to sustained growth and job creation".

Remember, this was in June 1988. Just to jog your memory, this was at a time when the fears of recession and even depression that initially followed the October 1987 stock market crash were starting to fade. Worries of a new inflationary outburst were becoming the main economic concern.

So what message was there for investors in that particular segment of the Summit communiqué? In the previous chapter, we saw how different economic conditions produce different investment strategies. The Summit leaders were issuing a warning to any investor contemplating a switch to an inflation-based strategy. By signalling their collective intent to fight any trend towards higher cost of living rates, they were telling us that a strategy based on rising inflation would be one of high risk. They would do everything they could to ensure its failure. There was no guarantee they would succeed. But the intent was clear and any investor who ignored it did so at his or her own risk.

There was also a message for conservative investors in that paragraph. The chief weapon used by governments to combat inflationary tendencies is interest rates. Higher rates put a damper on consumer spending and business investment, thereby slowing the pace of economic growth and creating some slack in the economy, preventing it from overheating.

However, higher interest rates are bad news for holders of bonds or fixed-income mutual funds because they lead to a decline in market value. So the message to bond holders from the Summit leaders was, "Sell. We're going to push up rates to keep inflation in check, so if you don't want to suffer a capital loss on your bond holdings, get out of them." It couldn't have been clearer, yet most people missed it, either because they didn't understand the significance of that paragraph, or because they didn't see it, or because the tone of the media reports had persuaded them that nothing the Summit leaders said for public consumption was worth paying attention to anyway.

Incidentally, within a month of the Summit wind-up, interest rates were raised in several countries, including the U.S., Great Britain and West Germany. Bond prices suffered accordingly. And the price of gold, which had been in the $450-$460 range, fell to below $430, reflecting a diminished belief in the likelihood of a significant increase in inflation. All of these important investment developments were foreshadowed in that single paragraph of the Summit communiqué.

Nor was that the only investment-related nugget in the torrent of words the Summit produced. In another paragraph, the leaders made reference to the fate of the U.S. dollar, which had been going through a lengthy devaluation process in a bid to make American exports competitive again internationally. Here's what the leaders said: "We endorse the conclusion that either excessive fluctuation of exchange rates, a further decline in the dollar, or a rise in the dollar to the extent that becomes destabilizing to the adjustment process could be counterproductive by damaging growth prospects in the world economy."

What did all that mean to an investor? First, that the Summit leaders, and in particular the U.S. administration, were satisfied that the dollar had fallen about as far as it should in order to restore American competitiveness. That meant investors would be unwise to make any moves which would depend on a further drop in the value of the U.S. dollar for success. Yeah, but that's stuff for currency traders, you may think. Not so. In recent years, international investing has become increasingly popular among investors. The easiest way to achieve this is by putting money into mutual funds with international holdings. The Canadian-based Templeton Growth Fund is perhaps the best known of these, but there are numerous others.

Many of these funds produced remarkable returns during the mid-1980s. Part of this was due to shrewd investing policies and to the spectacular boom in the Japanese stock market. But part of the gains were also due to the appreciation in value of such currencies as the yen, the mark, the Swiss franc and the pound sterling against the U.S. dollar. Even if a Japanese stock remained unchanged in its yen value during this period, the decline of the value of the U.S. dollar against the yen enhanced that stock's value to a North American.

So the message from the Summit to the effect that the dollar was not going to be allowed to drift much lower was important to anyone who held international investments or might be thinking of acquiring some. It sent the word that any gains based on the downward realignment of the U.S. buck would probably no longer occur. And it suggested that anyone contemplating an investment in an international mutual fund should look closely at the gaudy track record of the past few years to determine just how much of the gain had been created by the dollar's decline.

The other side of the coin was the statement that the dollar was not going to be allowed to appreciate significantly in value — that the Americans, having gone through the agony of bringing the value of the dollar down, weren't about to give up the economic advantage they had won. And sure enough, when the dollar started to rise after the conclusion of the Summit, central banks around the world did their best to knock it back down by selling dollar reserves into the market to keep the value within a tight range. They succeeded so well that by autumn the U.S. dollar was falling again and the effort had again switched to supporting the currency.

There were more messages in the Summit communiqué, but you get the idea. You didn't have to read between the lines to get some clear guidance as to what you should have been doing with your money. The directions were bold and clear: all you had to do was to pay attention.

Perhaps all of this still seems somewhat esoteric. You read the conclusions I drew from the communiqué and wonder how you could ever do the same thing — and, more important, if you would act on them.

Well, let me assure you, it is not that difficult. But you need to fine tune your antennae to statements and events which can have an impact on your investments. In short, you need a different mindset.

This point was brought home to me by a friend a few years ago. I had just returned from a trip to France with my family and I was telling him about how impressed I was with the way the French handled credit card transactions. There was none of the laboriousness that prevailed here at the time: the person behind the counter doing a manual check in a notice book to see if the card was stolen, entering the information into the register, running the credit slip through a machine to get the card imprint, filling out the detailed information in ink, perhaps doing a phone check for verification and then handing the slip to you to sign, demanding a phone number in the process just to lengthen the delay.

There was none of that nonsense in France. The French merchant simply punched in the amount of the purchase and ran the card through a magnetic strip reader. It did everything: verified the card, determined that the credit limit hadn't been exceeded, and printed out a receipt with your card number, the name of the merchant, the date and the amount. You didn't even have to sign. The whole process took about fifteen seconds.

When I finished telling my friend about the wonders of this process, he had only one question for me: "Who makes the machine?" When I said I didn't know, he looked at me sadly and shook his head. "When are you ever going to start thinking like an investor, Pape?" he asked. "That company could be one of the hottest investments around in a few years and you didn't even find out who it was." That one remark permanently changed my mindset. If you're going to be a successful low-risk investor, you have to *think* like one.

Let me give you an example of how I try to use this investment mindset in relation to developing events. As I write this book, I see the single most important change currently taking place in the world as being the *glasnost* phenomenon in the Soviet Union. I have no way of knowing whether this incredible experiment in social and economic change will work. I don't know if Mr. Gorbachev will be able to retain power in the face of opposition from conservative forces in his country. But I *do* know that if *glasnost* takes hold, the implications for investors will be enormous.

How? Well, consider these possibilities.

First, it is clearly one of the objectives of *glasnost* to reduce international tensions. The Soviet leadership appears to want to put its economic emphasis in the years ahead on the development and strengthening of its domestic economy. To do this, a significant amount of the country's production capacity must be shifted from weapons to heavy and light machinery and consumer goods. This change can only be achieved if the prospect of war with the U.S. and/or China is greatly reduced. So we've seen events that a few years ago would have been deemed impossible: a treaty eliminating an entire class of nuclear arms, the promise of a pullout without victory from Afghanistan that looks strikingly similar to the U.S. withdrawal from Vietnam, attempts at rapprochement with China, and efforts to cool tensions in a number of world hotspots.

I believe all this effort signals a basic change in international relationships that could last for a generation. If I'm right, it will mean a business slowdown for many of the companies which are prime suppliers of sophisticated weaponry. Therefore, I would not be inclined to invest in defense-related stocks over the next few years. They could be hard-hit if *glasnost* evolves in the direction it appears to be headed.

That's not all *glasnost* suggests to me. The Soviets are showing a willingness to inject some elements of free enterprise into their economy. The eastern European countries are going to follow this lead, and China is moving in a similar direction. This process is going to increasingly involve joint ventures with leading Western countries. As this is written, McDonald's of Canada has just concluded lengthy negotiations with the Soviets to set up operations in Moscow. Pepsi is already in the U.S.S.R. Other companies are going to be right behind.

Don't misunderstand me. Despite the size of these new markets, these deals aren't a license to print money. The Soviets, Chinese and eastern Europeans are tough bargainers and their countries are short of hard currency. So for a time, most or all of any profits generated are going to be held within the host country or re-invested there.

Eventually, that will change. Any firm gaining a strong foothold in these markets is going to have tremendous growth potential. McDonald's, for example, has just about saturated the North American market; there simply isn't any more room to grow. But the Soviet Union and China offer brand new possibilities. And it's not just North American companies that stand to benefit. The Japanese, Germans, French, British, Koreans and others will be competing for a stake, too.

What do I read from this as an investor? That there may be significant profit opportunities for some aggressive companies down the road. I'm going to scan the business pages for reports of new deals. I'm going to pay attention to the terms of the deals, looking for things like exclusivity and profit distribution. When I find something that looks good, involving a solid company, I'm going to acquire some of the stock as a long-term investment.

Here's another example. The European Common Market still has in place some significant trade barriers between member countries. But there are plans to eliminate these by 1992. That will create major new opportunities for those companies which move aggressively to take advantage of the situation. Some leading European brokerage houses have already begun to identify those firms best positioned to benefit from the disappearance of all trading barriers. They range from transportation companies such as British Airways to pharmaceutical firms such as Sanofi SA of France.

An alert investor will be acquiring positions in those companies now, either directly (many are traded on international exchanges) or through international mutual funds specializing in Europe.

Closer to home, the Free Trade Agreement with the U.S. is another example of world watching. The bitter 1988 election campaign on the issue showed just how important an international deal can be to the fortunes of individual investors. Every time the polls showed a surge in the fortunes of the Liberals under John Turner, Canadian stock markets dropped and the dollar softened. Polls favouring the Progressive Conservatives, champions of the FTA, produced the opposite effect.

Had the electorate rejected the deal, the result would have been an immediate general drop in the market, followed by several months of decline in the value of shares of those industries most negatively affected — steel, for example. Acceptance of the arrangement created profit opportunities for shareowners of companies best positioned to take advantage of it.

That's what I mean by watching the world. Look for investment opportunities in new developments. Pay attention to warning signals that tell you to dump a particular holding. Scrutinize the words of world leaders for hints on what they're planning and see how you can profit from those plans.

If you feel you need some further help in training yourself to think this way, I strongly recommend a monthly reading of *The Bank Credit Analyst*, a highly respected economic journal published in Montreal. Although it's somewhat technical, it regularly reviews international developments and points out some possible courses of action for investors. For instance, in the July 1988 issue it suggested that one of the most important developments for investors over the next few years will be the rebuilding of the U.S. industrial base as companies take advantage of the new export opportunities created by a lower dollar. That means stocks in heavy industries and export-oriented companies, which have not performed well for most of the 1980s, could do much better in the years ahead.

The Bank Credit Analyst isn't cheap — a one-year subscription costs US $545. That's one reason why few people have heard of it. But it's excellent reading for anyone who wants to become a real world watcher. If you can't afford the hefty price, see if your local library has it available.

However you do it, make yourself aware of what's going on. Develop your investor mindset and apply it liberally. You'll be amazed at the opportunities it reveals.

A Solid Foundation

Upon this rock I will build my church.
— Holy Bible

L ET'S PAUSE FOR a moment. I've kept you moving at a pretty hectic pace so far, what with time travel, mass psychology, summits and *glasnost*. Before we go any further, let's spend just a few moments reviewing the basics.

If you've read my book *Building Wealth*, you can skim through this chapter because it's simply a quick overview of the fundamental principles contained there. If you haven't, then I strongly suggest you give careful consideration to what follows.

As a first step, I'm going to ask you a question. I want you to stop reading for a moment and think about your answer. It's this: are you absolutely sure you have the proper foundation in place on which to build an investment portfolio?

If you don't, you may find yourself building your church on sand instead of rock.

I said in Chapter One that you shouldn't even consider starting to build a portfolio of non-tax sheltered investments until you've completed the initial steps towards achieving financial independence. So here's a checklist to follow. If all the following statements are true, then you're ready to extend your investing activities into other areas. But if you can't honestly say "yes" to any one of them, you should be applying your available funds to that particular goal.

1. *I have no long-term consumer debt.* One of the traps many people fall into is trying to build an investment portfolio while still carrying a heavy consumer debt load — credit card balances, a car loan, a furniture loan or whatever. That's a no-win situation, as a little basic math will quickly show.

The interest rate you're paying on your consumer debt is not tax deductible. That means your payments are being made in after-tax dollars. Let's assume you owe $10,000, perhaps on a car loan, and you're being charged interest at the rate of 13%. The loan has to be paid off over a three-year period, with monthly payments of $335.40, blended principal and interest.

The total amount you'll have to repay the bank is $12,074.40. Of that, $10,000 represents the principal; the other $2,074.40 is interest.

Let's assume you're in the middle tax bracket. Depending on your province of residence, that means your marginal tax rate will be in the 40% range. So you'll have to earn $3,457.33 to have the after-tax funds available to pay the interest on your loan.

Now let's say you have the $10,000 to pay for the car. But you decide to open an investment portfolio instead. You put it into something safe and solid (because you're a low-risk investor) that pays you a 10% return. What happens?

Now you've generated an income stream of $1,000 a year, which you plan to apply against reducing the car loan. That's $3,000 over the three years. But you need $3,457.33 in before-tax earnings just to pay the interest on the loan.

It doesn't look like a very smart move.

But, you may be asking, what would happen if you could find an investment that paid you a return of better than 13% (the interest rate on your loan). Wouldn't investing the money instead of paying off the loan then make some sense?

Probably not. By definition that will mean you'd have to put your money into a higher-risk investment — which means you could end up losing part or all of your principal if things go sour.

It would make more sense to pay cash for the car and then borrow $10,000 to invest. That way, the interest on the loan becomes tax deductible, at least in theory. There are some problems involved with that course as well, which I'll explain in detail in a later chapter.

You may also be asking yourself whether investing the $10,000 and paying down the car loan as you go isn't a good form of self-discipline. At the end of three years, you end up with a fully paid-for car plus $10,000 to continue investing. It's cost you a few hundred dollars more to do it that way, but it may be worth it.

True enough. But look at it another way. Suppose you'd paid for the car at the outset but then started putting aside $335.40 a month — the amount of the payment had you been carrying the car loan. At the end of three years, assuming you invested the money at 10%, you'd have amassed about $13,000 in principal and after-tax interest. In both cases, the car would be paid off at this stage. But now you'd have the car plus $13,000 to continue your investing program instead of the car and just $10,000. Sure, a greater degree of self-discipline is involved. But isn't a 30% gain in your capital worth it?

Any way you look at it, setting up an investment portfolio while you're still carrying consumer debt doesn't make much sense. So if you owe any money, pay off your debts first.

2. *I own my house.* I regard the family home as the cornerstone of any-one's lifetime wealth-building strategy. I've heard and read arguments to the contrary from highly respected financial advisors who suggest that at certain times, such as periods of low inflation, you're better off rent-ing. I just don't agree.

There are several reasons for my strong bias towards home-owning.

To begin with, your home is a wonderful tax shelter — one of the best around. Any profit that you make when you sell it is all yours to keep — the government won't take one cent of it. Over a period of many years, that can add up to a great deal of money — enough to make a big difference to your standard of living when you retire. In a country with fewer and fewer tax shelters, this is one you simply can't afford to miss.

Second, your home is an appreciating asset. Yes, it's true that residential real estate doesn't always go up in value. A depressed economy, either regional or national, can have a negative impact on the market value of your home. And if you're forced to sell for any reason during that period, you can sustain a loss. It happens. But over the long haul, your house, if it's well located and properly maintained, will rise in value, sometimes dramatically so. Someone recently remarked that there are now two economic classes in the Toronto area — those who owned homes before 1985 and those who didn't. In 1985, the average sale price of a Toronto home was just under $110,000. By mid-1988 it had doubled, to the $220,000 range. That dramatic increase turned some people who never expected to achieve the status into millionaires, at least on paper. Even without such quick price run-ups, your home is a valuable asset — one of the best you're ever likely to possess.

Finally, I like a home as an investment because it's functional. It's not a piece of paper like a stock or bond. It's where you live. You have to have shelter anyway. Why not own it instead of paying rent to someone else?

3. *I have paid down my mortgage.* It isn't enough just to buy a house. Once you've done that, your priority becomes paying down the mortgage as quickly as possible.

Building Wealth contains several examples of how early mortgage paydowns can save you tens of thousands of dollars in interest costs. I won't repeat them here. Let me just stress that, in the early years of a mortgage, there is no better use to which you can put your money. That's when the impact of a mortgage paydown is at its maximum.

Ideally, you should have the entire mortgage paid off before starting to build an investment portfolio. That's because, here again, your mortgage interest costs are not deductible for tax purposes. That means you have to invest your money in something that's giving you a higher return than your mortgage interest rate before it begins to make any financial sense.

Even more important, a mortgage-free home means you're not going to lose your house if your investments don't work out. There's no one hovering in the background, threatening to foreclose.

However, many people prefer to start diversifying their assets before the mortgage is fully paid off. If you're one of them, just be sure to take a close look at the net financial impact of what you're doing before you go ahead.

But I strongly recommend not going that route until you've paid down your original mortgage principal by at least 50%. That may sound ultra-conservative — but that's the way I am.

4. *I have emergency cash available.* You never know when something is going to happen. So before you plunge into stocks, bonds or mutual funds, be sure you have money put aside that you can tap into quickly and easily should the need arise. The equivalent of six months' family take-home pay is a good target. Canada Savings Bonds or Government of Canada Treasury bills are an excellent place to hold such emergency funds — they pay a fair rate of return and can be cashed at any time.

5. *I have a Registered Retirement Savings Plan.* This is the other great Canadian tax shelter, and it's one of the most powerful wealth-building tools available. Like the family home, it is one of the rocks on which personal fortunes should be built. If you aren't making the maximum possible contribution to an RRSP, you shouldn't be thinking about starting a non-tax sheltered investment portfolio. By the time the tax people get through with you, it's very difficult to come out ahead, unless you manage to generate very large capital gains.

This doesn't mean you can't start building an investment portfolio at a relatively young age. An RRSP is a great place to learn and practice the principles of low-risk investing. Instead of directing your contribution into deposit accounts or GICs, use your RRSP funds creatively to maximize your returns and to familiarize yourself with the wide range of securities that are available. I'll go into this idea in greater detail later in the book.

So that's the checklist. If you've met all five goals, then you've established a solid financial foundation for yourself and can go forward from there.

What if you haven't? Well, if you've said "no" to one of the points, then you should direct your funds there until you're satisfied you've dealt with the situation. If there are two or more points on the list you haven't accomplished, then you need to put together a plan with a firm timetable for achieving those goals. In that case, I strongly suggest you read *Building Wealth*, as it contains all the basic information you need.

However, that doesn't mean you shouldn't finish this book — and it's not an author's desire to retain his audience that makes me say so. The fact is that this book should give you a number of ideas about what to do with your money while you're saving for the downpayment on a house and/or building your RRSP. In both cases, you want your funds to bear as little risk as possible, while generating the best possible return. Some of the advice in subsequent chapters may help you achieve those objectives.

Don't be tempted to stray from your basic goals. Until you've met the five requirements I've set out in this chapter, you simply should not contemplate setting up a non-tax sheltered investment portfolio.

CHAPTER 7

Choosing Your Partners

Thou wert my guide, philosopher and friend.
— Alexander Pope

NOW THAT WE'VE dispensed with the basics, let's have some more fun. I want to go time travelling again, this time back to 16th century London.

If you're wondering why you're reading all this history, frankly, it's because the past intrigues me. The more I read of it, the more I'm convinced that everything that happens has happened before. Our technology and communications may be more sophisticated today, but our underlying motives and the actions that flow from them remain unchanged. So lessons from the past can be extremely valuable, if we take the time to consider them.

What follows is a story which I saw retold recently in a newsletter published by the brokerage firm of Rosenthal & Company.

The scene is London in 1524 — a time when a poorly educated population was easily misled by the hocus-pocus of soothsayers and astrologers. For some reason, these false visionaries collectively decided that the Thames was about to overflow its banks in a great flood that would devastate a large section of the city. This prophecy was spread among an increasingly terrified populace, with the predicted ravages of the roiling waters growing more frightening with each retelling. The date for this terrible disaster was fixed as February 1, 1524.

As you might expect, people began to flee the city as the date for the Great Flood grew nearer. Accounts from the time tell of roads jammed with people and carts piled high with family possessions. Many of those who stayed behind took the precaution of having a boat available — just in case.

Finally, the terrible day came. Those who remained in the city watched the Thames closely for the first signs of rising water. But nothing happened. The placid river continued to flow at its normal pace, totally oblivious to the doleful forecasts of its wrath. Sheepishly, the townspeople who had fled to the hills began to trickle back and, in time, normal life resumed.

Now, you would think that the reaction of ordinary Londoners would have been to toss the prophets of doom into the same river they had said would wreak such havoc. But the astrologers managed to wriggle off the hook by claiming they had rechecked their calculations and found that they were, in fact, correct. It was just their timing that was slightly off — the Great Flood would take place in 1624, not 1524. A small error, but of course understandable when one is interpreting the universal movements of the stars. Now, for our next prediction. . . .

I like that story because it says so much about relying on other people to guide your decisions. It's not just good advice that you want. It's good advice *at the right time*. It's not much help to know that a Great Flood is going to occur or that the stock market is going to drop. Both of those things will happen sometime; you need to know *when*. No one's perfect, but the best advisors are those who can at least make educated guesses.

Which brings me to the main point of this chapter. Every investor needs some good, trusted advisors — people who, as Pope says, will not only provide guidance but will also share your investing philosophy and why may even, in time, become friends.

What advisors do you need? Here's a list of possibilities. You shouldn't require the services of all of them, but you may need more than one.

A Financial planner

If you've completed the basic financial foundation I outlined in the last chapter, then it's highly doubtful you need the services of a financial planner. The thing these people do best is to organize your financial affairs and provide you with a basic program for achieving your strategic objectives. They are not, generally, good sources for specific investment advice.

If you do feel the need to consult a financial planner, be cautious. The profession is unregulated and there are some dubious practitioners around. A few years ago *The Wall Street Journal* carried a story about financial consultants in the States who based their advice on what they called "Christianomics". Their plans were drawn up according to their interpretation of Biblical verses relating to money. Don't get me wrong, I have nothing against the Bible. It's just that I doubt it was ever intended to be used for such purposes.

More recently, readers of the *Report on Business* followed with fascination the testimony before a panel of the Ontario Securities Commission by a woman who claimed she'd been misled by a financial planner who told her to sell her Canada Savings Bonds, borrow $75,000 and invest the money in mutual funds, for which he and his company received a commission. She had paid $600 for the "plan", and said she had no idea the planner was also going to be receiving a sales commission from the invested money.

So be wary of sharks in the financial planning waters. If you do need a planner, check with the Canadian Association of Financial Planners in Toronto for their brochure on how to select a one. You'll also find more detail on how to proceed in *Building Wealth*.

A Tax Consultant

This is a role that can be filled by an accountant, certain financial planners, or a tax lawyer. I'd be reluctant to rely on a tax preparation firm, as most of them are staffed by people with minimal training. At this stage in your financial life, you're likely to need more sophisticated advice.

I strongly recommend devoting some time to learning about the tax system, developing your own tax-saving strategies, and preparing your own return. You're the best person to look after your own interests; no one else cares about your money as much as you do.

However, it's a good idea to have a qualified expert review your plan and check your return once it's completed. He or she may come up with some wrinkles you hadn't thought of — which may both save you some money and give you new tax-saving ideas.

In choosing your advisor on taxes, you're looking for three key assets. One is a thorough knowledge of the tax regulations. You'd be amazed how many so-called "experts" don't have it. Perhaps that's not so surprising considering the insane complexity of our tax system, but if you start finding you know more than your tax advisor does in certain areas, it's time to consider looking for a new tax expert.

The second asset you want is practical knowledge of how Revenue Canada works. You need someone who can say with authority: "The regulations are ambiguous on that point, but in practice Revenue Canada will accept the claim if . . . ." Accurate advice of that sort can save you thousands of dollars.

Finally, you're looking for honesty. Most of us really don't want to cheat on our taxes. We simply want to organize our financial affairs in such a way that legally we can pay as little as possible. So unless you're a unrepentant risk-taker (in which case, why are you reading this book?) you don't want a tax advisor who's going to be constantly encouraging you to take chances. After all, who wants to go through the ordeal of an audit?

AN INVESTMENT COUNSELLOR

This is the person you consult if you have a lot of money which you don't want to manage yourself. For a fee (sometimes a hefty one) the investment counsellor will take over the entire decision-making process. You provide the general philosophy and objectives; he or she will take it from there. You'll receive regular reports on what's happening to your money and there will be a face-to-face meeting a couple of times a year. Apart from that, you don't need to know what's going on.

A couple of points here. First, not all investment counsellors are created equal. Some are better than others. When you're shopping around, ask to see some actual portfolios the advisor has managed for other people. Check the performance and how it was achieved. If the results look good but were gained largely through speculative mining stocks on the Vancouver Stock Exchange, ask yourself whether that sort of approach is consistent with your personal philosophy.

Also, keep in mind that investment counsellors have their particular specialties. I know of some who will hold nothing but stocks or cash in a portfolio — they never put money into bonds, mortgages or other fixed-income securities. If you want a balanced portfolio or you're investing for income, this is certainly not the route you want to go.

A BROKER

Finally, we come to the broker, the only one of this group who is absolutely essential to an investor. Many people think of brokers purely in terms of stocks. The reality is that they're your prime source for a variety of other investment vehicles, including bonds, mortgage-backed securities, mutual funds, and options. You can't get along without one, and you shouldn't try.

In *Building Wealth* I outlined in detail my Five Ps for selecting a broker: Personality, Philosophy, Patience, Prudence and Profits. I also explained how to interview a prospective broker and some of the things to watch for in the way your account is handled. For the sake of those who have already read all that, I won't go over the same ground again here.

One point from that book I would like to reiterate, though, relates to discount brokers. I am constantly asked whether discount brokers are for real, and whether they can actually give you the kind of savings on brokerage commissions their ads claim.

The answer is yes, they are for real and so are their savings. But it's like everything else in life — you get what you pay for.

In the case of a discount broker, you're getting an order taker — someone who will take your buy or sell order over the phone, execute the transaction and send you a confirmation. Nothing more.

I believe every investor, no matter how experienced, needs more than that. You need an advisor — someone who will recommend securities properly suited to your goals, whom you can bounce ideas off, who will provide you with solid research materials, who can intelligently discuss the state of the market, and who understands the importance of timing (remember the flood).

A discount broker will do none of these things for you. That's why I suggest you don't use one, at least not exclusively. A discount firm can be valuable as a second broker, to be used when you don't require any advice on a particular transaction. But to operate in the investment world without a trusted, full-service broker to advise you is akin to flying blind.

In dealing with a broker, always keep one point in mind: brokers will frequently tell you to buy; they will rarely tell you to sell. In fact, knowing when to sell is one of the most difficult problems facing any investor.

Ira Gluskin, the colourful, cigar-smoking Bay Street money manager who writes one of the most insightful investing columns you'll ever read, in *Financial Times*, has his own theories on why brokers are so reluctant to tell their clients to sell.

Buy recommendations can be acted on by everyone, he points out. Sell recommendations are limited to those who already own the stock — a much smaller client base. On top of that, sell signals may anger management at the company being dumped. They, in turn, may decide not to use the services of a particular brokerage house when the time comes for their next stock underwriting.

I have an additional reason, and it comes out of my own experience.

A few years ago, one of my brokers recommended the purchase of Torstar warrants. (Torstar is the company that owns *The Toronto Star*; the warrants gave me the right to purchase shares in the company at a specified price, regardless of what the stock was trading for on the TSE).

His rationale for the recommendation was good: the company was undervalued, earnings were improving, and the stock should begin to move up soon. By purchasing the warrants (which were cheaper) instead of the stock, I could get more bang for the same bucks. It sounded good, so on January 28, 1986, I purchased 1,000 warrants at an average price of $16.31, including commission.

Hardly had I made the purchase when Torstar began to move. Within weeks the company announced dramatically improved earnings, a share split and all sorts of other good things. "Hold on for $20," my broker advised. "Then sell."

On February 26, less than a month later, I sold out at $20.08 including commission. I had realized a return of just over 23% in that time. Annualized, that works out to an incredible 277%.

I should have been delighted, right? Well, I wasn't, because the price of the stock and the warrants kept shooting straight up. The warrants eventually passed the $40 level — twice what I'd sold them for.

So did my broker get credit for his great pick? No way. Although I never complained to him directly (after all, it was my decision in the end to get out), I haven't forgotten his premature sell advice to this day. What in fact was a profit of about $3,700 could have been more than $23,000 — if only that damned broker . . . .

That's why many brokers are reluctant to go out on a limb and tell you to dump a stock. They're in a no-win situation. If it's a stock on which you've taken a beating, they've locked in your loss. If it's one on which you've made a profit, they run the risk of incurring your resentment if it goes higher.

So in most cases you're going to be very much on your own when it comes to selling. Don't expect a lot of help from your broker.

Having said that, perhaps this is a time to give you a few tips on selling your securities.

One approach if you've done well is to take half your profits. This is a common practice among experienced investors. It involves telling your broker to sell half your holdings while keeping the balance in case the price goes higher. Had I done that with my Torstar warrants, I would have continued to benefit from the stock run-up.

Another approach is to set up *trailing stops*. These are stop-loss orders designed to protect your profits in case the price of your securities begins to fall. You place a stop-loss order by telling your broker to sell a security if the price falls to a certain level. For example, if a stock you bought at $5 is now trading at $10, you may enter a stop-loss at $8. If the stock drops to that point, it will be sold.

In the case of the Torstar warrants, I might have put in a stop loss at $18 instead of selling when the price hit $20. As the price moved up, I could have continued raising the level of the stops until I was finally convinced it was time to get out. This is what is meant by "trailing stops"; the stop-loss level keeps rising as the price increases.

The only real problem with this strategy is that you can't always get out at the stop price. In a market free-fall, such as we experienced on October 19, 1987, the price may fall too rapidly for you to get out — or there may not be any buyers. So it's not an infallible approach.

Finally, don't ever be afraid of taking a good profit. If a security has had a long run and you no longer feel there's much left in it, take your money and go. If you leave a little something on the table for the next person, that's all right. You've done okay.

The next problem is judging the quality of the investment advice you're receiving. After all, if you're going to pay a premium price for the services of a full-service broker, you want a pay off. You can find plenty of bad advice for free; you don't need to pay for it.

That brings me to one of the most important lessons of low-risk investing: learn from both your failures and your successes. If an investment goes sour, take the time to figure out why. Determine whose fault it was, if anyone's. Specifically, evaluate the particular advice you received from your broker; was it good or bad?

I admit, it's not always easy to do that kind of analysis, especially regarding a losing investment. The natural reaction when you've just taken a financial beating is to put the whole miserable experience out of your mind. It's natural — but it's a big mistake.

If you're going to invest successfully, you have to understand where and why something goes wrong. Find out where the buck stops. If you don't, you risk making the same mistake again and again — or relying on an advisor who does.

I suggest keeping a scorecard on your broker. Note every recommendation he or she gives you. For those you actually follow, your scorecard can look like this:

Security	Date Bought	Price	Quantity	Current/ Sale Value	Date Sold	Profit/ (Loss)
Alcan	Feb3/88	$33	100	$38	Jul15/88	$500

If you want to include more detail, you can add columns for the commission paid, net profit after commissions and annualized return. But this basic outline will give you a running report on the quality of the advice you're receiving.

To be fair to the broker, though, you should also keep a record of recommendations *not* acted on. After all, if you're unlucky enough to select all the dogs while passing up the big money-makers, it's not entirely the broker's fault. You can't expect a winner every time.

So keep a separate scorecard on the other recommendations you receive. See if it shows a similar pattern over time to those you actually put money into.

You should review your scorecard with your broker at least twice a year. If it's good, see how it can be made better. If it's bad, talk over your approach and philosophy again with the broker. Then, if it doesn't improve over the next six months, switch to someone else.

As I said earlier, it's especially important to pay attention to your losers. See where they went wrong. Here are three points to consider whenever you sell a security at a loss:

1. *Determine who made the recommendation.* The idea to purchase this dog had to come from somewhere. Did your broker suggest it? If so, enter it onto the scorecard.

If the advice came from some other source — perhaps an article in a financial newspaper or newsletter — make a note of that as well. The next time the same writer makes a recommendation, be more cautious.

But perhaps the idea was strictly your own. In that case, face up to it. Analyze why you chose that particular security and where your logic was faulty. Sure, it's painful. But the process may save you a lot of money in the future.

2. *Decide if your timing was at fault.* Often investment losses are strictly a matter of timing. If you hadn't bought when you did or sold when you did, the whole thing would have worked out just fine. I can't stress enough the importance of timing, and a broker who can give you good advice on that score is worth his or her weight in gold.

Let me give you another personal example. In August 1985 the Conservative Government of Brian Mulroney took a major step in its program to privatize a number of Crown Corporations. It decided to sell all its remaining shares in the Canada Development Corporation to the public.

The CDC was not typical of Crown Corporations, most of which were set up to fill a specific economic need. This was a hodge-podge of a company, with a broad, vague mandate to develop new resource-related industries in Canada. Its operations included a number of diverse activities, ranging from the manufacture of chemicals to genetic engineering.

When the terms of the Government's share offer were announced, the deal looked pretty attractive. Payment for the CDC shares was spread over two years. Total price was $11.50, with one installment of $5.75 payable immediately. A piece of paper called an installment receipt was issued to buyers once this first payment was made. The second payment, also of $5.75, came due on September 16, 1986.

On the advice of another broker, who recommended it highly, I bought

500 shares. We both liked the leveraged potential for a quick profit. If the stock moved up, I could sell the installment receipts before the second payment came due, get the full benefit of the price increase and walk away whistling.

The problem is that leverage works two ways. The price of the stock dropped instead of rising. The value of the installment receipts plummeted. By the following May, they were down to $2.25. I figured I'd be smart and buy 1,000 more, again with my broker's approval.

It was a great idea — but it didn't work. CDC stock kept weakening in price. Finally, with the deadline for the next installment payment rapidly approaching, I decided not to throw good money after bad. I sold all my holdings and took a loss of over $3,700 on the deal. The broker went along with that decision.

What has all this to do with timing? Simply this: if I'd hung in there for another 18 months, I'd be telling you about a big profit right now instead of a loss. Canada Development Corporation eventually became Polysar Energy and Chemical Corporation. In early 1988, a takeover bid for the company was made by Nova Corporation. Share prices climbed to almost $22. After a long mating dance, Nova eventually succeeded. Any investor who owned the old CDC shares ended up doing very nicely. If I had gone through with the second installment payment, my total cash outlay for 1,500 shares would have been $13,750 before brokerage commissions. I could have sold out early in 1988 for over $30,000!

Investing is a game of ifs and one of the key ifs is timing. So when an investment goes bad, keep watching it even after you've sold. It may be that your instincts, or those of your broker, were right all along — it was the timing that was off.

3. *Ask yourself if you did your homework.* Most investment decisions are made on the spur of the moment: a broker's call, a newspaper article, a tip at a cocktail party. Often there's no solid reason for the purchase, it just seemed like a good idea at the time.

Sometimes these things pan out. More often they don't.

You should never make an investment decision without knowing why. After all, how can you determine later where your reasoning was right (or wrong) if you didn't do any thinking about the investment in the first place?

Suppose your broker gives you a call and recommends a particular stock. Your immediate reaction, unless you're familiar with the security, should be to ask for more information: a research report, a copy of the latest company annual report, a prospectus. Before you give a buy order for anything, look over the information you receive. Write down at least three good reasons for your purchase decision. Then file them away for future reference. Applying some constructive hindsight to bad investment decisions can be invaluable later.

So far I've only talked about losses. But you should be analyzing your profitable trades too. You want to keep repeating whatever you and your broker did that was right. If every gain is offset by a loss, you aren't going to make much headway.

As with your losses, you should be acutely conscious of the source of winning recommendations. If your scorecard shows your broker doing well over a period of time, you know you're onto something good. Don't let him or her get away, whatever you do.

There are many ways in which brokers can abuse the trust placed in them. Some will "churn" their accounts — encourage clients to make unnecessary trades in order to generate more commissions for themselves. Others will recommend investments they don't understand themselves — the National Association of Investment Dealers heard some admonitions on that score at its 1988 annual convention. Still others may attempt to sell you dubious new stocks at inflated prices because their firm is underwriting the issue.

All of these abuses are grounds for switching your allegiance. But, in the end, much can be forgiven a broker who performs well for you. The bottom line, after all, is a profitable investment account. If your broker delivers that, forget about whether you like his smile or she returns your calls within 10 minutes. Good, profitable advice is hard to find.

The Asset Mix Recipe

All my available funds are completely tied up in ready cash.

— W.C. Fields

OCTOBER 19, 1987, is one of those days I will never forget. I compare it to the Kennedy assassination, or the first lunar landing by Neil Armstrong, or (and here I'm showing my age) the day Franklin D. Roosevelt died. Every detail is etched in my mind: my wife coming into my office to tell me something unusual was happening in the stock markets, sitting in front of the TV and seeing the growing concern on the faces of the announcers and guests on the Financial News Network, watching the numbers roll across the bottom of the screen telling us the Dow was down 200 points, 300 points, an astonishing 400 points, and finally an unbelievable 500+ points.

I recall my son arriving home from school in the midst of this financial carnage and sitting with us in a state of semi-shock (he was just starting an economics course), wondering whether he was witnessing the start of the new Great Depression. Both he and my wife were clearly worried about how the Crash would affect our own investment portfolio and whether it would make any difference in our standard of living. Neither, however, asked the question, perhaps fearful of what they'd hear. Finally I answered it for them: yes, we'd be affected by the Crash; no, I did not anticipate it would be serious.

As it turned out, it wasn't. At the end of that week, I did a re-evaluation of the worth of our total investment portfolio. It turned out to be virtually the same as it had been prior to Black Monday. The total drop was less than 1%.

Why? Because of something called Asset Mix. Prior to the Crash I had substantially reduced the percentage of my total assets that were held in equities. I had built up my cash reserves and maintained my bond holdings at about the same level.

The result was that, although I wasn't entirely out of the market, a much smaller percentage of my holdings was exposed to the effects of the Crash. On the other side of the coin, my bonds suddenly took a jump in value. That was because governments around the world moved immediately to sharply reduce interest rates in an attempt to restore business confidence. The decline in rates meant a big jump in bond prices — enough to virtually offset the losses I had suffered in the market.

I know a lot of people who took a big hit on Black Monday, although most won't admit it. One who does (in fact, he jokes grimly that to hear everyone else talk, it seems he was the only person left in the stock market on Black Monday) is Al Frank, one of America's most colourful investment newsletter writers. He was not only fully invested in the market, he was heavily margined (which means a lot of his stock was paid for with borrowed money). The value of his holdings fell about 60% in the Crash! He's since recovered much of that loss, but the experience was, as you might expect, traumatic.

So what does an investor do to protect a portfolio against such losses? The starting point is something called your Asset Mix. That's simply an investing buzz term for the old proverb about not putting all your eggs in one basket.

There are some investment experts who contend that Asset Mix is the single most important element in the success or failure of any portfolio. If your money is concentrated in the right assets at the right time, you'll win. If it's in the wrong assets, you'll lose.

The classic investment portfolio holds three main types of assets. I'll run through them briefly.

Cash or the equivalent. These are your holdings that are either in actual cash (e.g., deposit accounts) or in securities which can be converted to cash quickly and easily at their full face value. These securities would include such things as Canada Savings Bonds, government Treasury bills, money market mutual funds, and term deposits of under six months.

Fixed-income securities. These are your income-producing assets. Generally, they'll be conservative holdings and will be quite stable in value. Included here are such securities as Guaranteed Investment Certificates, regular bonds (not CSBs), mortgages, mortgage mutual funds, bond mutual funds, mortgage-backed securities and preferred stocks.

Growth securities. These are investments you hold primarily for long-term capital gain. Included here would be common stocks and a wide range of equity mutual funds.

There are other types of assets you can hold, of course — real estate is one that will come immediately to most people's minds. But these aren't usually included in Asset Mix calculations because of their comparative illiquidity — you can't move in and out of real estate as quickly and easily as you can acquire or dispose of stocks and bonds. So for purposes of this discussion, we'll confine ourselves to the three types of assets outlined above: cash, fixed-income, and growth.

The first point to bear in mind is that all three should be represented in your portfolio at any given time. This is called diversification, and it's a time-tested way of reducing your risk. In fact, it's a basic principle of low-risk investing that you never concentrate all your assets in a single area.

Applying that rule saved me from serious losses on Black Monday, as I've explained. But remember the story I told in an earlier chapter about the older woman who had phoned the hotline show I was appearing on two days after the Crash? The one who had everything she owned in the stock market? That's a classic case of failure to diversify. With everything she owned in equities, there were no cash or fixed-income holdings to cushion the shock. As a result, everything she owned went down in value. It's not something you want to happen to you.

Why always hold some of all three types of assets, you may ask. Surely if all the experts are forecasting a drop in the stock market, I should be out of equities entirely.

It sounds logical. It isn't. The reason is that the experts are often (some might say usually) wrong. In fact, some U.S. financial forecasters actually base their view of where the market is going in part on a reverse position to the consensus among investment newsletters in that country. If the majority of letters are bullish, these contrarians will factor in a bearish position. If the newsletter writer are bearish, this is seen as a bullish sign. I know it sounds ridiculous, and it certainly doesn't add to one's confidence level when it comes to investment letters. Yet this is what actually happens.

Consider the aftermath of Black Monday. I attended an investment conference in Fort Lauderdale, Florida, in January 1988, and the prognostications of doom and gloom were everywhere. As a speaker, I'd gone prepared to give the delegates my own dark view of what was coming. But after hearing so much talk about depressions and bank failures and further stock market drops, I lightened up a bit. It's been proven over the years that when the whole world is pessimistic about the future, that's the best time to invest. Hearing all the dire predictions in Fort Lauderdale actually made me a touch more optimistic (although prudently so) about the markets.

Nevertheless, many investors who attended that conference were probably so unnerved that they got out of equities entirely. And what happened? Over the next six months, the markets rebounded significantly. Those who had retired to the sidelines missed out completely on that rally. Those who had retained a portion of their Asset Mix in growth securities benefited.

You can't outguess the markets, and as a low-risk investor you shouldn't try. Your objective should be to place yourself in a position where your capital base will be relatively secure and you'll benefit from growth opportunities as they arise.

That's why you should always hold some of each type of asset in your portfolio. How you mix them will depend on a number of factors. These include your age, your family situation, your investment objectives, and general economic conditions.

Just to give you an example, a single man aged 32 with no dependants would want to hold a larger portion of his assets in growth securities than a married woman of 64 who has been in the workforce all her life and is about to retire. The younger you are, the more you can take advantage of the years ahead of you to maximize your return from growth securities. The closer you get to retirement, the more you will want to shift the emphasis in your Asset Mix to fixed-income securities which offer a higher degree of safety and a revenue source.

Some investment advisors contend that your age is the single most important criterion in determining your Asset Mix. Royal Trust, for example, advises its clients to be guided very closely by age considerations in working out their Asset Mix. Their formula looks like this:

Asset Type	Age			
	20-30	31-49	50-60	60+
Cash or equivalent	15-20%	5-15%	5-10%	15-25%
Fixed-income	35-55%	25-35%	45-60%	50-70%
Growth	20-40%	50-70%	30-50%	15-25%

These numbers are the recommended percentage range of your holdings in your particular age group. So, for example, if you're aged 31 to 49, Royal Trust is suggesting you hold not less than 5% and not more than 15% of your assets in cash, a minimum of 25% and a maximum of 35% in fixed-income securities, and a low of 50% to a high of 70% in growth assets.

Royal Trust's rationale for these ranges goes like this:

In your twenties, your emphasis should be on building a solid investment base. Hence the relatively low proportion of growth assets and the larger recommended holdings in cash and fixed-income securities.

In your thirties and forties, you should emphasize growth. You have plenty of earning years ahead to ride out any ups and downs in the stock market and to take advantage of the long-term upward trend in stocks.

When you reach your fifties, you pull back, reducing your risk and putting greater emphasis on income. And when you pass 60, your strategy becomes one based primarily on safety — you probably don't have a lot of time left to recover if you make a mistake.

These are good general guidelines within which to work. To make them even more applicable to your own situation there are other factors I believe you should also take into account.

Your family situation is one. If you have a number of dependants, you should lean to a more conservative investment approach. The reality is that you are less well-positioned to absorb a setback than a young single person without any major commitments. You don't want to place yourself in a position where severe losses could jeopardize a youngster's chance to attend university, for instance.

General economic conditions are another consideration in determining your Asset Mix. When times are good and the stock market is bullish, as it was from August 1982 to August 1987, you'll want to have a larger proportion of your holdings in growth assets to take advantage of the situation. When times are tougher and the markets are trending down, you'll want to emphasize cash and fixed-income securities.

The brokerage firm of Midland Doherty regards the general economic climate as being the critical element in asset allocation. It therefore takes a different approach from Royal Trust in advising clients how to divide their money.

Midland's research department looks at two key factors: the level of economic activity and the direction of interest rates. They divide each category into three groups, creating a series of cells. Their recommended Asset Mix ends up looking like this:

		INTEREST RATES		
		DECLINING	**STABLE**	**RISING**
E C O N O M I C A C T I V I T Y	**D E C L I N I N G**	**Cell 1** Bonds 55% Stocks 35% Cash 10% 100%	**Cell 4** Bonds 40% Cash 40% Stocks 20% 100%	**Cell 7** Cash 80% Bonds 10% Stocks 10% 100%
	S T A B L E	**Cell 2** Stocks 45% Bonds 40% Cash 15% 100%	**Cell 5** Stocks 55% Cash 30% Bonds 30% 100%	**Cell 8** Cash 60% Stocks 30% Bonds 10% 100%
	R I S I N G	**Cell 3** Stocks 60% Bonds 30% Cash 10% 100%	**Cell 6** Stocks 50% Bonds 25% Cash 25% 100%	**Cell 9** Stocks 40% Cash 35% Bonds 25% 100%

As you can see, this is quite a different approach to the Asset Mix concept. There are several ways of determining the right blend; you have to decide with which one you're most comfortable.

The final factor you must consider is your personal goals. If you're interested in maximizing returns, even at the sake of incurring greater risk, you'll increase the proportion of your growth assets. If you're conservative by nature and regard preservation of capital as your number one priority, you'll concentrate on cash and fixed-income assets.

The true low-risk investor will err on the side of prudence. That means that the percentage of growth assets held at any given time will usually be at the low end of the recommended range. The cash and fixed-income percentages will vary, with cash being dominant during periods of rising interest rates and fixed-income assets dominating when rates are in decline.

For low-risk investors, I recommend the following Asset Mix ranges. I've divided them into two groups, one for when general economic conditions are good, the other for when they're bad or uncertain. You should determine the most suitable position for you by taking into account your age, goals, and family circumstances.

	Good Times	Bad/Uncertain Times
Cash	10%-25%	25%-50%
Fixed-Income	20%-40%	25%-50%
Growth	35%-50%	15%-25%

Many investment advisors will look at these numbers and immediately criticize the growth portion as being too low. Certainly the ranges suggested by Royal Trust and Midland Doherty would allow for a larger percentage of growth assets under certain conditions.

However, I get uncomfortable when I have more than 50% of my holdings in any one asset group. There's too much risk exposure concentrated in one place in the event something should go wrong. So even in the middle of a raging bull market, I wouldn't have more than half my assets in equities. Yes, I'll give up some potential profits as a result. But if the bull comes to a sudden and unexpected end, as on Black Monday, the rest of my portfolio will help absorb the shockwaves.

Maintaining a proper Asset Mix in your portfolio is not easy. It requires a thorough knowledge of your holdings, a regular (say once a month) analysis of the percentage of your holdings in the various groups, and the discipline to buy and sell as required to adjust the balance to your changing needs.

However, once you've established a suitable Asset Mix, maintaining it is usually just a matter of fine tuning. Rarely are you going to be in a position where you have to make massive changes because a major realignment is required. About the only time this is necessary is when there are changes in your personal circumstances (you start a family or cross an age threshold or change your objectives) or when a dramatic shift occurs in the economic climate.

Otherwise, the best way to vary Asset Mix is simply to direct new investments into the area(s) where you feel you're light. If you want to increase the percentage of your cash holdings, use interest and dividend payments generated by other investments to achieve the goal. Your portfolio will be constantly producing income and you may well be adding more capital from time to time. Before you decide where to commit these new funds, take a careful look at the total picture of your holdings. If you're satisfied with the current balance, then distribute any new money equally between the three asset groups. If you're not, then decide which area needs strengthening and find a good investment that will do that for you.

In my experience, the Asset Mix concept is one of the simplest investing approaches around once you get the hang of it. Yet many people have never heard of it or, if they have, fail to practice it.

For a successful low-risk investor, this is an essential, and easy, starting point. Selecting the right assets to hold within a particular group is less simple. But it's not as hard as it's often made out to be either. I'll deal with securities selection later. But first, I want to look at the tax implications of an investment portfolio because it's another critical element to take into account in your initial planning. That's what the next chapter is all about.

Sheared, Not Skinned

Kings and governments ought to shear, not skin, their sheep.

— Robert Herrick

ANY WAY YOU look at it, Canada is a highly taxed country. Every year, Vancouver's Fraser Institute calculates what it calls Tax Freedom Day — the day on which all your taxes to various levels of government are paid off and you can keep the rest of your income for yourself. The actual date varies, depending on what province you live in, but for most of us, it falls in early July. That means you spend more than half the year just earning enough money to pay your tax bills!

Yet we accept this state of affairs without a murmur. Governments pile the taxes higher and higher and we docilely acquiesce. Unlike the Americans, who periodically become extremely agitated over taxes (after all, the American Revolution was launched on the battle cry: "No taxation without representation"), we go along with whatever our governments propose. To my knowledge, there has never been a successful, broadly based anti-taxation movement in this country. Special interest groups have been immensely successful in persuading governments to *spend* money on them. But no one has formed a powerful lobby group to convince governments to significantly *reduce* the tax burden. Since, collectively, we don't seem to care if governments raise taxes ever higher (or, if we do, we can't manage to do anything more than grumble ineffectively), we're in the sad position of being skinned, not shorn.

Nor is that situation likely to change. The best chance we had at reducing the level of government spending, and, as a result, our tax burden, was the 1984 election of the Conservative government of Brian Mulroney. All the ingredients were there: an overwhelming majority in the Commons, a party philosophically committed to less government, a capable Finance Minister in Michael Wilson, and four years to do the job. You know what happened: the government lost its nerve early on, mainly because of protests that arose when it announced plans to partially deindex Old Age Security payments. That set the pattern; rather than attempt to deal with the horrendously high cost of universality in our social security system, the government turned its back on the issue entirely. And without the big spending cuts that would have been achieved by taking a figurative meat cleaver to these bloated programs, all hope of reducing the tax burden was lost.

In fact, the Tories managed to find ways to make it much worse, through new massive spending programs (including billions spent or committed to such diverse but equally questionable programs as day care and nuclear-powered submarines) and an ever-increasing national debt which costs billions more to service each year. The so-called tax reform program implemented in 1988 was merely an attempt at political sleight of hand, an effort to draw voters' attention away from the Conservatives' dismal record on taxation during the 1984-88 period.

Since neither of the other major federal political parties has any tax-reduction program (quite the contrary, they're potentially even worse spenders than the Tories), the harsh fact of life for investors is that the high-tax regime in this country is going to continue for the foreseeable future. That means you must organize your investment portfolio in such a way as to minimize the tax burden on it.

To do that, you must first adopt a specific mindset: *The only profit that matters is your after-tax return.* Every investment you make must be looked at in this context. The nominal return doesn't matter a hoot; the only thing that counts is what's left in your pocket after Revenue Canada finishes with you. That's why I'd much rather have a security that produces a 10% capital gain than one that yields 15% interest. In the end, I get to keep more.

I wish I could tell you that it's easy to construct a portfolio that keeps the tax burden to a minimum. Unfortunately, that's generally not the case. There are so many variables to take into account that you have to plan very carefully. Even your income level will play a role in determining what you should emphasize when you invest.

There are three types of investment income, all treated differently by the government. They are:

Interest. Interest income from bonds, GICs, CSBs, deposit accounts, Treasury bills, mortgages or other interest-bearing investments is by far the most common source of investment income. Predictably, it's also the most heavily taxed. You'll pay at your marginal tax rate. So if you're in the middle income-tax bracket ($27,500 to $55,000 taxable income) any interest you earn will be taxed in the 40% range, with the exact percentage depending on your province of residence. And you pay that tax from the first dollar earned; the old $1,000 investment income deduction, which sheltered a nice chunk of your investment earnings, was swept away in the tax reform program.

Dividends. These are payments made to holders of common or preferred shares of corporations. Dividends used to be an excellent way to receive investment income, offering attractive tax incentives to investors. They're still good, and for investors who have used up their capital gains exemption they remain the most tax-effective way to receive income. But tax reform reduced their appeal considerably.

Capital gains. One favour the Tories did for investors was to announce a lifetime $500,000 capital gains exemption for every individual, to encourage more investment and risk-taking in this country. But they then decided that was too rich and partially reneged on their promise in the tax reform package by reducing the exemption to $100,000 and hedging it with all sorts of conditions. The capital gains exemption is still a useful tool for investors — but it's nowhere near as lucrative as originally proposed.

You may have gathered from the foregoing that tax reform hasn't been such a hot deal for investors. You're right — in fact, it was a disaster. The federal government's rationale was that the quid pro quo for stripping away some of the incentives investors had enjoyed was a general lowering of tax rates. But that's turned out to be more smoke and mirrors — the top rates may be lower but they cut in sooner. And more income is now subject to tax because of a variety of lost deductions. To cap it off, the provinces have moved quickly to fill at least part of the tax gap created by the federal government. The net effect has been to make investing in Canada much less attractive than it was before the whole process began. Any investor who's looked closely at the entire package wishes the Tories had left well enough alone.

Still, until someone changes it we either have to live with the system or move to some offshore tax haven. If packing up and moving to a sand-spit in the Caribbean isn't your thing, then as a low-risk investor you'll want to organize your affairs in such a way as to pay the least possible tax on your earnings.

The simplest situation is a completely tax-sheltered investment port-folio, such as within an RRSP. You don't have to worry about the tax consequences (at least not the short-term ones) of most investment deci-sions you make. Your income within the plan is generally received tax-free, so it doesn't matter whether it comes in the form of interest, divi-dends or capital gains.

(One exception is dividends received from some foreign stocks, such as U.S. issues, which are subject to a 15% withholding tax at source. That's money you'll never recover because of a quirk in the tax laws.)

You *do* have to think about the tax consequences of your RRSP earn-ings down the road, though (I told you nothing was simple here). When you withdraw funds from a plan, that money immediately becomes subject to tax. Part of those funds will represent your earnings over the years in interest, dividends and capital gains. When the money comes out, Revenue Canada will make no attempt to distinguish the original source. That means that any income you earned from dividends and capital gains within your RRSP will receive no special treatment; it will simply be taxed at your marginal rate. You lose the tax benefits you would have enjoyed had the money been received outside the RRSP. That's why many tax advisors tell you to hold only interest-bearing investments within an RRSP and those earning dividends and/or capital gains outside the plan. That's a nice theory. But I have three problems with it.

First, it's not always possible to separate interest-bearing securities from those generating dividends and capital gains. Bonds are an excel-lent example; although they're thought of primarily as interest-bearing investments, they can also produce substantial capital gains during periods of falling interest rates.

My second objection is based on financial reality. Many people simply don't have adequate funds to maintain large separate investment portfolios both inside and outside an RRSP. For years, the only portfolio I had was within an RRSP because the total value of any new investment money I was able to generate each year was just about enough to make my RRSP contribution. If I had confined myself to interest-bearing securities within my plans, I would have missed out on some great profit opportunities.

Which brings me to the third point. I believe that an RRSP, like any other investment portfolio, should be managed with the objective of maximizing profit. That means having a good Asset Mix and holding those securities which will produce the best return — regardless of what they are.

So my advice is to manage your RRSP without undue concern for the tax consequences that are years away. The plain fact is, the benefits you gain from tax-free compounding within the plan will more than offset the loss of any tax breaks.

A non-tax sheltered investment portfolio is quite a different matter, however. Here you need to be constantly aware of the tax treatment of the various forms of income you receive. As a starting point, take a look at the following table. It shows you how various types of investment income were treated in 1988, under the tax reform program. I've assumed a provincial tax rate of 50% of the federal rate in all cases. The capital gains rate applies only to income not sheltered under the lifetime $100,000 capital gains exemption.

Taxable Income	Federal/Provincial Tax Rate		
	Interest	Dividends	Capital Gains
Under $27,500	25.5%	6.87%	17%
$27,501-$55,000	39.0%	23.75%	26%
Over $55,000	43.5%	29.37%	29%

In 1990, the effective rates on capital gains will increase to 19.13%, 29.25% and 32.63%.

Study this little table carefully. It contains a goldmine of information about how to set up your investment portfolio in such a way as to reduce the tax bite.

Let's look at the three income groups, and see how the strategies will differ.

Taxable income under $27,500. Your strategy is clear, although perhaps somewhat surprising. Go for dividends. Minimize the interest you receive. Don't even be overly concerned about capital gains at this stage — save the use of your lifetime exemption for the time when you're in a higher tax bracket and it will be worth more to you. The plain fact is that the net tax on dividends is so low (under 7%) as to be virtually negligible. The investment income you earn from this source is almost tax-free.

Just to give you an example of the impact this quirky tax treatment produces, suppose you invested $10,000 in a guaranteed investment certificate paying 12%. Your $1,200 annual income would be subject to tax at a rate of 25.5%. That means your after-tax return would be $894.

Now suppose instead that you put that $10,000 into preferred shares paying 9.75%. Your before-tax return is much less — $975 compared to $1,200 from the GIC. But your after-tax return is actually better — $907.72 compared to $894 from the GIC. Even though you've given up more than two percentage points in yield, you've come out ahead when the tax consequences are factored in.

You'll have to do your own tax calculations to see whether the difference between interest rate yields and preferred share dividends at the time you make your investment makes the shares the better bet for the fixed-income portion of your Asset Mix. Generally, if interest-bearing securities are paying 3% or more above the yields on preferreds, the tax advantage will be wiped out. So make use of your calculator. And be sure to use the actual tax rates which apply in your province when you do your figuring.

Taxable income between $27,501 and $55,000. At this stage you must start to look more closely at capital gains, assuming you can shelter them under the $100,000 lifetime exemption. Since we're talking zero tax payable in that situation, capital gains now become your preferred source of investment income.

As far as dividends and interest are concerned, you remain slightly better off with dividends, if the spread in favour of the interest-bearing security is not more than about 2-1/4%. A $10,000 investment in a GIC paying 12% will leave you with $732 after tax ($1,200 x 39% = $468 tax). A preferred stock with a 9.75% dividend will leave you with $743.44.

Taxable income over $55,000. Capital gains should clearly be your number one priority, and both your growth and fixed-income assets should be chosen so as to maximize the potential for such gains. That means emphasizing bonds or bond mutual funds over GICs and mortgages in the selection of your fixed-income assets, because of the gains potential from bonds when interest rates drop. In the choice of stocks, don't lose sight of quality. But there are some quality issues with greater capital gains potential than others, as we'll see in a later chapter. There's $100,000 in tax-free money to be earned here, so you should make every possible effort to take advantage of it, especially since, given the fickleness of politicians and the reality of Tax Risk, it may not be around forever.

Surprisingly, interest income becomes slightly more attractive in this bracket, even with a 43.5% tax rate applied. That's because the spread between the tax rate on dividends (29.37% at this level) and interest is actually slightly reduced. The $10,000 GIC I've been using as an example now yields $678 after tax. The 9.75% preferred share yields $685.72.

Before I end this chapter, a word about tax shelters.

The true low-risk investor will stay clear of tax shelter deals. That's because, by definition, tax shelters are generally high-risk ventures. The government wouldn't be offering a tax incentive to put your money into mineral exploration, the oil and gas industry, films or whatever if these ventures were attractive enough to raise sufficient capital without such artificial supports.

That being said, the fact is I have personally had excellent returns from the tax shelters I have invested in. I referred in Chapter One to the phenomenal after-tax profit I made from Western Pulp Limited Partnership. Since then I have also had very good returns from some flow-through share investments and a seismic data venture into which I put a small amount of money. Furthermore, I have never yet lost money on a tax shelter deal — something I can't say about most other types of investments I've made. So my admonition about avoiding tax shelters is tempered by the fact that I've done all right with them. Many people haven't, however — I've heard several stories about tax shelter investments that went sour. Many of the early tax shelter movies, for instance, lost substantial sums for their backers.

Even more important, however, is the fact that changes to the income tax regulations have made tax shelters much less attractive now than they used to be. The more exotic shelters — yachts, houseboats, recreational vehicles and the like — were dealt a severe blow in 1985 when Finance Minister Michael Wilson decreed that Capital Cost Allowance (CCA) incurred by participating in these shelters could no longer be used to write off income from other sources. In practice, that meant investors couldn't use depreciation on their yachts or other items to reduce the tax payable on their regular incomes. Since many tax shelters had been structured to produce exactly that result, a great deal of scrambling ensued among the shelter promoters. You can still find deals for yachts and RVs around, but they're nowhere near as attractive as they once were.

The same is true of flow-through shares. For a brief, heady period, which ended with the onset of tax reform, these tax shelters were almost sure-fire money makers. They not only delivered substantial tax deductions; many of them also turned out to be extremely profitable as investments, sometimes with after-tax returns of well over 100% in a year.

The concept of flow-through shares is quite simple: companies in the mining or oil and gas industry carry out exploration and development work, within the areas defined by the federal government. The tax write-offs created by these expenditures are then passed on (or flowed through) to the investors who put up the money in the first place. They are permitted to write off these tax savings against income from any source.

What made flow-throughs so popular was syndication. Large financial groups such as CMP were formed to use investor money to purchase flow-through shares in a variety of companies — in effect creating a flow-through mutual fund. These funds took in hundreds of millions of dollars in tax-sheltered cash during the mid-1980s. The combination of generous tax write-offs (Quebec residents could claim up to 166-2/3% of their investment in some cases; other Canadians 133-1/3%) and the booming stock markets that buoyed the value of the flow-through issues created big profits for lucky investors.

For example, an analysis was done by the brokerage firm of Mac-Dougall, MacDougall and MacTier in mid-1988 of the performance of various flow-through share issues. It showed that investors who had put money into CMP, one of the biggest and most popular of the flow-through syndicators, did remarkably well during the 1984-87 period. By the middle of 1988, those who had purchased the 1984 offering and had left their holdings in the fund had a 150% return on their original after-tax investment. Those who bought the 1985 issues were 232% ahead. The 1986 issue was up by 142%, the 1987 resource issue by 44%, the 1987 oil and gas issue by 56%, the first 1988 issue by 53% and the second 1988 issue by 70%. No wonder investors liked CMP!

The stock market crash of October 1987 and tax reform took some of the bloom off this particular rose, however. In fact, flow-throughs were almost wiped out by the tax reform program; it was only some after-the-fact adjustments by Mr. Wilson in the face of strong pressure from the mining industry that saved them from extinction.

Even with these improvements, the new-look flow-throughs are a pale imitation of the pre-tax reform version. If you are contemplating putting some money in them, keep the following points in mind:

Your capital gains exemption will be eroded. Revenue Canada says that, for tax purposes, the purchase price of any flow-through share (technically referred to as the adjusted cost base) is zero. That means that when it comes time to sell your holdings, the entire sale price will be deemed to be a capital gain. With a lifetime exception of only $100,000, it won't take too many flow-through investments to eat it all up.

Some of your flow-through profits may not be eligible for the capital gains exemption. As part of tax reform, the government introduced a dreadful concept known as Cumulative Net Investment Loss, or CNIL. I'll explain how it works in detail in the next chapter. For now, it's enough to point out that the impact of CNIL may well mean you'll have to pay income tax at the capital gains rate on part of the proceeds when you sell your flow-through units.

Your money will be locked in for a time. There are legal restrictions on the resale of flow-through units which mean that you won't be able to get your money out for at least a year. If you think you might need the funds before then, you shouldn't be considering this type of investment.

Flow-throughs only work if all the money you're sheltering is in the top bracket. All the financial calculations in the prospectus (which contains all the details of the offer and should be read carefully) are based on the assumption that every cent you shelter in this way would be subject to tax at the highest applicable rate in your province. That means you must have taxable, not total, income well in excess of $55,000 to take advantage of these deals. If all or any part of your sheltered income does not fall within the top bracket, you will end up having a lower tax write-off than is shown in the prospectus and, consequently, more of your own money at risk.

Your province of residence will have an influence on your decision. Flow-through shares (or any tax shelter) become more attractive the higher your tax rate. In 1988, that meant that residents of Quebec, Manitoba and Saskatchewan stood to do best tax-wise from such shelters (and, therefore, have the smallest amount of their personal funds at risk). The units were least attractive to residents of Ontario, British Columbia and Alberta.

If you've used up your lifetime capital gains exemption, your risk is considerable. In fact, I'd go so far as to say that if you don't have any capital gains exemption left, you should forget flow-throughs entirely. The risk level is just too great.

There are other types of tax shelters being marketed. I'm constantly bombarded with solicitations to purchase units in everything from containers (the kind used to carry cargo on ships) to townhouses. Generally, I suggest you be wary of such deals. If you *must* have a tax shelter, start by making your maximum RRSP contribution. If there's room left after that, look at the deal you're being offered extremely carefully. Note some of the warnings about flow-throughs and see if they apply in the case of the particular venture you're contemplating. Also check on:

The percentage of "soft costs". This is the amount of your investment that goes towards such things as commissions, administration fees and the like. They're deductible immediately, which is why many tax shelter deals are based on unusually high soft costs. The problem is that these payments on your part are usually going into someone else's pocket, not towards the direct purchase of an asset. So watch out for them. If they're in excess of 20% of the total amount, they're too high, both for you and, probably, for Revenue Canada.

Cash flow projections. Every prospectus should provide detailed information about how much money the investment is expected to return over the years. Study these very closely. See what assumptions have been used in arriving at the projections. If the forecasts seem unrealistic, they probably are — many tax shelters are sold on the basis of income and profit projections that never materialize.

Personal use. Some tax shelters offer attractive sweeteners to make up for mediocre profit projections. Often these relate to some personal benefit that will accrue to you as a participant. Promoters of shelters based on yachts or recreational vehicles, for instance, sometimes tell prospective buyers they'll be able to use the boat or RV themselves for a certain amount of time each year. The problem is that Revenue Canada takes a dim view of this practice, especially if personal use seems extensive. If you are attracted by such bonuses, don't plan on using your live-in tax shelter for more than two weeks a year at peak times. And keep careful records of your personal use in case you're questioned by the tax people.

The fact is that most tax shelter deals of this kind are borderline in their acceptability. Study them carefully and chances are you'll decide to put your money elsewhere.

Investing with Borrowed Money

Getting into debt is getting into a tanglesome net.
— Benjamin Franklin

F OR THE TRUE low-risk investor, this is a very short chapter. I can sum it up in a single phrase: never borrow to invest. That's it. Skip to Chapter Eleven.

You're still here? Then either you don't yet consider yourself a genuine low-risk investor or you suspect there may be more to this borrowing business than a simple admonition to avoid it.

Well, you're right. In fact, I confess to being somewhat ambivalent on this whole question of investing with other people's money. There is absolutely no doubt that wise use of borrowed funds can tremendously enhance the profit potential of your investments. It is equally true, however, that such practices greatly increase your risk exposure.

Certain types of investment borrowing are essential for most of us. I put mortgages into that category. Very few people can afford to pay cash for a home, so a mortgage is a necessary stage most of us must pass through on the way to greater wealth.

At this point, your mortgage stage is presumably behind you, or nearly so. The question you have to deal with now is whether you should borrow money to build your investment portfolio more quickly.

Many people dramatically increased their net worth in this way during the great bull market of 1982-87. Let me explain how.

Let's suppose that you allocated $25,000 of your total assets during that time for the purchase of a portfolio of top-quality equity mutual funds. This represented one-third of your total investment portfolio, which was worth $75,000.

You spread this money over four mutual funds, which collectively increased in unit value by 18% during the first year (this was quite attainable during the bull market). You also collected dividends totalling 3% of your original investment. Let's see where you stood after one year.

Original investment	$25,000
Market value after one year	29,500
Dividends received	750
One-year profit	5,250
Return on investment	21%

Now let's suppose that you'd decided to be more aggressive. You went to a financial institution and asked them to match the money you were putting into equities. The $25,000 loan (for which you paid 12% interest) brought your mutual fund investment to $50,000, or 50% of your total portfolio (which now totals $100,000 — your original $75,000 plus the loan money). You also got a tax break, because you were able to deduct the interest paid on the loan. We'll assume you were in a 50% tax bracket. Here's how it would have worked out:

Your original investment	$25,000
Borrowed money invested	25,000
Total investment	50,000
Market value after one year	59,000
Dividends received	1,500
One-year gross profit	10,500
After-tax cost of loan interest	1,500
One-year net profit	9,000
Return on your original investment	36%

As you can see, by borrowing to double your mutual fund holdings, you increased the return on your original $25,000 from 21% to 36%.

That's a pretty strong argument for using leverage (the technical term for borrowing to invest).

Now let me show you the other side of this coin. Let's suppose you decided to make this move in 1987 and were holding the equity funds when the market crashed on October 19. Let's also assume your funds held up reasonably well, and the total loss for the full year was only 5%. First, here's what would have happened if you hadn't borrowed any money:

Original investment	$25,000
Market value after one year	23,750
Dividends received	750
One-year loss	500
Return on investment	-2%

You lost money, but the amount was minimal — your dividends partially offset the drop in the unit value of your funds. Now let's see what would have happened if you'd borrowed the additional $25,000.

Your original investment	$25,000
Borrowed money invested	25,000
Total investment	50,000
Market value after one year	47,500
Dividends received	1,500
One-year investment loss	1,000
After-tax cost of loan interest	1,500
Net loss	2,500
Return on your original investment	-10%

See what's happened? The borrowed funds have magnified your losses considerably. Instead of the modest $500 loss you would have incurred if you hadn't borrowed, you're now out of pocket $2,500. The percentage of your original capital lost has jumped from 2% to 10%.

That's the two-edged sword of investment borrowing. It's great when you win. It's hell when you don't. Now you understand why I said at the outset of this chapter that the true low-risk investor won't go into debt to build a portfolio. The dangers are too great.

That's not the whole story, however. When I selected the Benjamin Franklin quote as the theme of this chapter, I did so with tax reform in mind. Our new tax system has certainly made borrowing to invest a tanglesome net.

In Chapter Nine I made reference to the Cumulative Net Investment Loss (CNIL) and said I would explain it in more detail at this point. Well, here goes. Hold on tight, because this is bureaucracy at its worst.

Each individual investor has his or her own CNIL account. Technically, this is defined by the government as "the amount by which the aggregate of (a taxpayer's) investment expense for years ending after 1987 exceeds the aggregate of his investment income for years ending after 1987".

In other words, your CNIL account is a lifetime thing. Think of it as a perpetual credit card statement. Every investment expense or loss adds to your total bill. Every dividend, interest or rent cheque you receive constitutes a credit.

What makes this relevant in deciding whether to borrow to invest is the fact that interest charges on your investment loans are considered to be expenses for purposes of CNIL and are therefore added to your account. As the government put it in the December 1987 Notice of Ways and Means motion tabled in the House of Commons:

> A taxpayer's investment expense for a taxation year (shall) be defined to include the following items that are deducted in computing his income for the year:
> - deductions, including interest, with respect to property acquired for the purpose of earning interest, dividends, rent or other income from property . . . ,
> - carrying charges, including interest, with respect to an interest in, or a contribution to, a partnership or co-ownership arrangement where the taxpayer is not actively engaged on a regular and continuous basis in its business, or a limited partnership,
> - the taxpayer's share of a loss of any co-ownership arrangement or partnership referred to above,
> - 50% of the taxpayer's share of Canadian exploration and certain other resource expenditures that are attributed to a resource flow-through share or were incurred by a partnership or co-ownership arrangement where the taxpayer is not

actively engaged on a regular and continuous basis in its business or by a limited partnership, and

- any loss from the renting or leasing of a real property owned by the taxpayer or a partnership, not otherwise included on his investment expense.

I've bored you with this whole long recital to show you just how all-encompassing the CNIL concept is. Any deductions you make relating to your investments or any investment losses you incur are going to get caught in this net somewhere.

What's the significance of it? If your CNIL account is in the red — that is, the aggregate of all your expenses and losses exceeds the aggregate of your investment income — then you start to lose access to your lifetime $100,000 capital gains exemption. Let's go back to the examples of investment borrowing I used earlier in this chapter to see how this works in practice.

In the first case, we assumed a capital gain of $9,000 on a $50,000 mutual fund investment, half of which was financed by borrowed money. Under the pre-CNIL rules, all of that gain could have been tax sheltered by using part of your lifetime capital gains exemption. With CNIL in play, it's a different story.

Let's look at this specific investment in isolation and assume for the sake of simplicity that this is Year One of your CNIL account. You borrowed $25,000 to finance half of the investment. Loan interest cost you $3,000. Partially offsetting that was dividend income of $1,500. So your CNIL account looks like this:

	Debits	Credits	Total
Dividend income		$1,500	
Interest cost deducted	$3,000		
Aggregate			($1,500)

This means you have to use $1,500 worth of your capital gains to bring your CNIL account balance to zero. So instead of a $9,000 tax-free profit, only $7,500 can be sheltered under your capital gains exemption. The other $1,500 is subject to capital gains tax. Two-thirds of that amount is actually taxable. If you're in the top bracket, your marginal rate for capital gains is about 29%, so you owe Revenue Canada $435. CNIL has struck!

Now let's look at what happens when a leveraged investment loses money. Going back to our example, the capital loss incurred on the $50,000 investment made just before the stock market crash was $2,500. If you had sold your mutual funds at that point, that loss would have been "recognized" for tax purposes. (You can't have a tax loss until you sell or otherwise dispose of the property.) If you had some capital gains that year, you could write off that $2,500 against those gains. You can also go back three years or carry forward the $2,500 loss until you can use it sometime in the future. You cannot deduct the loss from other income.

Because of these restrictions, this type of capital loss won't affect your CNIL. But certain losses will have an impact — reread the Notice of Ways and Means motion to see which ones.

So in this example, your CNIL account will still be in the red by $1,500 at the end of the year, even with the capital loss. The difference is that you don't have any gain against which to apply that negative CNIL balance, so it carries forward. Obviously, a few more years like this, with the CNIL account continuing to accumulate on the minus side, will make it pretty difficult to make use of the $100,000 capital gains exemption.

With CNIL coming into play, getting into debt to invest really is a "tanglesome net".

If, despite all these warnings, you still want to borrow to finance your investment portfolio, you should look for the least expensive way to do it. If you've paid off most or all of your mortgage, you probably won't find any cheaper source of money than a home equity loan. These are now available through a number of banks, trust companies and credit unions. Typically, they allow you to borrow up to 75% of the value of the equity in your home, although 66-2/3% is more common. The interest rate you're charged is usually prime or slightly higher. In most cases, you can repay the loan at your own pace, as long as you pay at least the monthly interest charge.

The difference between a home equity line of credit and remortgaging your home is the flexibility involved. A line of credit simply gives you the right to borrow up to a certain amount. You can use as much or as little of that borrowing power as you wish, and you pay interest only on the actual loan.

The flexible repayment schedule means you can reduce your loan balance at a pace that suits you. You're not locked into a fixed monthly payment as you are with a regular mortgage.

The only real drawback to these lines of credit are the set-up charges. Since your house is the collateral, you have to place a new mortgage on it. That will set you back between $500 and $1,000, depending on the legal fees involved.

If the idea of putting a new mortgage on your home doesn't appeal to you, even if it is just for purposes of setting up a line of credit (and some people find this psychologically difficult to do, having worked for years to pay off the mortgage), then talk to your broker about setting up a margin account. It's relatively simple and there are no up-front costs. However, you'll pay a higher rate of interest — prime plus 1-1/2% to 2% is typical.

Finally, to minimize the risk of investing with borrowed money, follow these rules:

1. Borrow when the markets appear to be close to or at a cyclical bottom, or in the initial stages of an uptrend. Don't borrow when the markets have had a long upward run and you're starting to hear speculation about an impending correction.

2. Borrow only when the potential gain justifies the risk.

3. Don't pay more interest on your loan than you absolutely have to.

4. Never borrow if you'd be jeopardizing your financial stability in the event things don't work out as you'd planned.

5. If possible, try to generate enough investment income to offset your deductible borrowing costs so you don't start accumulating a large CNIL account.

There's no doubt that you can enhance the return on your investments through the intelligent use of other people's money. And in certain circumstances, it may make sense. Nevertheless, there are major risks and tax complications involved. As I said at the outset, if you're a true low-risk investor, you'll probably decide this is a route you don't want to follow.

Getting Started

What's past is prologue.

— Vincent Massey

THAT'S IT FOR the basics. Now it's time to get started on building a low-risk investment portfolio.

Before we do, though, I would ask one thing: if you've had any bad investment experiences in the past, put them out of your mind. Start fresh. If you learned anything from your previous ventures, that's fine, but don't let them intimidate you in any way. You've got a clean balance sheet.

Okay, let's go. Start by applying the principles I outlined in the previous chapters. Here's a step-by-step approach.

STEP ONE: *Assess the economic climate.*
Before you put any money into an investment, take the time to make sure you really understand what's happening to the economy at this moment. You don't have to transform yourself into a financial expert, but a basic knowledge of the trends that are currently in place will greatly increase your chances of getting off on the right foot. Look especially at the following:

The interest rate trend. This is one of the key elements in determining where you should put your initial investment emphasis. It's important to understand that it is not the actual level of interest rates that's critical — it's the direction in which they're moving.

If interest rates are heading up, you should be very cautious about committing a large portion of your funds to fixed-income securities, such as bonds. The market value of these securities will decline as rates rise, and the last thing you want is to start your portfolio with an immediate capital loss.

You should also be cautious about stocks when interest rates are in an uptrend. Often, although not always, a rising interest rate scenario is a tip-off that the people who run the central banks are concerned about the economy overheating and the prospect of growing inflation. That was the case during the spring and summer of 1988, when virtually every country in the western world moved interest rates higher. The usual outcome of this interest rate tightening is an eventual slowdown in economic growth. That's bad news for the stock market, which thrives on prospects for greater sales and higher profits. It's not a situation in which you want to be committing large amounts of money to equities.

One word of caution here, though. On occasion, the Bank of Canada will jack up interest rates in an effort to defend the Canadian dollar, which is coming under one of its periodic attacks on world currency markets. In those situations, the economy may be perfectly healthy and stocks may be an excellent investment. That's why it's important to look beyond our borders to see what's happening to interest rates in other countries. If they're moving up in the U.S. and the U.K. as well, then you'll know you're not just witnessing an aberration brought on by a weakened buck.

An international rising interest rate picture should tell you to be very cautious about where you put your money. High-yielding short-term notes, such as Treasury bills or bankers' acceptances (a form of short-term financing used by chartered banks) are good alternatives. So are money market mutual funds.

A stable interest rate pattern tells you that the economy is in pretty good balance. Growth is at a level with which the politicians and bankers feel comfortable. There are no perceived disasters on the immediate horizon; everything seems to be ticking along nicely.

If that's the situation when you're starting your low-risk portfolio, it's a positive sign. It suggests you should commit less of your money to cash-type investments and more to bonds and stocks. Whether you decide to emphasize stocks or bonds will depend on several other factors. Generally, though, the higher interest rates are in relation to the inflation rate, the more I tend to favour bonds.

And what if the interest rate trend is clearly down as you read this? That often suggests we're in an economic slowdown, or just beginning to climb out of one. Governments are moving to reduce rates in an effort to restore business and consumer confidence and to get the economy moving again.

For the low-risk investor, this is frequently a time of exceptional opportunity. If the slowdown has been serious, perhaps producing a recession, there will be a great deal of pessimism around. You may hear talk of hard times lasting for several years. Fear will be the dominant emotion among investors. Scare stories will predominate.

All of this doom and gloom will encourage people to stay out of the stock market and hide their money under the mattress. That means a smart investor will be able to find genuine bargains, especially in stocks, gold, and real estate.

A declining interest rate picture will tell you to give careful consideration to significantly increasing the proportion of stocks in your portfolio. Bonds also can be attractive, depending on how long the down trend has continued. If it's just starting, you'll make some nice capital gains by purchasing bonds now and selling when rates drop lower. On the other hand, if the downward trend has been in place for some time, it may be close to bottoming out. In that situation, bonds are not a good choice. Cash should be kept to a minimum if interest rates are moving down, because you'll receive less interest with every downtick. And you have no prospect of any capital gains.

I believe that the interest rate trend is your single most important economic indicator as you prepare to make your investment decisions, but you may want to look at a few other things as well.

The stock market trend. The direction in which the market is moving and how long it has been going that way is an important factor in deciding what proportion of your funds to commit to equities. There are bull (up) and bear (down) markets, and you should be aware of which phase we're in right now. You should also know that bull markets generally last much longer than bear markets — the last big bull ran for five years to the month, from August 1982 to August 1987.

If we're in a bull market and it has been running for some time, it's a signal to be cautious. Be doubly so if everyone around you is talking about how much money they've made. The higher the level of optimism, the greater the likelihood that a bear market is just around the corner.

On the other hand, if the market is in a bear phase, pay attention — especially if it's been wallowing for a year or more. At that point, most small investors have fled, brokers are opening bookstores to occupy their increasing spare time, and prices are gradually sinking lower. There's a philosophy known as Value Investing that thrives on these situations. It's the investment equivalent of rag-picking on garbage dumps, but it works. It amounts to seeking out companies whose stock is greatly undervalued and buying as many shares as possible. The deeper the bear market, the more value investing opportunities there are. So a down market may not be bad news at all. It may offer an excellent opportunity to add to the growth component of your portfolio at bargain-basement prices.

(Incidentally, if you want to learn more about this investing approach, the classic book on the subject is *The Intelligent Investor* by Benjamin Graham. It was first published in 1950 and has been revised and updated several times since.)

The inflation rate. The other economic factor you should take into account is the inflation rate and the direction in which it is moving. It's often an excellent tip-off to the investment climate down the road, as I explained in Chapter Four.

A declining inflation rate, such as we saw from 1982 to 1987, is considered healthy. Disinflation suggests that interest rates will likely drop, that wage increases will be moderate, that the rate of increase in business costs will slow, and that the economy generally will be solid.

If disinflation tips into deflation, however, that's bad. As I pointed out in Chapter Four, we haven't seen any generalized deflation since the 1930s. But we have experienced what's called *sector deflation* — a sharp drop in prices in a particular segment of the economy. One recent example was the decline in oil prices in the 1980s. The failure of the OPEC cartel to maintain its production quotas created a world oil glut. As a result, prices, which had at one time been over US$30 a barrel, dropped to the low teens. That meant a slowdown in exploration and development activity, an indefinite postponement of many oil-related mega-projects and, most important to investors, pressure on oil company profits, which kept stock prices at relatively low levels.

A generalized deflation, such as occurred in the 1930s, creates a similar impact throughout the economy. But even that situation can create opportunities for the smart investor.

A rising inflation rate, of course, produces an entirely different set of circumstances to consider, as I also explained in Chapter Four.

Once you're satisfied you know enough about the current economic climate, there are a few other steps to go through before you start putting your money on the line.

STEP TWO: *Determine your objectives.*

Never begin an investment program without knowing clearly in your own mind exactly what you intend to achieve. Without a firm goal in view, you'll inevitably founder.

To set your objectives, you must determine the relative importance to you of three elements: safety, income and growth. As a low-risk investor, obviously you will rank safety high on your priority scale. The relative emphasis you place on income and growth will be determined by your personal situation. Generally, the younger you are, the more important growth should be to you. The income element usually becomes of major importance as you approach or attain retirement age and want to use your investments to supplement your cash flow.

STEP THREE: *Determine your initial Asset Mix.*

Using the information in Chapter Eight, your personal objectives and your reading of the economy, decide on your initial Asset Mix. If you're unsure, tend towards the conservative. You can become more aggressive later if you wish.

STEP FOUR: *Do your tax planning.*

Take another look at Chapter Nine. Make sure that your investment plans will allow you to benefit as much as possible from the tax breaks available. Be shorn, not skinned.

STEP FIVE: *Make sure you're comfortable with your advisors.*
If you have a broker, don't put your money into the first thing he or she suggests. Wait. Monitor the recommendations, see how well they perform. Decide whether you're comfortable with the types of investments being recommended. See how closely they conform to your personal goals. I've dealt with brokers who have nodded sagely as I explained my objectives and then phoned the next day with a stock tip that was so far off the mark I couldn't believe it. Make sure the advice you're getting is in line with what you want to do. If it isn't, now's the time to switch. It's essential to get off to a good start in investing. It builds your confidence and encourages you to go forward. If your initial investments lose money, you'll tend to doubt yourself and to become tentative and uncertain. So do yourself a favour and make sure you're truly prepared before plunging in.

When you're confident you're ready, begin gradually. Don't feel you have to invest all your money at once. Start with cash holdings that give you the best possible return and move your money out into other areas gradually. This will give you an opportunity to get a better feel for what you're doing. If the whole process takes six months, don't be concerned. You're embarking on a course that will probably last the rest of your life. Consider this first phase the warm-up.

Now let's look at some basic investment strategies.

You've probably already heard a lot about a buy-and-hold approach versus a trading approach. It's one of the basic decisions you're going to have to make in managing your portfolio: are you going to trade actively or sit on your securities come hell or high water?

Almost every investment book you'll read will encourage small investors to adopt a buy-and-hold strategy. The idea is to gradually accumulate a portfolio of solid assets over time, while keeping commissions and load charges to a minimum. Numerous studies have been done proving that this approach is best, and many advertising claims are based on it.

Well, I'm sorry, but I don't like the buy-and-hold approach — at least not as a steady diet. Investing is like everything else in life: you should always be prepared for change. Any suggestions that you read in this or any other book should be regarded as guidelines only. As I pointed out in Chapter Four, flexibility and willingness to adapt to an evolving situation are among the keys to investment success.

A buy-and-hold approach does not, by definition, encourage flexibility. On the contrary, it is a strategy of rigidity, the investment equivalent of trench warfare. A diehard buy-and-holder will maintain virtually the same investment portfolio at all times, in all situations. I think that's just plain silly. There are times when you must be ready to move in a new direction or risk seeing your investments left behind.

That doesn't mean you should go to the other extreme and turn over your entire portfolio every year or so. There's a happy medium and you have to find it.

I use what I call a gardening strategy. That means that most of my investment portfolio stays the same from one year to the next. I perform regular weeding, selling off poorly performing securities or those that seem to have reached a profit peak. I retain and cultivate those that are healthy and doing well. I add new plants through the purchase of additional securities from savings or the proceeds of sales. Very rarely, if ever, would I consider ripping out the entire garden and starting all over again. Only a major change in the economic climate would cause me to do that.

Let me carry the gardening analogy a step further. Every garden contains two types of plants, annuals and perennials. You make the decision on how they will be mixed and in what proportion. Similarly, every portfolio will contain two types of securities — Holders and Traders.

The Holders are those you buy for the long term — not forever, though, because every security should be sold at some point. The Traders are those you expect to dispose of in the short to medium term — say within three years. Here's how I'd divide them up:

Holders

Canada Savings Bonds: A solid core investment for any portfolio, combining reasonable interest rates with total flexibility. I always have some.

Regular government or corporate bonds: Buy them when bond yields are high and sit back and enjoy the steady income flow.

Stripped bonds: I'll explain in greater detail how these work in the chapter on bonds. They're especially good for RRSPs, and provide you with a guaranteed yield until their maturity — something few other investments will do.

Mortgage-backed securities: A relatively new investment form based on residential mortgages, these are issued by financial institutions and guaranteed by Canada Mortgage and Housing Corporation. They're excellent income vehicles if you're looking for cash flow but their capital gains potential is limited.

Guaranteed investment certificates: You really have no choice. GICs are normally locked in until maturity. So by definition, they're Holders.

Mutual funds: Most investment funds should be considered Holders, including equity funds. They'll perform best over the long haul, especially if you use a dollar-cost averaging approach that I'll explain in a minute. The one exception: money market funds.

Gold: I always believe in having a little gold in my portfolio, just as insurance. I'll explain why in more detail later in the book.

TRADERS

Treasury bills: By definition, these are short-term notes. You can't hold them because they'll mature; all you can do is roll them over at prevailing interest rates.

Money market funds: these are a short-term place to park cash profitably while you're waiting for economic trends to clarify or making an investment decision. They should never be used as long-term holds.

Options and warrants: These are bought to trade, never to hold.

Commodities: Ditto.

Stocks: Consider all your equities as Traders, but especially the cyclical ones, such as resource stocks. A broker I had lunch with recently told me how appalled he was at the number of cyclical stocks people hold in their portfolio over the long term. Cyclical stocks are bought to sell;

I'll explain the strategy in a later chapter. What about the classic widow and orphan stocks, such as Bell? Many people consider these to be Holders, but if there are clear signs the market is peaking, I'd be inclined to sell and buy back later.

Why, you may wonder, do I classify equity funds as Holders and the equities themselves as Traders? The reasoning stems from the management. The managers of a good equity fund should know how to exercise damage control in a declining market. And, in fact, an analysis I did for *The MoneyLetter* in spring 1988 identified a number of funds that had actually made money for their investors when their performance during the tough market years of 1981, 1984 and 1987 was averaged out.

On the other hand, it is unlikely that you, as an individual investor, will be as astute as the professional money managers during hard times in the stock market. Nor is it likely your portfolio will be anywhere near as diversified as that of a major mutual fund. All that suggests greater risk to individual stock investors than to those holding equity funds. Thus the difference in where I categorize them on my Holder-Trader scale.

Finally, a word about dollar-cost averaging.

There are a number of investment formulas used to try to beat the problem of market timing. Some of these are quite complex, involving the maintenance of portfolio ratios between conservative and speculative investments. Dollar-cost averaging, however, is easy to understand and simple to manage, and it's the only strategy most people really need to know.

The principle behind dollar-cost averaging is to smooth out the peaks and valleys of price movements, reducing your risk in the process. It's a conservative technique, perfect for the low-risk investor. Here's how it works.

You select one or more securities you want to own on a long-term basis. That means they must come from the Holder group; Traders are not suitable for this strategy. You then commit yourself to purchasing the same dollar value of the security at periodic intervals. You may decide to invest $100 a month, or $250 each quarter, or $500 every six months, or $1,000 a year. The amount you invest and the time frame you choose aren't important. What counts is consistency over a long period of time — say five years, minimum.

By investing this way, you acquire more shares or units when prices are low; fewer when the cost is high. Assuming the securities you select will gradually rise over time, you'll come out ahead. You must be disciplined enough to keep putting in money even when times are bad and everyone is predicting the economic end of the world. That sometimes requires a lot of guts; it's hard to keep cool and hold your strategy in the face of what looks like irresistible logic that disaster is looming. All you can do is take consolation from the fact the world economy hasn't collapsed yet, despite centuries of predictions that the end was nigh. It's unlikely that will change in your lifetime.

In fact, the internationally famous Templeton Growth Fund bases its advertising claims on the principle of dollar-cost averaging. You may have noticed the ads in the financial pages, typically reading something like: "If you had invested $2,000 in Templeton Growth Fund every year since 1957 . . . you would be able to retire now with over $1.8 million." Now that's what dollar-cost averaging can do!

Here's an example. I've assumed an investment in a no-load mutual fund of $250 every three months over a two-year period.

Purchase Date	Amount	Unit Price	Number Purchased	Total Held	Value
March 31	$250	$5	50	50	$ 250
June 30	250	4	62.5	112.5	450
Sept. 30	250	6	41.7	154.2	925.20
Dec. 31	250	5	50	204.2	1,021
March 31	250	3	83.3	287.5	862.50
June 30	250	4	62.5	350	1,400
Sept. 30	250	5	50	400	2,000
Dec. 31	250	6	41.7	441.7	2,650.20

Total Investment	= $2,000
Market Value	= $2,650.20
% Increase	= 32.5%
Average cost per unit	= $4.53

In this particular example, the market was quite volatile so the value of the units fluctuated between $3 and $6 during the two-year period. Obviously, if you'd been astute enough to hold your funds in cash and invest everything when the value was down to $3, you'd have improved your profit. But picking the low is extremely difficult, even for professional traders.

Your total investment using dollar-cost averaging increased in value by 32.5% over two years. And you achieved this even though the actual change in the unit value during that time was only 20% (you started at $5, ended at $6). If you'd invested the entire $2,000 at the outset, the value at the end of two years would have been only $2,400.

Obviously, if the unit value had been below $4.53 at the end of the second year, you'd have been showing a loss. But that shouldn't concern you since you're in for the long haul. You just keep on making those $250 contributions every quarter and as long as you've selected good securities, the process will pay off.

Does it work in the real world? Judge for yourself. Using basic information from *The Financial Times Mutual Fund Sourcebook*, I've calculated below the effect of $1,000 invested annually over 10 years in Royfund Equity, one of the biggest of the no-load funds investing in Canadian stocks. I have not taken into account any dividend distributions during this time, which could have been used to purchase more units. The period covered is from March 31, 1979, to March 31, 1988, a time of major ups and downs in the stock market.

Date of Purchase	Amount	Unit Price	Number Bought	Total Owned	Market Value
March 31/79	$1,000	$ 8.85	112.99	112.99	$ 1,000
March 31/80	1,000	10.39	96.25	209.24	2,174
March 31/81	1,000	14.09	70.97	280.21	3,948.16
March 31/82	1,000	8.34	119.90	400.11	3,336.92
March 31/83	1,000	11.01	90.83	490.94	5,405.25
March 31/84	1,000	12.18	82.10	573.04	6,979.63
March 31/85	1,000	14.92	67.02	640.06	9,549.70
March 31/86	1,000	19.84	50.40	690.46	13,698.73
March 31/87	1,000	22.73	44	734.46	16,694.28
March 31/88	1,000	20.18	49.55	784.04	15,821.93

Total investment	= $10,000
Market value	= $15,821.93
% Increase	= 58.2%
Average cost per unit	= $12.75

As you can see, dollar-cost averaging would have worked quite effectively here. But you would have to have shown a lot of self-discipline to keep putting money in after the disastrous fall in unit value between 1981 and 1982. It's at such times that many investors lose their resolve. Don't make that mistake.

Remember too, the above results do not allow for any dividend distributions. Those would have increased your holdings significantly over the ten-year period.

For dollar-cost averaging to work, however, you must choose the right securities. I've seen several articles on the subject that use stocks as an example. Frankly, I don't think you should ever use dollar-cost averaging for straight stock purchases.

There are several reasons for this. First, you shouldn't be putting so much money into one stock, no matter how solid it appears. The risk is just too great. You'd need to diversify your investment over several stocks, to spread the risk, and that would require a very large commitment of funds on your part.

Even if you were willing to do that, there are a number of practical problems involved. To begin with, to achieve a true dollar-cost average you would end up buying odd lots of shares — maybe 36 one year, 22 the next, 47 the next. Odd lots are difficult and expensive to acquire; if you can find them you usually have to pay a premium. Plus, if you're only buying small amounts each time, brokerage commissions will be proportionately higher.

Mutual funds are the ideal vehicle for a dollar-cost averaging program. You can buy any number of units at a time, providing it's more than the fund's minimum investment, which typically ranges from $100 to $1,000 initially and $25 to $100 thereafter. You'll even be able to get fractional units. The fund will provide you with the diversification you won't get with an individual stock. And if you purchase a no-load fund, you won't have to pay any commissions.

Remember: you're investing for the long haul. That makes the initial selection of your fund extremely important. So do your research and make sure you're comfortable with the fund before you commit yourself. I'll explain how to choose a good mutual fund in a later chapter.

That's it for the preliminaries. You're ready to start building your investment portfolio. Now let's look at what you should put into it.

CHAPTER 12

Making
the Most
of Cash

Ready money is Aladdin's lamp.
— Lord Byron

W HEN THE BRITISH feared invasion during the months after the fall of France, they changed all the direction signs at rural crossroads. The idea was to befuddle Hitler's armies by sending them down blind alleys, thereby creating confusion and uncertainty in the ranks.

Investors frequently find themselves in the kind of situation the Germans would have encountered had they crossed the Channel. More often than not the economic signposts generate conflicting signals. In mid-1988, for example, the prognosis for the next one to two years ranged from continued prosperity to economic slowdown to severe recession, depending on whom you listened to. You could find a strong, cogently argued case for an economy dominated by accelerating inflation, and equally persuasive opinions for the onset of a 1930s-style deflation.

Advice to investors was equally divergent. I sat at conferences listening to goldbugs forecasting huge rises in the price of gold because of inflationary expectations and encouraging people to put as much money into gold stocks or bullion as they could afford. Then the very next speaker would argue with that whole idea and tell people to buy bonds because interest rates were about to peak and they could make good capital gains as they started to come down.

Opinion on the stock market was equally divided, with some experts counselling buying while prices were low while others insisted the bear market still had many months to run and better bargains would appear.

With the benefit of hindsight, it's easy to see who was right and who was wrong. But in the midst of such uncertain times, the average investor can become pretty confused.

That's one reason why cash-type investments are so important in your Asset Mix strategy. What else provides you with maximum flexibility, universal acceptance, a decent return, and immediate or near-immediate liquidity (liquid assets are those that are easily converted to cash)? Substantial cash reserves also give you some built-in protection against most financial disasters, the one exception being hyperinflation — a runaway type of inflation in which paper money loses purchasing power almost by the hour. Cash also enables you to take advantage of new investment opportunities as events unfold and the economic picture clarifies.

If you follow the Asset Mix formula I set out in Chapter Eight, you'll have between 10% and 50% of your holdings in cash at any given time. The exact amount will be determined by a number of factors, as I've outlined.

Normally, you'll pay two prices for the protection and flexibility of cash. One is a low rate of return — cash will generally be the least productive of your assets. The other is a lack of diversification — until recently, there haven't been many alternatives for your cash assets.

However, this situation is changing. Hot competition in the financial industry has produced the largest choice of cash or cash-equivalent options the ordinary investor has ever seen. And that same competition means the interest paid on your cash holdings is more attractive than ever before.

That means it's now possible to build a diversified portfolio of cash-type investments which will provide you with an acceptable return on your money.

This is an important development. Since the cash component of your Asset Mix will usually produce the lowest return, the effect will be to reduce the total gain on your investments. The greater your cash holdings and the less interest they earn, the more difficult it will be to attain your goal of an average return at least two percentage points higher than a five-year GIC.

The examples below make this point clearly. Each assumes a total investment portfolio of $25,000.

Example 1

Asset Type	Value	% of Total	Expected Return	Annual Profit
Cash	$ 2,500	10%	6%	$ 150
Income	10,000	40%	10%	1,000
Growth	12,500	50%	15%	1,875

Total profit = $3,025

Return on investment = 12.1%

If we assume the return on the income portion of the Asset Mix is about equal to the five-year GIC rate, the overall portfolio profit of 12.1% is in line with our objectives. Since this is a "good times" Asset Mix, the 15% return on the growth assets is not unrealistic.

Now let's look at what happens when the cash component is increased.

Example 2

Asset Type	Value	% of Total	Expected Return	Annual Profit
Cash	$ 6,250	25%	6%	$ 375
Income	6,250	25%	10%	625
Growth	12,500	50%	15%	1,875

Total profit = $2,875

Return on investment = 11.5%

As you can see, adding to the cash component at the expense of the income component, has made the total return on this investment portfolio drop below the target level. This suggests one of two things has to happen. Either the cash portion must be kept low, with the resulting loss in flexibility, or the return on the cash holdings has to be improved. Let's see what happens when the return is increased to 1-1/2 points below the yield on the income holdings.

Example 3

Asset Type	Value	% of Total	Expected Return	Annual Profit
Cash	$ 6,250	25%	8.5%	$ 531.25
Income	6,250	25%	10%	625
Growth	12,500	50%	15%	1,875

Total profit	= $3,031.25
Return on investment	= 12.1%

The actual dollar return in Example 3 is slightly higher than in Example 1, even though the total cash holdings in the portfolio are substantially larger. In this case, we've attained our target return while maintaining flexibility within the portfolio in the form of large cash reserves.

Now, it won't always be possible to position your cash holdings in such a way that they'll yield only 1-1/2 points less than your income investments. But there are times when it can be done fairly easily — in fact, you can even do better. In August 1988, for instance, 91-day Treasury bills were yielding about 9-1/2% while 90-day banker's acceptances were paying close to 10%. At the same time, the yield on medium- to long-term Government of Canada bonds was only in the 10-1/4% to 10-1/2% range. So at that point in time, it was possible to generate a yield on your cash assets very close to what was available on a typical income asset.

The effective management of your cash assets is critical to the overall performance of your investment portfolio — and the higher your proportion of cash, the more important good management becomes. If you consistently maximize the return on your cash assets, your prospects for attaining your targeted return will be greatly enhanced.

So begin your investing program by finding the best possible places to put your cash reserves. Here's where to look.

DEPOSIT ACCOUNTS
Fierce competition in the financial industry has resulted in the creation of a wide range of high-interest accounts bidding for your money. The names vary — T-bill savings accounts, investor accounts, money maker

accounts — but all have one thing in common: they pay top interest rates for high deposits. Typically, you must have over $25,000 in one of these premium accounts to get the best rate. However, some banks have introduced a new wrinkle by paying special bonus interest on the balance in excess of $60,000 (which, not coincidentally I suspect, is the point beyond which you're not protected by deposit insurance). The promotions for these bonus accounts can be deceiving, however. Many of them pay the high rate on *only* the amount over $60,000. So if you have $61,000 on deposit, you'll get the bonus interest on $1,000 and ordinary interest on the rest. There are a few financial institutions that pay the maximum rate on the entire balance, however, so if you're interested in premium accounts you should seek them out.

Most of these accounts are limited in their chequing and withdrawal privileges, so they should be used strictly as a place to park large amounts of money. They're convenient, but they have two major disadvantages. One is that the interest rate is adjusted frequently, often on a weekly basis. That means you have no guarantee your money will continue to earn interest at the rates that applied when you made your deposit. The other is the amount of money required to earn the best rate. Unless you have a very large investment portfolio, this could result in your holding more assets in cash than you may wish.

TERM DEPOSITS

An alternative to the premium deposit account is the short-term deposit. Here you're sacrificing some flexibility in return for a guaranteed interest rate over the life of the investment contract. This type of term deposit typically matures in 30 days to a year, with the interest rate for the longer term slightly higher. You can usually cash them in earlier if you need the money, but be prepared to pay a penalty.

Contrary to general opinion, term deposits won't always pay you a better return than a premium savings account — in fact, the return can actually be less. The main advantage of term deposits is the guaranteed rate — your investment won't be subject to the whims of the marketplace.

If you're putting money into term deposits, I strongly advise going for the best rate you can find, as long as your funds are protected by deposit insurance. Usually you'll find these at smaller trust companies, and sometimes the spread can be significant. In August 1988, for example, you would have received only 6-1/2% on your money if you'd placed it in a 30-day term deposit at one of the major chartered banks. A large trust company, such as Canada Trust or Royal Trust, would have given you 7-1/2%. But a smaller trust company, such as Guardian or Household, would have paid 8-1/2% to 9%. That's a spread of 2-1/2 percentage points between the lowest and highest. Obviously, where you put your money will have a big impact on the return you receive on the cash portion of your assets.

CANADA SAVINGS BONDS

Don't let the word "bond" mislead you; these aren't real bonds at all. They should be more properly called "savings certificates", and in fact some financial institutions are now offering something similar under exactly that name. But just because CSBs have been misnamed doesn't mean they aren't a good place for your cash reserves. In fact, I recommend you always have some in the cash section of your portfolio.

Until late 1988, it wasn't possible to find any other investment with the advantages CSBs offer. No other security had its interest rate adjusted upwards if it became uncompetitive yet protected you if rates declined, while allowing you the flexibility to cash in at any time. That's a pretty good combination for a cash asset.

There are other alternatives now available, which I'll outline later in this chapter. Yet CSBs remain an excellent alternative, especially for very small or very large amounts of money.

The main thing you have to watch in your CSB holdings is that the government doesn't allow the rate to fall too far behind that offered by other cash vehicles. By mid-1988, for example, the CSB rate of 9% was starting to look a bit puny compared to the 9-3/4% to 10% returns on T-bills and banker's acceptances. When the government made no move to increase the CSB yield, some people with large holdings cashed in and switched. In the past, when CSB issues carried a guaranteed minimum rate for all years after the first, that could be risky. Those who held on to the 1981 issue, for instance, collected 10-1/2% interest in 1988 because of that guarantee. But Ottawa abandoned the policy with the 1987 issue. So if you have a lot of money invested in CSBs, you should keep monitoring the situation to see if you can get a better return elsewhere. Don't lose sight of the importance of the flexibility offered by CSBs, though; you shouldn't switch unless you can get at least a half point more for your money.

Most people think of CSBs as straightforward and uncomplicated, but there are a few points to consider before you buy.

First, be sure to select the right type of bond for you. There are two kinds of CSBs, regular interest (R) bonds and compound interest (C) bonds. The interest on R bonds is paid annually, either by cheque or direct deposit to your bank account if you've made the appropriate arrangements. The interest on C bonds is added to the principal each year, enabling you to earn interest on interest. R bonds should be your choice if you need a steady income stream; C bonds are best if you're looking for long-term growth.

If you make the wrong choice, you do have an escape hatch. Most people don't realize it, but you can switch your R bonds to C bonds at any time up to August 31 of the year following purchase. C bonds can be switched to R bonds at any time.

Many people give little or no consideration to the denominations of the CSBs they buy, but it can make a difference. If you think you may have to cash some of your bonds before maturity, you should give yourself some flexibility, since partial redemptions aren't allowed. For example, two $500 bonds may suit your requirements better than one $1,000 bond.

You should also consider the tax implications of CSB purchases. In the case of R bonds, you'll have to declare the interest annually, as it is received, and you'll be taxed at your marginal rate.

Holders of C bonds, however, have more options. In this case, you can declare the interest each year, even though you haven't actually received the money. Or you can defer your tax liability for up to three years, and declare your accumulated interest at that time. Remember, if you go the latter route, you'll be paying three years' worth of tax at once.

If you have C bonds, try to declare your interest during years when you're in a lower tax bracket. An acquaintance of mine recently asked for some advice about planning for his retirement, which is about two years away. At the time, he was planning to buy the 1988 issue of CSBs. I suggested he purchase C bonds, and not declare the interest for three years. By then he would be retired and in a lower tax bracket, and Revenue Canada's share of his return would be reduced.

One other point: if you have to cash in a CSB before maturity, be sure to do so on the first of the month. If you cash the bond mid-way through a month, you'll only receive interest to the previous month-end.

TREASURY BILLS

T-bills are the short-term equivalent of CSBs. They're issued by federal and provincial governments with maturities of 91 days, 182 days and 364 days. Provincial T-bills normally pay a slightly higher rate and are worth considering, if you can find any.

Unlike CSBs, you buy T-bills at a discount and collect the full face value when they mature — that represents your interest. Your interest rate is guaranteed until maturity, but if you want to get out before then you can usually do so. However, you may have to sell at a slight discount if interest rates have risen in the meantime.

There was a time when T-bills were the exclusive preserve of the super-rich. If you didn't have at least $100,000 to invest, no one was interested. But the brokerage industry changed all that in recent years, making T-bills available to their clients for as little as $10,000 and sometimes even $5,000. The brokers aren't getting rich by providing this service — far from it; the paperwork involved makes T-bills loss leaders most of the time. So if you want to use T-bills as part of your cash component, be nice to your broker. He or she is doing you a favour by providing them.

Treasury bills have become one of the favourite methods of holding cash, especially when short-term interest rates are high. They're safe, competitive, and easy to buy. I recommend buying a mixture of maturities; that way you can take advantage of the higher rates available on the longer bills (182 and 364 days), which can be more than half a point. At the same time, you'll have funds becoming available for reinvestment on a regular basis.

BANKER'S ACCEPTANCES

Many people are now using these as an alternative to T-bills because of the higher interest they pay. Banker's acceptances are promissory notes issued by companies borrowing short-term funds from Canada's major chartered banks. Instead of holding these, the banks offer them to investors with their own guarantee of repayment. Thus, while banker's acceptances may not be quite as safe as Government of Canada securities, they're not far behind. They're a good option for people who want to squeeze a little bit more out of their cash holdings; they'll generally pay a better return than most of the alternatives mentioned in this chapter. Like T-bills, you can usually sell them before maturity if you need the cash. They're available through brokers, with a minimum of $10,000 usually required.

GMACs

General Motors Acceptance Corporation offers high-interest, short-term deposit certificates to investors, but you need at least $50,000 to take advantage of them. The return is somewhat higher than from T-bills, so if you have that much money for temporary investing, ask your broker about them.

Savings Certificates

These are the private sector's answer to CSBs, and they're worth looking at. Counsel Trust became the first financial institution to offer them nationally (except in Quebec) in September 1988. However, by the time you read this book, more companies may have jumped in. Savings certificates function very much like CSBs: the interest rate is set for one year and they can be cashed in at any time for full interest after an initial holding period (60 days in Counsel Trust's case). Your investment is protected by deposit insurance up to the $60,000 limit.

In many ways, these certificates offer advantages over CSBs. If you compare interest rates when CSBs are on sale, you'll probably find the savings certificates are paying slightly more. And since these certificates are on sale all year long, you can roll them over into new ones if interest rates go higher. If rates drop, your rate is protected for a year, as with CSBs. Savings certificates can also be bought by corporations; CSBs can only be purchased by individuals.

The main disadvantages of savings certificates affect small and large investors. The minimum purchase offered by Counsel Trust is $1,000, so if you have only a few hundred put aside you'll have to stick with CSBs. If you have over $60,000 to invest, you should limit your holdings in savings certificates from any one financial institution to that amount, otherwise you won't be fully protected in case of trouble.

T-BILL FUNDS

This is an alternative for those who don't have enough cash to buy the T-bills themselves. They're mutual funds invested almost entirely in federal and provincial T-bills. These funds generally won't provide as good a return as the bills, but you can buy into most of them for a minimum of $1,000. That makes them more accessible to people with limited amounts of cash. And they're highly flexible; you can cash out any time without penalty. Just be sure you don't pay any load charge (commission) to get into one of these funds; the relatively low rate of return and the fact these are short-term holdings won't justify it.

CANADIAN MONEY MARKET FUNDS

These are also mutual funds specializing in short-term money. However, they hold a wider range of securities, including banker's acceptances and short-term commercial paper. As with T-bill funds, you can get your money out quickly, usually within 24 hours. During the first half of 1988 money market funds were just about the hottest investment ticket around, with stock-shocked investors switching to them at a record pace while awaiting the fallout from the crash of October 1987. That was because the combination of safety and high short-term rates made them especially attractive.

If you're considering money market funds as a cash alternative, here are some things to watch for:

1. Current yield. If you check the mutual funds section in the business pages of your newspaper, you'll see a number of funds bearing the initials MMF. This stands for money market fund. In brackets beside the initials will be a number. This represents the return the fund is currently paying.

The differences can range up to 2-1/2 points. All other things being equal, opt for the best return, especially since your money will probably only be there for a few months.

2. Load. As with T-bill funds, don't buy a money market fund that carries a load fee. The return isn't high enough.

3. Timing. Generally, money market funds lag the market. That means their current yields will be somewhat behind those you can receive for T-bills. That's because the assets of the funds will contain a mixture of securities, some of which were acquired several months ago. Therefore, money market funds are not a good place to be when short-term rates are rising. You'll get a better return from T-bills or banker's acceptances. When interest rates are declining, however, these funds are a good spot for your cash since you'll continue to benefit from securities that were issued when rates were higher.

INTERNATIONAL MONEY FUNDS

Relatively new to Canada, these funds invest in international short-term notes, such as T-bills issued by foreign governments and other high-grade securities. Their objective is to generate a better return than domestic money market funds by taking advantage of higher interest rates in other parts of the world and by profiting from currency fluctuations.

These funds are worth considering during periods when the Canadian and U.S. dollars are declining against other currencies. In this situation, the value of your cash investments will be shielded from the full impact of the decline. When North American currencies are strong, however, you're better off sticking with domestic funds.

If you have substantial funds available, I would suggest a mixture of cash assets something like the following when interest rates are stable or rising:

25%	Canada Savings Bonds or savings certificates
40%	90-day banker's acceptances (staggered maturities) or GMACs
20%	182-day provincial or federal T-bills
15%	364-day T-bills

This combination will provide you with an excellent return plus first-rate flexibility. All these securities are highly liquid.

When interest rates are declining, you may want to switch your strategy to keep your return at as high a level as possible. In that case, a mix like this would be more appropriate:

25%	Canada Savings Bonds or savings certificates
25%	182-day T-bills
25%	364-day T-bills
25%	T-bill fund or money market fund

This formula locks in the higher rates for a longer period, while still providing good liquidity if you need it.

If your cash balance doesn't allow for the purchase of T-bills and banker's acceptances, you could try an alternative plan:

35%	Canada Savings Bonds or savings certificates
35%	T-bill or money market funds
30%	Term deposits

Let me stress, however, that these formulas are not to be followed slavishly. There will be times when circumstances require some drastic changes to keep your return at maximum levels; for example, if the interest rate on your CSBs falls significantly below the yield on other types of cash investments. It's up to you to stay on top of the situation and to adjust your cash assets accordingly.

Finally, don't fall in love with your cash. There are times when your cash reserves should be high, other times when you should be all the way down to the 10% level. If you hold too high a proportion of cash during boom times in the stock and bond markets, you'll miss the big profit opportunities. Times of uncertainty and rising interest rates are good periods for building cash reserves. But when rates start to turn around and confidence is showing the first signs of making a comeback, start moving your money elsewhere.

Getting Started with Mutual Funds

There is a tide in the affairs of men which, taken at the flood, leads on to fortune.

— Shakespeare

AT SOME POINT in your life, I'm sure you've stared into a fire or across a lake and thought about all the things you would have done differently if only you'd known then what you do now.

It's a natural desire to want to turn back the clock: to take a course that might have changed your career path, or to say different words to a special person, or to go on the trip that never happened.

Of course, it's impossible. But we all daydream about what might have been.

I sometimes think about where I'd be today if I'd learned some basic lessons about investing early in my life. Nothing complicated, just a few fundamentals. Like the fact that mutual funds are a long-term hold.

You see, I didn't really understand that until I didn't have a long term left. I can't invest on a 30-year horizon any more; if I'm still alive at that point I'll be well into my 80s.

But I had the opportunity once. I let it slip away because I didn't understand it.

I bought my first mutual fund in the late 1960s. It was AGF Special Fund, a fund specializing in U.S. growth stocks. I put in about $1,000 and held on to it for a few years while it went nowhere. In 1973 I sold out, for virtually the same price I'd paid originally.

If I'd understood how mutual funds work, I would never have sold at that point. In fact, I would have adopted a dollar-cost averaging program instead. Since I wasn't making a great deal of money at that time, it would have been fairly modest — say $100 a month.

Had I gone that route in 1973 and stuck to it all these years, I would have invested $19,000 in AGF Special Fund by the end of 1987 — my original $1,000 plus $1,200 a year for 15 years. The market value of my holdings at that time would have been worth in the vicinity of $100,000. I can think of a lot of nice things I could do with that money today.

But of course I don't have it. Sigh.

Enough of daydreams. Back to the reality of building a low-risk portfolio.

Once you've stashed your cash where it will earn the best possible return, it's time to begin the process of putting together a portfolio that suits your objectives. Mutual funds are an excellent place to start. In fact, if you so choose, you don't have to go any further. You can build a well-balanced portfolio, perfectly geared to your Asset Mix requirements, entirely with mutual funds.

Before I explain how, a bit of history. Mutual funds are simply a pool of money put up by a number of investors and managed by professionals. They've been around for a long time — their origins can be traced back to Europe in the early 19th century. But it's only been since the Second World War that they've become popular with ordinary investors. Through the 1950s and 1960s, they were the fastest-growing investment form in North America. It's estimated that between 1955 and 1972, total fund assets under management in the U.S. increased 7-1/2 times, from $8 billion to $60 billion, fuelled largely by the combination of a long bull market and increasing personal wealth. The growth in Canada during this period was even more dramatic, from $252 million in 1956 to $2.7 billion.

But in the 1970s, this heady growth came to a sudden end. The Dow-Jones Industrial Index plunged from a high of 1,052 in 1973 to 578 in 1974 — a drop of 45% in about a year. That wiped out the profits of many mutual fund investors and sent them into a panic, scrambling to redeem their units while they still retained some value.

Between 1972 and 1974, total assets of Canadian mutual funds dropped almost 40%, from $2.7 billion to $1.6 billion. Mutual funds became a dirty word. Many people had lost a great deal of money, having bought in just when the market was approaching its peak and then selling out at the low. Of course, had they held on they would have recovered their losses and a lot more, assuming they were in a well-managed fund. But at the time, all they could see was the fact they'd taken a terrible financial beating.

The image of mutual funds wasn't helped by some highly publicized scandals that erupted during this period, which included the collapse of some well-known funds, including those run by the high-flying Bernie Cornfeld.

It took almost a decade for investment funds to come back into favour, with the bull market of 1982-87 one of the primary catalysts. Growth during the mid-1980s was mind-boggling. In 1983, members of the Investment Funds Institute of Canada had about $5.8 billion in assets; by the end of 1987 the figure was $20.4 billion. Once that five-year market run came to an end on Black Monday, however, mutual funds began to slip back into the doldrums. In the first half of 1988, equity fund redemptions in Canada exceeded new sales by a considerable amount, and many of the smaller funds merged or were sold as the industry went into a period of downsizing and consolidation.

So when it comes time to make your investment decisions, you may find a general mood of euphoria relating to mutual funds. Or you may hear a litany of woe from people who have lost money. Don't be influenced by either. Properly selected and monitored, mutual funds can be one of the building blocks of a low-risk portfolio. The good ones have an excellent record of profitability over the long haul. They offer built-in management skills at a level far beyond what most individuals can hope to achieve. They provide excellent diversification. And — as a car dealer might say — they come in a wide range of colours and models. As you may have guessed by now, I am a firm believer in the value of mutual funds for the individual investor.

Before we move to the heart of the issue — how to pick a quality mutual fund — let's review a few basics. If you read the chapter on mutual funds in *Building Wealth* you can skim through this quickly. If not, here's everything you need to know to get started.

First, there are different types of funds available. They can be categorized in several ways; the following is the most basic:

Equity funds: These invest in the stocks of publicly traded corporations. A broad-based equity fund will hold shares in a large number of corporations. These may be concentrated in one country, generally Canada or the U.S., although Japan-based funds have done well in recent years. Or they may spread their holdings among a number of nations, in which case they're called international or global funds. You will also encounter different types of specialized equity funds. Some concentrate their investments in a particular sector of the economy — energy funds and resource funds are examples. Others invest only in a particular type of stock — preferred shares, convertibles, or those with high dividend yields. Still others use a specific investment approach, for example, only buying stocks that trade below book value.

As you can see, the term "equity fund" covers a variety of investment options. That means you have to look beyond the generic categorization when you're considering an equity fund. Before you do anything else, find out what type of equities that particular fund invests in. If its holdings are of no interest to you (perhaps it specializes in U.S. stocks and you're looking for a Canadian-based fund for your RRSP), you can move on to something else.

Fixed-income funds: These funds invest in securities which pay a fixed rate of return, hence the term "fixed-income". Typically, these will be bonds and mortgages. But, again, the type of securities held will vary from one fund to another. Some invest in mortgages exclusively. Some concentrate on Government of Canada bond issues. Some hold international bonds, denominated in different currencies. Some blend bond and mortgage holdings in varying proportions.

What fixed-income funds share is an emphasis on income flow and a more conservative investment approach than the typical equity fund.

Balanced funds: These funds combine both equity and fixed-income holdings in a single fund. This is the Asset Mix approach at work; the idea is to vary the allocation among the types of securities held, depending on economic conditions. Generally, a balanced fund will adopt a more conservative approach than an equity fund, but will be more aggressive than a fixed-income fund.

Money market funds: We already looked at these in Chapter Twelve. They're funds that invest in short-term securities, such as T-bills and banker's acceptances. They provide a safe harbour for your money, but generally pay low returns.

Precious metals funds: These are mainly gold funds, although some hold silver and platinum as well. Their investments may be in the form of shares, bullion, or, at times, hard cash. By their nature, these funds are considered higher risk than the more conservative fixed-income or balanced funds.

Real estate funds: These can range from highly conservative investments in prime residential real estate to speculative holdings of raw land. Most, however, concentrate on commercial properties. There are only a few around and most are still quite young.

Commodities funds: These are highly speculative funds that concentrate on commodities futures. In most cases, they won't fit with a low-risk investing strategy.

Fund of funds: This is a relatively new concept: a mutual fund that invests in other funds. The idea is to enable the investor to attain his or her desired diversification and Asset Mix in one place. Instant portfolio, if you like.

Royal Trust has been one of the leaders in popularizing this concept in Canada, through its three Advantage Funds. Here's how they work:

The Advantage Growth Fund puts the emphasis on above-average returns. To achieve that, the majority of its assets consist of units in other Royal Trust funds specializing in Canadian, American and Japanese stocks, plus the company's energy and global funds.

The Income Fund, as you might expect, invests primarily in the Royal Trust Bond Fund and the Royal Trust Mortgage Fund.

The Balanced Fund has a little bit of everything in it, with the goal of achieving a balance between growth and income assets.

In principle, the fund of funds concept looks attractive for low-risk investors. But it hasn't been around long enough to prove itself; none of the publicly offered funds has had sufficient time to establish a track record. So while it may be tempting to take the easy route by handing over all your money to a fund of funds that matches your goals, I don't recommend it. Add a fund of funds to your portfolio if you wish. But don't rely on it exclusively, at least until it's had time to establish a performance record that satisfies you.

The next thing you must be aware of is cost. Every fund will cost you money — the sales people and managers are in business, after all. But the way in which you pay for their services will vary considerably. Here's what to look for:

Front-end loads: These are sales commissions that you pay up-front when buying units in a fund. They can range from a low of 2% to a high of 9%. The cardinal rule is never to accept the quoted fee as being hard and fast. A few funds do discourage discounting. But in most cases, you should be able to negotiate the commission down to half or even less of the quoted rate — even if you're only making a small investment. In the case of money market funds, which generally quote a 2% maximum, you should be able to buy in for no commission at all. If the fund salesperson or broker you're dealing with doesn't want to negotiate, take your business elsewhere.

I can't emphasize strongly enough the importance of paying the lowest possible front-end load when you buy fund units. The difference between a 9% and a 4% commission on a $10,000 purchase is $500. If you'd bought into Industrial Growth Fund in March of 1978 and paid a 9% load (the maximum posted rate), your $10,000 investment would have purchased $9,100 worth of units. By March 1988, the value of your holdings would have increased to $50,105.83. If you had paid only 4%, however, you would have started with $9,600 and ten years later your units would be worth $52,858.90 — a difference of more than $2,700. So it's not just the up-front hit you take on the higher load that's important; it's the compounding effect it has on the value of your investment over the years.

If a fund is designated as a no-load fund, you'll pay no sales commission, of course. But you'll pay in other ways.

Back-end loads: As investors have become more conscious of the impact of front-end loads on their overall returns, the mutual fund companies have developed canny new techniques for earning money. One of these is the back-end load. These funds don't charge you anything to get in — only to get out. When you redeem your units, you're hit with a redemption fee.

These back-end loads come in a number of forms. Some funds — Industrial Horizon is an example — reduce the redemption fee payable the longer you own the fund. In Horizon's case, the fee drops from 4-1/2% in the first year to zero after nine years.

The method by which these fees are calculated also varies. Some funds base it on the original purchase price; others on the value at the time of redemption. That may seem like a detail, until you see the bill. Suppose that 10 years ago you invested $5,000 in a fund with a 3% back-end load, based on the original purchase price. The fund performed well, with an average annual compound rate of return of 15%. Now, with your original units worth $20,227.79, you decide to sell. If the 3% redemption fee is based on the original book value, your cost is a mere $150 ($5,000 x 3%). But if it's based on current market value, you're going to hand over $606.83. So if you're considering a back-end load fund, find out how the redemption fee is calculated. If it's on the basis of market value, look for alternatives.

Management fees: These are hidden fees, the ones you never see. But they can erode the returns on your mutual fund investments. They're usually calculated as a percentage of the total assets of the fund and paid annually to the fund managers as compensation for their services. Some funds also pay incentive bonuses to the managers if performance exceeds a target level. Most investors aren't aware of these payments — which can total several millon dollars a year for large funds — because they aren't charged against individual accounts. Instead, they're withdrawn from the fund's assets.

Management fees can range from less than 1% of assets to 3%, but most funds charge in the 1% to 2% range. There isn't much you can do about them — they're part of the fund's structure. Nevertheless, you should be aware of how much the managers are receiving and decide for yourself if the performance of the fund justifies the rate. By the way, there's no apparent correlation between the management fee and a fund's performance. You'll find some funds with a 1% management charge that generate far better results than those with a 2% fee.

Trailer fees and prizes: Here are two more examples of fees you never see, but which may have an influence on your mutual fund investments. Trailer fees are paid to a broker on the basis of the amount invested in a particular fund by his or her clients. These are in addition to the up-front load charge, and typically amount to 1/4% to 1/2% of the total invested. Payments are usually made quarterly and continue in perpetuity as long as the broker keeps his or her clients in the fund. The sales rationale is twofold: it encourages more sales of a particular fund and it provides an inducement for brokers to discourage their clients from selling and switching their money elsewhere.

Trailer fees are a relatively new phenomenon in Canada, but they're catching on quickly. Obviously, they're popular with brokers looking to increase their sources of revenue. But for you, as an investor, they represent a problem.

Trailer fees place your broker in a conflict of interest situation. On the one hand, he or she should be giving you unbiased investment advice. But it's sometimes hard to be unbiased when the result takes money out of your pocket — especially when the brokerage industry is going through hard times, as it was in 1988 following the stock market crash.

My own view is that trailer fees should be banned outright. By allowing them to multiply, the mutual funds industry risks a serious erosion in public confidence as more and more investors question the integrity of the advice they're receiving. However, as of mid-1988, no action to outlaw these fees appeared imminent.

Another potential conflict of interest is created by the ambitious incentive programs offered by some mutual funds. In addition to the normal commission, a sales person can earn points from every sale, which can be redeemed for anything from a clock radio to an exotic south seas vacation. The more points accumulated, the better the prize. These incentive programs have also created a great deal of controversy, but so far nothing has been done about them other than a requirement that fund promoters disclose this information in their prospectus.

All this means that you, the investor, must be even more critical when assessing the advice you receive on mutual funds purchases. The broker or sales representative you're talking to may stand to benefit in three different ways: from the load charge you pay, from the trailer fees your account will generate and from the prizes he or she may win as a result of your purchase. You may find a broker who will be able to put all that aside and make mutual fund recommendations strictly on the basis of the best investment for your needs. But the temptation to allow a little self-interest to creep in is worrying. I suggest that you review the prospectus and ask the broker whether any trailer fees or awards are attached to the particular fund being recommended before making a purchase. If they are, be very sure the fund is really a good one before proceeding. That means doing a fair amount of homework. But it's the only way to protect yourself.

Next, a few words about closed-end and open-end funds.

Open-end funds are what you'll normally encounter. These funds place no limit on the number of shares or units outstanding. Anyone wanting to buy in can do so at any time, at the fund's current net asset value (NAV). That's calculated by dividing the fund's total assets by the number of units outstanding.

Closed-end funds, on the other hand, issue a limited number of shares at the outset and then close the books. You can't buy into them after that unless you purchase shares from another investor or on the stock exchange.

Generally, you should *never* buy shares in a closed-end fund at issue. The reason is that, for reasons no one has ever satisfactorily explained to me, these funds almost always trade at a discount to their NAV after they come out. And sometimes that discount can be very deep, up to 30%. That means if you pay $10 a unit for shares in a closed-end fund at issue, you may find six months later that it's trading for only $7 on the stock exchange — even though its true NAV is still $10. Don't ask me to explain it, that's just the way it is.

A number of closed-end funds were started up in the early to mid-1980s. But this situation became so distressing to investors that many of those funds have since converted to open-end status or have been wound up.

So if you come across a closed-end fund you like, wait until it's been publicly traded for a time before buying in. You'll probably pick it up at well below the issue price.

Finally, here are a few more things to watch for when buying into mutual funds:

RRSP/RRIF eligibility: Some funds can be included in a retirement plan without limit. Others — those investing mainly in U.S. securities are one example — are considered foreign property, which means they cannot exceed 10% of the book value of your RRSP.

Volatility: This is a measure of a fund's stability, based on its average monthly return. A fund with a high volatility rating will show some sharp peaks and valleys in its performance over the years, and will probably be more susceptible to a sharp market decline. A low-volatility fund will show a more consistent pattern of earnings and will likely be more stable. Low-risk investors should favour funds with lower volatility. You'll find volatility information in the mutual fund rankings provided by *The Financial Post* and *Financial Times of Canada* under the column heading "Variability".

The Financial Post takes the volatility measurement one step farther by providing its readers with a "reward/risk ratio". It divides the compound rate of return of a fund by the variability factor to produce a measurement of reward relative to risk. It's a useful extra tool in selecting a fund.

Dividends: Mutual funds, like stocks, can generate dividends. These can be paid to you directly, or reinvested in new fund units. Check the dividend record and distribution policy of any fund that interests you before investing.

Finally, the hardest part of all — when to get out of a fund. As I said earlier, mutual funds should generally be regarded as a long-term investment. Redeeming your units after a few years or switching frequently from one fund to another is usually counter-productive unless you're a very skilled market timer. But there are circumstances in which you and your fund should part company:

When your objectives change. As you grow older or your family situation changes, the goals you had when you originally invested in a particular fund may evolve. For example, you may come to a point where income needs supersede growth potential as your primary concern. At that stage, you should review your mutual fund holdings and make whatever moves are necessary to bring them into line with your revised objectives.

When your fund consistently underperforms. Funds change. The manager may be hired away or economic conditions may no longer suit the overall investment philosophy. If you've been careful in your fund selection, you shouldn't abandon ship if things go bad temporarily. Certainly don't bail out on the strength of a single setback — it may be that all funds are having problems and, in fact, yours is holding up better than most. But if your fund underperforms the industry average for a lengthy period of time — say, more than two years — it's time to look for alternatives.

When there's a major change in the market cycle. Even the most dedicated low-risk investor would not have wanted to be completely out of equity funds during the great bull market of 1982-87. When it become apparent the economy was starting to recover from the 1981-82 recession and that a major turnaround was in progress, a move of some assets into equity funds would have been in order. That doesn't mean you should be trying to catch every little swing in market direction. But when the flood tide appears, as it may once in a decade, you should be ready to ride it.

CHAPTER 14

Picking the Right Funds

The more alternatives, the more difficult the choice.
— Abbé d'Allainval

THE FIRST THING you'll be faced with in selecting a mutual fund is the dazzling array of alternatives. There are now over 500 mutual funds in Canada and the number is growing all the time. That makes choosing the good ones a real challenge — especially since your broker may not be in the best position to provide you with objective advice.

That means you must do a lot of the research yourself. There's a saying in the industry: "Mutual funds are sold, not bought." Don't let that be true in your case. If you allow yourself to be sold a fund rather than carefully selecting your own, you may end up with a dog that will make no one rich but your broker.

How do you go about it? Here's my Surefire Six-Step Selection Strategy for buying mutual funds.

STEP ONE: *Decide what you want.*

Before you do anything else, sit down and think through your precise objectives for a mutual fund investment. Take into account your desired Asset Mix, the relative importance of safety and growth potential, income needs, and RRSP/RRIF eligibility. Once you've completed this exercise, you'll have a clearer fix on what type of fund or funds you require, and you'll probably have eliminated a couple of hundred from the list.

Let's suppose, for example, you're building a retirement portfolio and your goal is to combine long-term growth with reasonable safety. You might want to look especially closely at balanced funds with RRSP eligibility. On the other hand, if you're investing outside an RRSP and you want to go for maximum growth, a Japanese-based fund or a fund specializing in U.S. growth stocks would suit your needs better.

The following chart gives you an idea of the type of funds to look at most closely, depending on your goals. The RRSP-eligible funds must be based at least 90% on Canadian securities.

Objective	In RRSP	Outside RRSP
Maximum safety	T-bill Money Market	T-bill Money Market
Income	Bond Mortgage	Bond Mortgage
Modest Growth, Safety	Balanced	Balanced
Maximum Growth	Canadian equity	Canadian equity U.S. equity Japanese equity International equity
Speculative	Precious metals Real estate	Precious metals Real estate Commodities

Most low-risk investors will select their funds from the first three groups. If you want to add any growth funds to your portfolio, look for those with relatively low volatility and a consistent performance record over a long period.

Once you've identified the types of funds that best meet your goals, find those with an investment philosophy that closely parallels your own. There can be significant variations in approach among funds in the same group.

For example, the highly successful Mackenzie Mortgage and Income Fund has an investment policy that allows it to put money into preferred and common shares as well as mortgages, bonds and debentures. As a result, its volatility rating is considerably higher than many other fixed-income funds, which limit themselves to debt securities exclusively. If that makes you uncomfortable, you'll cross Mackenzie Mortgage and Income off your list despite its good track record.

You'll find a mutual fund's investment policy set out in its prospectus. If you don't want to take the trouble to obtain and read through a couple of hundreds of these, try to find a copy of the *Financial Times Mutual Fund Sourcebook*. It's the most comprehensive source of such information I've come across to date and is available either in a printed version or on computer disk. It's expensive to purchase, however, so see if you can refer to a copy at your library. If not, your broker should have one available; ask if you can come in and browse through it. When you've identified the funds that seem to best fit your objectives (and don't despair if you have a full page of them, we'll narrow it down), you're ready for Step Two.

STEP TWO: *Check out the track record.*

Whenever you see a performance claim in a mutual fund advertisement or brochure, you'll find a line in small print that reads: "Past performance does not necessarily reflect future results."

It's something to always keep in mind. A fund may have done extremely well in the past, but its prospects for the future may be bleak. Remember the investment in the carriage manufacturer we were considering in Chapter Four? The same thing can happen to a mutual fund.

Yet although a fund's track record isn't the whole story, it is a valuable indicator. If it hasn't performed well in the past, why should you think it's going to do better from now on? Conversely, a consistent record of solid returns in both good and bad economic times suggests the managers have known what they were doing up to now.

In considering a fund's track record, there are a number of factors to take into account. The first is the average annual compound rate of return over a period of time. These numbers tell you what return you could have expected from an investment made several years ago, assuming you reinvested all dividends, interest and capital gains.

This information is easy to find. Both *Financial Times of Canada* and *The Financial Post* include it in the mutual fund performance reviews they publish every month. Both papers provide three-year, five-year, and ten-year results, so you can see how any given fund has performed over time.

The differences can be dramatic, even within the same fund group. The *Financial Times* report published in July 1988 showed that among Canadian equity funds, the average annual compound rate of return over ten years ranged from a low of 1.9% to a high of 19.2%. That means that a $10,000 investment made in mid-1978 in the worst-performing fund would have been worth only $12,070.96 a decade later. That same investment in the top-performing fund would have grown to $57,911.20. See why it's so important to find a quality fund?

The range when five-year averages were looked at was even more dramatic. Investors in the weakest equity fund would have actually *lost* an average of 5.7% a year. But if you'd picked the best performer, you would have enjoyed an average annual gain of 19.7%.

The three-year record showed a range of -9.8% to +22.4%.

Even in the less volatile bond and mortgage funds you'll find a wide divergence. The best ten-year average was 13.3%; the worst was 8.1%. The five-year range was 7.5% to 15.7%; the three-year was 5.8% to 14.7%.

Clearly, although mutual funds may be created equal, they don't stay that way very long.

The next thing to look at is the simple rate of return over the past year. The *Times* provides one-month, three-month and one-year results; the *Post* gives you six months and one year. These figures tell you how the fund is doing at present. You shouldn't place too much emphasis on them, however, because they can be distorted by specific events.

In mid-1988, for example, you might have been impressed that Investors Canadian Equity fund went up 6.6% between May 31 and June 30. But when you looked at the one-year column, you'd have seen it had actually dropped 7.2% during the 12-month period. The explanation is simple: the one-year performance reflected the result of Black Monday while the one-month jump was made possible by a late spring market rally.

A classic example of the danger in relying on short-term results is the case of RealGrowth Canadian Equity Fund. This small fund began operations in 1983, but few people ever heard of it until 1986 when the managers astonished the investment world with a 54.5% gain in a single year. That led to a big advertising campaign, which saw the fund more than triple in size in 1987. And what happened? RealGrowth units dropped 14.3% in value that year and the fund ended up ranked 86th out of 88 Canadian equity funds by the *Financial Times Mutual Fund Sourcebook*.

So don't be overly influenced by short-term results. The record over several years is more significant.

Now that you've looked at the raw numbers for the funds in which you're interested, compare them with the industry averages. These figures are shown at the end of each fund section in the tables published by the financial papers. Here's where you get out your red pencil. Cross off your list any funds that have consistently done worse than the average, in both the short and long term. Circle those that have consistently done better — these are your prime prospects. Put a question mark beside those showing a long-term average or below-average performance, but which have been above average over the past one to three years. These are your secondary prospects.

You've now reduced the size of your list and identified the primary and secondary funds you're interested in. The next step is a bit more difficult.

STEP THREE: *Consider the future prospects.*
Now that you know the history of your candidate funds, you want to do some intelligent guessing about their future prospects. Admittedly, that's not easy and there are no guarantees. But there are some signposts to guide you.

The first is the trend line. Which way is the fund's performance going, up or down? And if it's relatively stable, what can you learn from that?

One easy way to assess this is to find out some information about rankings — how has a fund performed over time compared to the others in its group? Is there a discernible pattern emerging?

Unfortunately, you won't find that information in the tables published by the *Post* or the *Times*, although both papers occasionally carry stories on the subject. Here again, the best place to go is the *Financial Times Mutual Fund Sourcebook*. It provides a detailed breakdown of how every fund has performed compared to the total group for a number of years. You can glean a great deal from that information.

For instance, take a look at the following examples and see what you can learn about each fund. All of them are real, by the way.

Fund A

Year	Performance Ranking	Number in Group
88	55	93
87	51	83
86	36	73
85	22	70
84	16	67
83	14	65
82	13	64
81	7	63
80	9	63
79	6	63
78	4	63
77	4	63

Fund B

Year	Performance Ranking	Number in Group
88	88	93
87	81	83
86	71	73
85	66	70
84	63	67
83	62	65
82	59	64
81	58	63
80	61	63
79	59	63
78	58	63
77	58	63

Fund C

Year	Performance Ranking	Number in Group
88	4	93
87	2	83
86	3	73
85	3	70
84	3	67
83	10	65
82	4	64
81	13	63
80	30	63
79	46	63
78	51	63
77	48	63

Fund D

Year	Performance Ranking	Number in Group
88	5	93
87	10	83
86	5	73
85	5	70
84	6	67
83	11	65
82	8	64
81	11	63
80	8	63
79	11	63
78	6	63
77	6	63

Just that small amount of information tells you a great deal about each of these funds, doesn't it? If I were you, I wouldn't put a dime into either Fund A or Fund B.

Fund A was a solid performer for several years. And, in fact, its long-term averages may still look pretty good. But around 1982 something went terribly wrong. We don't know what that was; maybe the manager was replaced or perhaps the investing style wasn't right for the strong bull market of the '80s. Whatever the reason, Fund A went into a steady decline from which it still hasn't recovered. From being consistently one of the top ten equity funds in Canada, it's now fallen to the point where well over half the other Canadian equity funds are outperforming it. The trend line seems to be continuing down. That's not promising for the future.

Fund B is in a different situation. It hasn't fallen back; it's just never been very good. Oh, it's a model of consistency — but lousy consistency. Any fund that manages to finish near the bottom of the heap so regularly for so long simply isn't worthy of your attention.

Funds C and D, on the other hand, look promising. Fund C started off slowly, but look what's happened since 1982 — only once has it been out of the top five, and the trend line seems to be continuing up. Somebody there seems to have discovered the secret of successful fund management. Fund D has a flat trend line — but it's flat across the top of the scale whereas Fund B was flat across the bottom. Fund D has been a stellar performer all along — always in the top 10 or close to it.

Of course, the trend lines can always change. But right now I'd be comfortable putting my money into either Fund C or D.

The trend line is just part of the story, however. You must also bring some of your world-watching intuition to bear in deciding which funds have the best future prospects.

For example, mutual funds based on Japanese stocks have enjoyed spectacular growth over the past decade. People who put money into AGF Japan Fund in 1977 had a compound rate of return of 25% a year for the next 10 years. No other mutual fund could match that, although Investors Japanese Growth Fund came close, with a 23.1% return.

These are amazing results. But what about the next decade? It seems unlikely that Japan's growth can continue at the same pace, given the strengthening of the yen, the growing pressure on the Japanese to open their markets to more foreign goods, and the strong push by the U.S.

to reduce its huge foreign trade deficit. Japanese-based mutual funds may continue to do well. But anyone who expects returns similar to those of the 1977-87 period may be disappointed.

On the other hand, some of the other Pacific Rim countries, such as Korea and Taiwan, are starting to flex their economic muscles. Some analysts believe investments in mutual funds based in these areas could have greater growth potential than Japanese funds over the next ten years.

Funds based in the U.S. could also have potential. The argument is that as American industry moves to exploit the export opportunities created by the currency realignment of the 1980s, which saw the value of the U.S. dollar drop dramatically, share prices of many of these companies will strengthen. Well-managed mutual funds will take advantage of that upward trend.

Long-term trends in interest rates will influence your thinking about fixed-income funds. If rates appear to be heading up, you'll be very selective about where you put your money. You'll search out funds that show flexibility in their holdings. Often, you'll find these by a careful reading of the business pages. In August 1988, for example, when interest rates were moving up, the *Globe and Mail Report on Business* quoted a bond fund manager as saying he was going to stay primarily in cash until rates peaked and began to drop. At that point he would aggressively buy bonds, which would appreciate in value as rates continued to drop. If you were shopping for a fixed-income fund at that time, this information would have been extremely valuable to you in making a selection.

If you're considering gold funds, the prospects for rising inflation will help you decide whether to go ahead. Rising inflation will have a positive impact on gold prices; disinflation will be negative.

Obviously, you can't predict the future. But by carefully considering the factors that will affect a fund's future, you'll improve your odds of selecting those funds with the best growth potential.

STEP FOUR: *Study the management team.*
The management of a mutual fund is the single most critical element in its ultimate success or failure. Some fund managers are financial geniuses.

Others would do better selling cars. If you select a fund with a well-established, proven management team behind it, your chances of success will be enhanced immeasurably.

Identifying the good managers is extremely difficult, however. Very few of these people are public figures; in fact, most avoid the spotlight and prefer to remain virtually anonymous. You have to work at finding out who is good and who isn't.

Most investors have heard of John Templeton, for example. His Templeton Growth Fund, which is Canadian-based, has become synonymous with success in mutual fund investing. What most people don't realize, however, is that the performance of the Templeton Growth Fund has fallen off in recent years. In fact, it doesn't even make the top 50 in the *Financial Times Mutual Fund Sourcebook* based on three-year averages to March 31, 1988.

On the other hand, very few people have ever heard of Alex Christ. You rarely read about him in the press and he isn't listed in the *Canadian Who's Who*. But insiders on Bay Street regard him as one of the most astute mutual fund managers in Canada. Of the top 20 performing funds between March 1985 and March 1988, he was involved with seven of them as a senior member of Mackenzie Financial Corporation. This company, which markets the Industrial group of funds as well as serving as advisors to others, has established a track record which is second to none in the industry.

So just because a fund manager is well known doesn't necessarily mean he or she is the best around, or even particularly good. You'll find some with reputations that far outweigh their actual performance.

To pinpoint the top managers, check out the top 25 performing mutual funds over the past five years. See who is actually running them — again, the *Financial Times Mutual Fund Sourcebook* will be of great value. If you find the same name or group of names appearing several times, see if they're involved with any of the funds still on your list. If so, that's another plus.

You can also gather intelligence on the top fund managers by a careful reading of the business press and by talking to brokers and other investors. It won't all come at once — you'll form your impressions by dribs and drabs. But over a period of time, you should be able to zero in on the best people and what funds they're involved with.

STEP FIVE: *Review the costs.*

By now your list of potential funds should be down to only a few. Before you make the final selection, take a close look at the costs involved for each fund.

Cost should never be your primary consideration in choosing a mutual fund. It's penny wise and pound foolish to select a mediocre no-load fund over an outstanding load fund because you don't want to pay a 4% commission.

But if your choice has come down to three or four funds with little to differentiate them, cost may be the deciding element. Look carefully at all the cost elements, as I outlined them in the previous chapter. See if one fund appears to be a clear-cut winner on this score. If so, you have completed your search.

If not, there's one more area to look at.

STEP SIX: *See who's best when the going gets tough.*

A low-risk investor hates to lose money. Even a few hundred dollars here and there is unacceptable. It's not just the capital base that's being eroded. It's the compound earning power those lost dollars would have generated over time.

So, all other things being equal, you should select a mutual fund with a history of doing well in tough economic times. In the case of equity funds, that means a better-than-average performance during bear markets. For fixed-income funds, consider those that held their own during periods of rising interest rates.

In order to determine which funds have performed best under pressure, you'll need to gather some intelligence. First, you have to determine which periods during the past 10 to 15 years were especially tough. In the case of the stock markets, 1981, 1984 and 1987 were bad. For bond markets, 1980 was particularly difficult.

Armed with that knowledge, use the information in *The Financial*

Post, Financial Times or the *Financial Times Mutual Fund Sourcebook* to see which funds on your short list stood up best. Look especially at the following factors:

1. Good overall performance in relation to comparable funds. If everyone was down (and most Canadian bond funds were down in 1980; equity funds were down in 1981) see if any of your funds were down less.

2. Performance relative to the TSE. If you're considering a Canadian equity fund or a balanced fund, see if it managed to outperform the Toronto Stock Exchange 300 Index during the years you're considering.

I did an analysis like this on Canadian equity funds for *The Money-Letter* in May 1988. Here are the funds that emerged at that time as the best performers during stock market slumps. I chose 1981 and 1984 because the TSE 300 declined in those years. The index was actually up on a year-over-year basis in 1987, but many equity funds suffered losses because of the stock market crash.

Fund	Performance Record*			
	1981	**1984**	**1987**	**Average****
Industrial Dividend	-3.7%	8.2%	17.6%	7.37%
Universal Savings	-2.8%	2.7%	17.1%	5.67%
Cundill Security	-1.7%	7.0%	7.5%	4.27%
Industrial Growth	-7.8%	5.5%	11.7%	3.13%
Mackenzie Equity	-6.6%	1.4%	12.3%	2.37%

* Simple annual rates of return

** Average rate of return for 1981, 1984 and 1987

Source: *Financial Times Mutual Fund Sourcebook*

As you can see, with any of these funds you would have ended up making a small average annual gain for the three down years in question. If that doesn't leave you overly impressed, consider that many mutual funds actually *lost* money in all three of those years. AGF Management's

Growth Equity Fund is an example; it had an average annual drop of 13.7% per unit during that time.

So that's the Surefire Six-Step. Yes, there's a fair amount of work involved in finding the right fund. But the payoff can be terrific. It's worth the effort.

The Specialty Funds

MUTUAL FUND PROMOTERS are nothing if not innovative. The more you learn about funds, the more you'll be impressed by the diversity of the offerings available.

Many investors see funds in one-dimensional terms: "mutual fund" and "stock fund" mean the same thing to them. Well, as we've already seen, that's not so. But the diversity goes far beyond even the basic categories I outlined in Chapter Thirteen. There are a variety of specialty funds available, designed to serve specific investor needs. And some of these are of particular interest to low-risk investors.

I've selected the most important of these specialty funds for inclusion here. Take a careful look at each type; you may well find some that fit perfectly with your personal goals and standards.

Value Funds. In an earlier chapter, I mentioned the concept of Value Investing, developed by Benjamin Graham. In a nutshell, this involves seeking out those stocks which are significantly undervalued, preferably trading well below book value (the actual net asset value of each share, based on the company balance sheet). When the price of the stock is above book value, the theory goes, you're paying a premium for it. The greater the premium, the more speculative the stock becomes.

Disciples of Graham therefore spend a great deal of time and effort combing the stock markets for issues that are trading below book value.

That, as you can imagine, requires a great deal of work. If you have the time and the inclination, fine. But if you'd rather use a short cut, take a close look at some of the mutual funds that use the Value Investing approach. They're excellent vehicles for low-risk investors.

Two of the best known in Canada are the Cundill Value Fund and the Cundill Security Fund. They're based in Vancouver and managed by Peter Cundill, a slim, academic-looking chartered accountant. He travels the world looking for ways to buy a dollar for forty cents; in mid-1988, for example, he was concentrating his attention on the West German stock market, which he felt was greatly undervalued. The big Volkswagen company was one of his special favourites; it was then trading at about 50% of its book value.

Cundill's approach is designed to construct an investment portfolio with a built-in safety net. By purchasing stocks trading well below a company's break-up value, he seeks to limit the downside risk while maximizing the growth potential. When market conditions change or investors discover the bargain-basement share price, the value of the stock will begin to appreciate, he reasons.

His nose for a bargain has paid off handsomely for investors in the Cundill Value Fund. It hasn't had a losing year since 1974 (based on calendar year results), and has consistently ranked among the top performers in the balanced fund group, according to the *Financial Times Mutual Fund Sourcebook*. In 1981, a year when many funds recorded major losses, the Value Fund showed a profit of 18.5%. In 1987, the year of the greatest stock market crash in history, it was ahead 12.9%.

The Value Fund's major drawback is that it is not RRSP-eligible, except as foreign property. Since foreign property holdings cannot exceed 10% of the total book value of your RRSP, that severely limits your ability to hold this fund in a retirement savings plan.

Cundill does have an RRSP-eligible fund, the Cundill Security Fund, which was set up in 1979. It specializes in Canadian securities. But that limits the investing options considerably — the Canadian market is very small by international standards. As a result, the Security Fund doesn't have as outstanding a track record as its international counterpart, although it has consistently been in the top third of the Canadian equity group on a calendar year basis. It has also stood up well in bear market conditions, as I pointed out in the last chapter.

There are other funds around that use Value Investing techniques as the basis for their investment decisions, but so far I haven't come across any that can match the consistent performance record of the Cundill funds over a long period of time.

Protected Funds. These mutual funds are designed for investors who want to participate in the stock market while minimizing their risk. To achieve this, they use a concept known as portfolio insurance. This is based on complex mathematical formulae which vary the Asset Mix of a fund so as to protect it against sharp declines in the stock market. The idea is to participate in bull markets while shielding investments from the full impact of a decline. It's all done by computer, and the concept came in for heavy criticism after Black Monday, when the programmed trading in insured portfolios that was triggered by the market drop was blamed at least in part for the exaggerated severity of the fall.

The managers of Protected Funds use differing techniques to achieve their objectives. Some, especially in the U.S., rely on stock index futures to provide the insurance component. Many of these were badly battered on Black Monday, sending the theoreticians back to the drawing board. Others use a more conservative approach, relying on Treasury bills to provide the protective component. As the market drops, more money is shifted out of stocks and into T-bills. When the market is rising, the proportion of stocks in the total Asset Mix is increased. Investors in these funds therefore won't enjoy the full benefit of rising stock values. But neither will they experience the full impact of a drop.

In theory, these Protected Funds should be attractive to low-risk investors. In the real world, however, there are two problems. First, these funds do not have a lengthy track record. As the October 1987 market crash proved, the theory behind them may be faulty. Second, there are not many Protected Funds available yet in Canada. You'll have to do some homework to find them.

One into which I've put $5,000 of my own money, basically to see how well it works, is operated by National Trust. It's called the PRO Fund (for Protected Risk Option) and it's one of the few Protected Funds available to the ordinary investor which has full RRSP eligibility.

Actually, there are two National Trust PRO funds: a "January" fund and a "February" fund. They're open only for a limited period each year, during RRSP season; if you miss the window you're out of luck. They were started in 1984 and the results for the first four years of operation indicate they're achieving their objectives.

	1984-85	1985-86	1986-87	1987-88
January Fund	+4.72%	+10.22%	+19.09%	+0.1%
February Fund	+6.82%	+10.95%	+22.26%	0

As you can see, the PRO Funds performed reasonably well during 1984-85, which was a tough period for the stock market. In 1985-86 and 1986-87, two years in which the markets were strong, they registered good returns. You could have done better in top-quality equity funds, but the results are quite respectable by industry standards.

In 1987-88, the period that saw the stock market crash and the end of the great bull market, the PRO Funds broke even. They didn't make any money, but they met their stated objective: to protect investors' principal in a market downturn.

There are also some Protected Funds available based on bonds rather than stocks. One is Protected Bond Fund, run by Toronto-based Guardian Timing Services. It's a no-load fund, but they aren't interested in your money unless you have at least $150,000 to put up.

Index Funds. This may surprise you, but there are a lot of Canadian equity funds that fail to outperform the TSE 300 index over the long term. In other words, the fund managers — professional money people — can't even match the average performance of the stock market.

That simple fact has led to a new type of mutual fund: Index Funds. These are stock portfolios that mirror precisely the composition and weighting of a major stock market index. The concept is simple: your Index Fund will perform exactly as the stock market performs. Since the long-term trend of the market is up, if you buy and hold you'll eventually make money. And since no high-powered portfolio decisions are involved, management fees are low.

The chartered banks are aggressively moving into this area. Toronto-Dominion Bank has two such funds: Green Line Canadian Index Fund is based on the TSE 300 Index; Green Line U.S. Index Fund is based on the Standard and Poor 500 Index. Neither has been around for very long, but the results of the first two full years of the Canadian fund are interesting. It was up 8.1% in 1986 (ranking it 37th out of 81 funds) and 4.9% in 1987 (26th of 88). Ironically, in both years it slightly underperformed the TSE 300, even though its holdings were exactly the same as the stocks that made up that index.

Bank of Montreal also has an Index Fund based on the TSE 300 and I expect others to appear over the next few years.

I don't particularly like Index Funds. They're an easy route to go if you want to be involved in the stock market, but by definition they're only going to produce mediocre returns. There are plenty of equity funds that consistently outperform the market indexes. A good investor will search them out.

Preferred Funds. As I pointed out earlier in this book, the low-risk investor should always look at his or her return in after-tax dollars. Nothing counts until the tax department has claimed its share. Preferred funds are designed to maximize after-tax dollars; they specialize in preferred shares paying better-than-average returns which are eligible for the dividend tax credit.

Because of the nature of these funds, they should never be held within an RRSP. Much of their attraction is based on the tax break they provide; that's lost within a retirement plan. Preferred Funds work best for investors whose priority is income and who can take maximum advantage of the dividend tax credit. You don't have to be in a high tax bracket to benefit from them; as we saw in Chapter Nine, dividend income is almost tax-free if your taxable income is under $27,500 a year.

One of the top-performing Preferred Funds in recent years has been the Vancouver-based Phillips, Hager and North Dividend Income Fund. Until 1987, it had never ranked worse than second among funds of this type since its establishment a decade earlier. Performance slipped in the first half of 1988, though, so if you're considering it, check how it's doing now.

You'd expect funds of this type to be fairly steady performers. They can display some wide swings, however, mainly due to interest rate movements. For example, Investors Dividend Fund, the oldest in this group, dropped 8.4% in value in 1981, as interest rates reached their pre-recession peak. It more than made up for that in 1982 and 1983, however, post- ing returns of 27.4% and 22.4% as interest rates retreated. So the time to buy into a Preferred Fund is when interest rates are high. The payoff in the ensuing years can be substantial.

Convertible Funds. Low-risk investors have always been attracted to con- vertible securities. That's because they're less risky than common stocks, while providing a better cash flow.

Convertibles are generally bonds or preferred shares paying a speci- fied rate of interest or dividend. That rate is normally more than you'd receive from a common stock dividend but less than you'd get from an ordinary bond. What makes a convertible unique is the privilege to con- vert the security to a predetermined number of common shares of a com- pany within a certain time. So if the share price moves up, you can switch to the common stock or sell the convertible, the price of which will reflect the increased value of the common stock. Either way you realize a nice capital gain. If, on the other hand, the share price remains low, you hold on to the convertible and continue to draw interest or dividends.

That distinction is important to your after-tax return. If the convert- ible is in the form of a preferred share, you'll receive dividends, which will be eligible for the dividend tax credit. If it's a bond, you'll be paid interest, which will be taxed at a higher rate.

Some mutual funds have been set up to specialize in convertibles. They're especially appealing in uncertain times, when investors don't know which way the markets are going and want to hedge their bets. But, again, this is a relatively new concept so these funds have not had time to establish a long track record. The oldest Canadian entry, Noram Convertible Securities Fund, was established in January 1985. It had a good year in 1987, with a 21.5% return. But it's still too soon to know how it or any other Convertible Fund will perform in comparison to other fund alternatives over the long haul.

Ethical Funds. If you don't want to put money into companies that invest in South Africa, or manufacture arms, or pollute the atmosphere, or profit from the porn trade, then Ethical Funds may be for you. They've become a hot trend in the U.S. and more of them are springing up in Canada.

The managers of Ethical Funds are essentially selling peace of mind. You can rest easy at night, knowing your money is not contributing to the maiming of innocent people or the exploitation of children.

There are two considerations in selecting an Ethical Fund. One is to find the fund that coincides most closely with your particular beliefs. That's not easy; different funds stress different priorities. The Vancouver-based Ethical Growth Fund, for example, excludes companies that do business with racist states, practice poor industrial relations, deal with weapons or the military, or are involved in the nuclear industry. The Summa Fund, managed from Winnipeg by the Investors Group, is more interested in avoiding companies involved with alcohol, tobacco, gambling, and pornography. The two Environmental Investment Funds (one invests in Canadian stocks, the other internationally) are closely tied to the Toronto-based Energy Probe Research Foundation and concentrate on companies that support the principles of environmental protection, conservation, and Canadian self-sufficiency in energy. By the time you read this, there will probably be more of these Ethical Funds around, each with its own set of investment criteria.

The other consideration when choosing an Ethical Fund is to find one that will give you a reasonable return on investment. Here again, we're dealing with a new concept so the track records aren't in place yet. Ethical Growth Fund's initial results are encouraging, however. For the year ending June 30, 1987, it realized a return of 9.1%, ranking it 16th of 83 Canadian equity funds. The year ending June 30, 1988, was even better. Ethical Growth Fund returned 12.3%, mainly because the manager, Larry Lunn, saw the stock market crash coming and was 73% in cash on Black Monday. That performance propelled the fund into the number two position in the Canadian equity fund rankings for that period — a pretty heady spot for a fund barely two years old.

So Ethical Fund investing doesn't necessarily mean sacrificing a good return on your money. Just be sure you find one with a manager who has instincts like Larry Lunn's.

Country-Specific Funds. American investors finally discovered the rest of the world in the 1980s. Canadians have been much slower to do so, however; many are even reluctant to venture as far afield as Wall Street.

However, there have been some tremendous profits made from international investing and this has spawned a new type of mutual fund, the Country-Specific Fund. These funds invest entirely in the securities of one nation.

The most familiar are the various Japan funds, which have achieved some spectacular results. The number one Canadian-based mutual fund for the five-year period ending June 30, 1988, was the AGF Japan Fund, which produced an almost-unbelievable average annual compound rate of return of 30.4% during that time. Over a ten-year period, it averaged 21.7%, second best in the country.

Unfortunately, Canadian investors are not very well served when it comes to Country-Specific Funds. Your only choices are funds specializing in Japan or the United States. If you want to participate in rapidly growing economies in other parts of the world, you have to look south.

A number of funds have been set up in the U.S. enabling investors to participate in the growing economies of other countries. Generally, these are closed-end funds that trade on the New York or American Stock Exchange. Some concentrate on nations with highly-developed economies: the France Fund, the Germany Fund and the Scandinavia Fund are examples. Others specialize in emerging countries: the Malaysia Fund and the Mexico Fund are examples. In some cases, these funds are the only way the average investor can participate in a booming economy because of foreign investment restrictions within the country. The Korea Fund and the Brazil Fund fall into this group.

Investing in Country-Specific Funds can be profitable, but it can also be risky. A politically unstable nation may be subject to changes in government which dramatically affect the business climate and, hence, the value of shares in its companies. If this sort of investing appeals to you, I suggest setting up a diversified portfolio of Country-Specific Funds to limit your risk. Eric Kirzner, a contributing editor to *The MoneyLetter*, monitors these funds on a regular basis and his recommendations may help you in deciding where to concentrate your investments.

Real Estate Funds. These were among the hottest performers in the year following Black Monday. Investors, nervous about the future of the stock market, rushed to put money into something with more perceived stability, such as real estate. The largest of these funds, Investors Real Property Fund, more than doubled in size in the 12 months following the crash. And fund managers responded to this vote of confidence with good results; two real estate funds made it to the top 10 for the year ending September 30, 1988, and not one lost money.

There are a number of problems with Canadian Real Estate Funds, however. To start with, they're all relatively young. None has been around long enough to be tested during a real estate slump. Until that happens, the degree of risk involved in such funds can't be properly assessed.

Size is another concern. Some of these funds are very small. As a result, all their assets may be tied up in two or three projects. Such a lack of diversification leaves a fund vulnerable to regional market drops.

Liquidity is another consideration. While all mutual funds should be regarded as long-term investments, this is especially true in the case of Real Estate Funds. Most of these funds are valued just once a month, and some only quarterly, which could mean a lengthy delay when you want to redeem your units.

Real Estate Funds do have an edge in one area, however. Their financial structure gives them a tax advantage over other types of mutual funds. Units designed for non-tax sheltered portfolios take advantage of Capital Cost Allowance (CCA) to effectively reduce the tax payable on the income generated. This means that annual income of, say, 11.5% could produce an after-tax return of between 10% and 10.5%. For low-risk investors in search of good after-tax returns, that can be very attractive.

But there is a catch. It's called recaptured depreciation, and it comes into play when a building is sold. Suppose your fund owned an office complex and, over a five-year period, claimed capital cost allowance of $250,000 against the building. At the end of that time, it is sold for more than its original value. The CCA is deemed by Revenue Canada to have been "recaptured", and tax is now payable on it.

Real Estate Funds treat this situation in different ways. Some will deduct a certain percentage from the value of your units when you redeem them, in recognition of this recaptured depreciation. Others will issue a tax information slip showing an amount which must be included on your next tax return. Before you invest in a Real Estate Fund, ask about their policies in this regard and make sure you understand them.

Also make sure you buy the correct units. Most funds have RRSP and non-RRSP shares, with the A units being suitable for retirement plans and the B units for non-tax sheltered portfolios.

If you do decide to put money into one or more of the specialty funds, just remember the principle of diversification. Don't overconcentrate; specialty funds should be just a small part of your total portfolio.

CHAPTER 16

Blending in Bonds

Neither a borrower nor a lender be.
— Shakespeare

THERE ARE TIMES I think nobody likes bonds except me. As an investment, they have a terrible long-term track record. Virtually every study I've seen on the real after-tax returns from various types of investments shows that, over the long haul, bonds are dreadful. For example, a recent report done by the Canadian Institute of Actuaries concluded that if you'd invested $1,000 in Government of Canada bonds in 1924, the real value of your investment in 1986, after inflation had been accounted for, would have been only $2,959.83. That's an average annual return of 1.76%. I don't know many investors who would be happy with that.

Even though it raises huge amounts of money with them, the federal government obviously doesn't like bonds. Certainly it does everything it can to discourage investors from putting money into them; why else would it tax interest payments at a higher rate than any other form of investment income?

The social stigma against being a money lender that prevailed in Shakespeare's time, and which is reflected in the quote from *Hamlet* that begins this chapter, has faded away. Nevertheless, the label of bond holder still manages to convey an image of stodgy conservatism which is somehow out of sync with the yuppie philosophy of the 1980s.

So, in the face of all this opposition, why do I persist in liking bonds?

Two reasons. First, because they're a relatively simple investment form. My life has enough complications; I don't need to add more. Second, and more to the point, I've made a great deal of money from them.

In the first chapter, I told you about the 73% capital gain I made when I purchased Government of Canada stripped bonds when interest rates were high in the summer of 1984. The bonds that I didn't sell continue to earn money for my RRSP at a rate of 13.6% a year.

And, as I told you in Chapter Eight, it was my bond holdings that saved my life on Black Monday. The gains in the market price of my bonds, which resulted from the massive drop in interest rates that followed the crash, just about offset my stock losses.

So I have a soft spot for bonds. But you have to treat them with respect. Get careless and this seemingly safe, dull investment can cost you a lot of money.

You can, of course, avoid bonds entirely in your investment portfolio. The income portion of your Asset Mix can be made up of other types of securities, such as mortgages. Yet I don't advise taking that course. Bonds are a relatively easy investment, much simpler for the ordinary investor to succeed with than stocks, for example. And they're highly liquid; you can always find a market for a quality bond. That's not always the case with fixed-income securities.

The biggest drawback of bonds is their tax treatment. There are no special breaks for interest income, no equivalent to the dividend tax credit or the $100,000 capital gains exemption. The one small tax break that was available vanished under tax reform when the federal government did away with the old $1,000 investment income deduction.

That means you have to look closely at the tax consequences of any bond investment before proceeding. If you're buying the securities for an RRSP or RRIF, there's no problem. However, if you're investing outside a retirement plan, review the alternatives first. You may find you'd be better off using preferred shares instead of bonds as your income assets, because of the effect of the dividend tax credit. Or you may decide on a bond strategy that emphasizes capital gains over income flow. Whatever decision you make, be sure you understand all the tax implications first.

If you want to make money from bonds, repeat this cardinal rule over and over again until it becomes fixed in your mind: *I will only buy bonds when interest rates are high.* Don't ever violate it. If you do, you risk being hammered.

Psychologically, this is not an easy rule to follow. It means buying bonds when interest rates are starting to frighten people. In 1981, when prime was over 20%, many people were afraid to buy bonds, thinking rates would go higher still, to 25%, even 30%. Those who had bought in at 15% were scared to death as they watched the market value of their holdings erode with every upward tick in rates.

As it turned out, those who had the nerve to get in when rates were in the 15% to 20% range made a fortune when interest rates started to fall sharply in 1982. The losers were those who had continued to hold off, expecting rates to move higher still. They ended up missing the boat entirely.

The corollary to my cardinal rule is this: *Never buy bonds when inflation is rising.* You'll lose two ways in that situation. First, rising inflation generally means that higher interest rates are coming as the central banks try to take some of the heat out of the economy. So your strategy should be to wait until those rates have taken hold and inflation appears to be at or near its peak before moving in. Second, inflation means reduced purchasing power for the dollar. That translates into the steady erosion of the real value of your hard-earned capital. So you lose on two counts: the market value of your bonds declines, along with the purchasing power of your invested money. It's not a situation you want to get into, but it's one you can profit from once the inflation cycle has run its course.

For the low-risk investor, who is constantly looking for ways to minimize the potential downside in a portfolio, there are three good times to buy bonds. I'll describe them in a few moments, but first we have to get some basics out of the way. If you already know about bond investing, you can skip the definitions that follow. If you don't, here are some terms you must understand:

Coupon rate: This is the amount of interest a bond pays. It's expressed in percentage terms and based on a $1,000 face value. So a bond with a 10% coupon will pay interest at the rate of $100 a year. This is usually paid semi-annually. The coupon rate is usually fixed, although there are some bonds with a variable rate.

Maturity: The date at which the bond comes due.

Redemption: Some bonds allow the issuer to redeem them before the maturity date, at a specified price. Redeemable bonds are generally not good investments because if interest rates drop, the issuer will probably call them in. That reduces the market value of the bond, which then becomes based on the first redemption date rather than the maturity date.

Retraction: Bond issues that allow the purchaser to sell them back to the issuer before maturity at a predetermined price are called retractables. These work in favour of the investor because they allow you to sell the bonds back, usually at par or slightly over, if interest rates rise after you've made the purchase. This adds downside protection to the investment, something low-risk investors always like to see.

Yield: This is the actual rate of return you'll receive on a bond you buy in the market. In its simplest form, it is calculated by dividing the annual interest paid by the current selling price of the bond. The yield can be quite different from the coupon rate and will vary depending on the bond price. For example, a bond with a $1,000 face value and a 10% coupon may be trading at $950 (you'll see it quoted at $95; bond prices are always based on $100). That gives it a current yield of 10-1/2% ($100/$950). If, on the other hand, it was trading at $1,100 (quoted as $110), the yield would be 9.1% ($100/$1,100).

When you look at the bond tables in the business pages, you'll see a column showing yield. This can be misleading because it represents *yield to maturity.* This tells you what return you could expect from the bond if you held it to maturity and all the interest payments were reinvested at the current yield. Obviously, that will be very difficult to do in most cases. So in real life, your yield to maturity will likely be somewhat less than you see in the paper. The longer the life of the bond, the less accurate the yield to maturity will be.

Some bond reports issued by brokerage houses provide you with greater detail, including current yield, yield to maturity, yield to redemption and yield to retraction. Before you make a bond purchase, it's a good idea to try to review such a report.

Rating: There are two bond rating services in Canada, the Dominion Bond Rating Service and the Canadian Bond Rating Service. They assign a safety sticker to every publicly traded bond. The higher the rating (AAA or A + + is the top), the safer the investment. Most low-risk investors will avoid any bond with a rating of less than A. You can find out the rating of any issue you're interested in from your broker.

Incidentally, these companies also rate preferred shares if you're planning any such investments.

So much for the fundamentals. Now on to the investment strategies. When you see any of these situations developing — I call them Opportunity Periods — be prepared to move quickly and aggressively into the bond market.

OPPORTUNITY #1: *The end of a business cycle.*
The typical business cycle ends with industrial capacity strained to the limit, rising commodity prices and labour shortages. The newspapers are full of warnings about the economy overheating and of growing inflationary pressures. The central bankers try to cool things out by ratcheting up interest rates. The theory behind this action is that higher borrowing costs will discourage consumer spending and business expansion, thereby reducing the building pressures within the economy.

Although the bankers and politicians try to manipulate their fiscal and economic policies to keep the economy stable, the usual end result of jacking up interest rates late in a business cycle is an economic downturn leading into a recession. That produces a policy switch. The main concern is no longer an overheated economy but a stagnating or declining one. As part of the program to get the economy moving again, interest rates are reduced to encourage more consumer spending and business investment.

For the bond buyer, the last gasp of a business cycle therefore represents a great opportunity. Interest rates are high, as the central banks try to squeeze out inflation. They may edge higher still, as they did in 1981. But you know the peak is near.

By purchasing bonds at this stage, you achieve two desirable results: you lock in high yields over the life of your bonds and you set yourself up for a healthy capital gain when the recession hits and interest rates start coming down. That's because bond prices move inversely to interest rates: when rates move down, bond prices go up and vice-versa.

The timing of your bond purchases in this situation is important. In 1981, everyone who bought bonds when the prime was in the 15% to

20% range eventually made money. But those who bought at 20% made a lot more. So the ideal situation is to buy in just when interest rates reach their peak. The difficulty is that even professional bond traders can't call that point exactly.

So you need a strategy. Here are two to consider:

1. Averaging up. This involves setting a target entry level as you see the end of the business cycle approaching. Let's say, for example, that your cash reserves are high in anticipation of moving into the bond market. You decide you'll start accumulating bonds when yields on long-term Government of Canada issues hit 11%. When they reach that point, start buying. But don't invest all the money you've set aside at once. Commit no more than 20% at this point. Then set a new target entry level — say 12%.

If rates continue to move up and reach your new target, commit more funds — say 25% of the remainder. Keep repeating the process until you see clear signs that rates have peaked and are starting to drop. At that point commit the balance of your available funds.

This system allows you to keep averaging up the yield on your bonds. But it will only work effectively if you set target entry levels that are realistic. If your entry level is too high, you could miss out entirely. If it's too low, you may exhaust the bulk of your cash reserves while interest rates are still well below their peak. Obviously, this becomes a judgement call, but a good rule to remember is that the higher the inflation rate, the higher interest rates will have to go to bring the economy back into line. If you're dealing with a relatively low inflation rate, say under 5%, entry levels of 10-1/2% to 11% are realistic. If inflation is high, say 8% or more, you probably won't want to start committing funds until long-term yields are in the 13% to 14% range. If you're faced with runaway inflation, don't buy bonds at all until you see clear signs that the cost of living index is coming under control.

2. Downslope buying. This strategy involves sitting on your cash reserves until you see clear signs that the interest rate cycle has peaked and is starting back down. You then move in with everything you've got.

The idea is that since no one knows where the top will be, you shouldn't try for it. Instead, aim to buy in within 20% of the peak. You can only do that with confidence if all the signs tell you the top has been reached and the slide down has begun.

There are two dangers with downslope buying. The first is that rates may fall so fast that you miss your buying opportunity. That's what happened in the aftermath of Black Monday. Normally, however, interest rates don't move that quickly, so this risk is minimal.

The other danger is that you'll receive a false signal from the interest rate market. It may look like rates have peaked, so you commit your money. Then the upward trend resumes. This is a real danger and there's no easy solution to it. But your key indicators should help you here. If there are no clear signs that inflation is starting to abate, any downturn in interest rates is likely to be temporary. Hold off until the indicators leave no doubt.

OPPORTUNITY #2: *Sustained disinflation.*

The second major bond buying opportunity arises during periods of sustained disinflation, such as we experienced between 1981 and 1987. During such times, interest rates are in a clear downward trend, although there will be occasional blips along the way. Bond prices during such periods will continue to strengthen as interest rates decline. So if you invest in bonds in the early stages of a disinflation cycle, they will perform well. However, if the economy has been going through a disinflationary phase for some time, avoid bonds unless you can purchase them during temporary upward spikes in rates.

OPPORTUNITY #3: *Temporary blips.*

No interest rate chart goes straight up or down. There are zigs and zags along the way, reflecting temporary changes in direction due to specific events. For example, when the Canadian dollar comes under one of its periodic sieges, the Bank of Canada will crank up interest rates in an effort to defend it by attracting more foreign capital into the country.

These blips in the trend sometimes generate bond-buying opportunities. The summer of 1984 was one such occasion and astute bond investors took advantage of it to lock in excellent yields in the 13% to 14% range.

The key to profiting from these blips is to look carefully at what's happening to long-term bond yields. Often they'll move very little. Short-term rates will rise, but long-term bonds will hold fairly steady. That means the professionals believe rates will drop again very soon, so they aren't about to start offering bargains.

If the yields on long-term bonds do move up, as they did in mid-1984, then you *may* be looking at a buying opportunity. Think it through carefully before committing funds. Make sure you're satisfied the upward move in rates is really due to temporary forces and does not represent the first leg in the last phase of a business cycle. If you're convinced you're right, then go ahead with the investment.

What do you purchase? These are the key things to take into account:

Maturity. The longer the bond has to run until maturity, the more inherent profit (or loss) it contains. That's because any movement in interest rates has a much greater impact on a bond that matures in 25 years than on one that comes due in six months. If you want to lock in your yield for a long time while at the same time maximizing the capital potential of the bond, you'll go long. Remember, though, that if interest rates go up, the market value of long-term bonds will decline more than on short-term bonds. So the longer the term, the greater the risk.

Low-risk investors generally stick to bonds with medium maturities (say up to 10 years out). This reduces the potential capital gain, but also cuts any potential losses if you were off in the timing of your purchases.

Safety. The low-risk investor will stick to bonds with a high rating. That doesn't mean you're limited to Government of Canada issues and nothing else. Provincial government bonds pay a higher rate of interest and most are A rated or higher. You'll also find corporate bond issues from blue-ribbon companies with A or better ratings, paying a full point or more than the Canadas. As long as the rating is respectable, go for the better return.

Yield. Obviously, you want to get the best return you can, consistent with the other key factors. Check this out carefully — you'll sometimes find yield variations among similar bonds. If there's no apparent reason for this, try to buy the one with the better return. Don't be surprised if you can't get it, though. Typically, brokers will sell you bonds from their own inventory. That means you may see one listed in the bond tables that looks attractive but when you place an order you'll find it's not available. That's because your dealer doesn't have it in inventory and can't find anyone who does. If that situation arises, you'll either have to place a standing order and wait or accept the closest available substitute.

Sweeteners and Sourers. Some bonds come with added inducements that reduce risk and add to their attractiveness. Retractables and convertibles fall into this group. You may also come across some extendibles, bonds for which the maturity date can be extended at the owner's option. See if any of the issues you're considering has these qualities.

On the other side, some bonds have conditions that make them less attractive to buyers — a redemption clause is one. These sourers, as I call them, make a bond less attractive in the marketplace.

So find out all the terms and conditions attached to a bond before making a purchase.

Strips. You can buy conventional bond issues. Or, if you prefer, you can buy strips. These are based on Government of Canada issues or highly rated provincial issues and come in two forms: bonds and coupons.

Stripped bonds have had all the interest coupons removed. You buy them at a discounted price and hold them until maturity, when you collect the full face value. No interest is paid in the interim; your return all comes at the end.

Stripped coupons are the interest coupons that have been removed from the bonds. Again, these are purchased at a discounted price and held to the date the interest was to be paid, when they're cashed in.

In both cases, the interest rate you receive is calculated on the discounted price you pay and the number of years to maturity. So a $1,000 stripped bond maturing in eight years and yielding 10% annually could be bought today for about $466. The higher the imputed interest rate, the lower the price.

Stripped bonds and coupons have one major advantage over ordinary bonds in that the yield to maturity is guaranteed. You don't have to worry about reinvesting the money at the same rate or better; the annual compound rate of return is calculated in the quoted price.

Stripped bonds and coupons are excellent RRSP investments. You can buy them to mature at the time you plan to retire, secure in the knowledge that your rate of return is fixed and you won't have to worry about reinvesting the interest. Being in an RRSP also eliminates tax problems. Outside a retirement plan the government insists you pay tax on the accrued interest once every three years, even though you haven't received a cent. That's something you should avoid at all costs.

Obviously, you don't buy strips if you require a steady income stream. Conventional bonds are the route to go if that's what you need.

So much for when and what to buy. Now for the much tougher question. When, if ever, should you sell?

I can make a plausible case for never selling a bond. I can also show you why trading in bonds makes excellent sense. Which route you go depends on your personality and your objectives.

Buy and hold. If you purchase bonds only during my Opportunity Periods, you'll acquire a portfolio of high-yielding bonds that will generate an excellent cash return. If income flow is your main concern, then you should only sell these securities in exceptional circumstances. Even though you might make a nice capital gain when interest rates are low, you wouldn't be able to replace the cash flow you're relying on.

For example, in late August 1988 the 13-1/2% Government of Canada bond maturing December 1, 1999, was selling for $116-5/8. In other words, you could have received $1,166.25 for every such bond you owned. If you'd bought the bond at par ($1,000), you'd realize a nice capital gain.

But when you turned around to reinvest that money, you'd run into problems. Your bond was paying $135 a year in interest. But short-term interest rates in August 1988 were around 10%. So your reinvested money would only generate about $116 in annual revenue — significantly less than your bond was paying. If you were living on the income from your bonds, you'd suffer a revenue loss.

In a situation like this, a buy-and-hold strategy makes the most sense. You time your purchases so as to maximize your return and then live off the proceeds.

About the only time I would counsel selling off a portfolio of high-yielding bonds where income was a paramount consideration would be in the face of possible runaway inflation. During hyperinflation, fixed-income investments of any kind are highly vulnerable; as the purchasing power of money collapses so does the real value of your holdings. But we haven't seen hyperinflation in Canada in our lifetime and I don't think we will. We flirted with it during the late 1970s but managed to pull back from the brink. I doubt our politicians and central bankers will allow this generation to come that close again.

Buy and trade. This approach works best when your objective is to maximize capital gains and minimize taxes. It involves buying during the Opportunity Periods and selling off when interest rates appear to be near their next cyclical low.

The advantage of the trading approach is that it channels part of your bond revenue into capital gains, where you get a significant tax break as long as you haven't used up your $100,000 lifetime exemption. That's why trading is especially appropriate for bond holdings outside an RRSP; inside a plan the tax benefits of a trading strategy are lost.

If capital gains are important to you, consider buying bonds nearing maturity that are trading below par. These are bonds with a low coupon rate compared to current market levels. You'll sometimes find them trading below $90 or, occasionally, in the low $80s. In August 1988, for example, you could have purchased an Ontario Hydro 7% bond maturing in less than four years for $891.25. What makes these bonds tax-attractive is that, regardless of what happens to interest rates, the price will rise towards par as the bonds approach maturity. This particular bond was showing a yield to maturity of 10.42%. But part of that yield included the $108.75 capital gain the bond would produce at maturity — a capital gain which, for most people, would be tax free.

As I said at the outset of this chapter, I like bonds. Every low-risk investor should own some, either to hold or trade. Forget all those gloomy analyses of how poorly they've performed in the past. You *can* make money from investing in them — if you do it right.

Other Income Investments

A large income is the best recipe for happiness I ever heard of.

— Jane Austen

T HE SINGLE MOST popular investment vehicle in Canada is the Guaranteed Investment Certificate (GIC). Every year we pour hundreds of millions of dollars of our savings into these supposedly safe and secure securities.

We do so for a number of reasons, all of them related in one way or another to our inherent conservatism as investors. The prime consideration is, of course, the apparent riskless nature of a GIC. As long as its value is $60,000 or less, the term is not more than five years, and the GIC is issued by a financial institution that's a member of the Canada Deposit Insurance Corporation or, in the case of credit unions, a provincial deposit insurance plan, your principal and interest are fully protected. If the issuing firm goes belly-up, the CDIC will step in and give you back your money.

Competitive interest rates are another attractive facet of GICs. There are few other low-risk investments available that provide as attractive a return — at least on the surface.

Finally, there's the matter of convenience. You can invest in a GIC at any branch of a bank, trust company or credit union in the country. And the whole transaction takes just a few minutes; it's not much more complicated than making a deposit.

No wonder GICs have become so popular.

Well, I hate to be the bearer of bad news, but there's some smoke and mirrors involved here.

As I pointed out in Chapter Two, things are not always as they seem in the investing world. Despite all the good things going for it, that GIC you're about to purchase may be a terrible place to put your hard-earned money. Unless you're very careful, you could end up with a real return of far less than you're expecting. And the purchasing power of your capital will be eaten away without your even realizing it.

You'll recall that in Chapter Two we looked at the combined effects of Tax Risk and Inflation Risk on a typical GIC. These twin killers can combine to turn a supposedly risk-free investment into a dead-certain money loser. The table below shows what happens to the value of a $10,000 GIC, in terms of real purchasing power, at various rates of inflation. I'm assuming that the income from the certificate is used to live on and is not reinvested.

Inflation rate	Real Value of GIC after:		
	5 years	10 years	15 years
5%	$7,738	$5,987	$4,633
7%	6,957	4,840	3,367
10%	5,905	3,487	2,059

Scary, isn't it? Even at a relatively modest 5% inflation rate, if you buy a five-year GIC and roll it over twice, your purchasing power will be less than half the value of your original investment when you redeem the certificate after 15 years. If inflation is running at 10% — which, I hope, is unlikely — the real value of your original $10,000 investment would be reduced by 80%. Not exactly the result you anticipated when you made the investment, is it?

Of course, inflation is not the only problem, as we saw in Chapter Two. Because interest payments are taxed at your highest marginal rate, Revenue Canada grabs a big chunk of all your GIC earnings.

Perhaps now you understand why I don't share the general enthusiasm for GICs. There are certain circumstances in which they can be a valuable investment alternative, however. You just have to follow some basic ground rules:

Hold GICs only in a tax shelter. If you limit your GIC investments to RRSPs, RRIFs, and deferred profit sharing plans (DPSPs), you immediately eliminate the Tax Risk aspect, at least until your plan matures. That's extremely important because it changes the entire GIC equation. Instead of handing over a large chunk of your interest to the government, you can now keep it all for yourself.

Allow the interest to compound. This is the key to staying ahead of inflation. By receiving 100% of the GIC interest and allowing it to accumulate, you'll build your capital base at a faster rate than inflation can erode it.

Stagger your maturities. As we saw in Chapter Two, one of the other dangers of GICs is Interest Rate Risk — getting caught holding low-yielding certificates as interest rates rise. One way around this is to stagger your maturities so you have some GICs coming due every year. That way, you'll have funds to roll over into new certificates. If rates are rising, you'll increase your average return by doing this. Of course, if they're falling, the opposite will happen. The best approach is to lock in for longer periods when rates appear to be at cyclical highs and select shorter maturities when they're low. That way you'll continually generate above-average returns on the GIC portion of your investments. Of course, that means you have to constantly watch the marketplace, but that's part of being a good investor anyway.

A word of explanation here. You'll often find the terms GIC and term deposit used interchangeably. Even the financial community can't seem to agree on the distinction between the two. You'll frequently see "term deposit" applied to a certificate with a maturity of less than one year, while GIC is used for those of a year or more. However, just to confuse you, you'll also find term deposits for up to five years.

I understand the correct differentiation to be one of cashability. The true GIC is a locked-in investment: you cannot get your money out before maturity under any circumstances (unless you sell it through a broker; more on that later). A term deposit, on the other hand, gives you the flexibility to remove your cash early, albeit with a penalty. As a price for this convenience, a long-term deposit will carry a lower interest rate than a GIC of corresponding length. The terminology can vary from one financial institution to another, however, so make sure you're on the same wavelength as the person from whom you're buying.

When you purchase GICs or term deposits, keep in mind they don't all come in the same size and shape. Increased competition has led to a number of variations on the GIC theme. Here are the main ones that existed in autumn 1988; there may be more by the time you read this:

High principal bonus: Some financial institutions will pay a premium (typically a quarter-point higher than the normal rate) if you invest a large amount of money with them. Often this sweetener is kept secret unless you ask, however.

Senior's bonus: If you're over 60, you'll find some places will add an additional quarter-point to your GIC rate.

Monthly income plans: If you need a regular income stream, there are GICs available which offer monthly payment options. I don't advise using them, because I think there are better ways to invest for income, but they're available if you want them.

Tax deferral GICs: You may see promotions for GICs which defer your tax liability for two or three years, if you expect to be in a lower tax bracket at that time — perhaps because you're planning a sabbatical or to have a baby. There's nothing special about these; they're ordinary compound interest GICs with a maturity date two or three years out. Tax laws allow you to defer declaring interest on this type of GIC for up to three years. At the end of that time, you must declare all interest earned to that date and pay the tax due.

Charitable institution bonuses: If you're involved with administering the funds of a charity, you may be interested to know that some banks and trust companies will pay a bonus rate on the charity's GIC deposits.

Diversified plans: There are certificates available which are designed to improve your rate of return by blending a standard GIC investment with a higher-yielding mutual fund. Royal Trust, for example, offers a plan which directs 75% of your investment into a GIC. The other 25% goes into their mortgage fund, which traditionally has a somewhat higher yield. Your return is therefore slightly better than with a normal GIC. As with a standard GIC, your principal is guaranteed.

Indexed GICs: These are really more of a gamble than an investment. The return on your investment is determined by what happens to one of the indexes you select during the term of your GIC. Typical options are the TSE 300 index, the New York Stock Exchange Composite Index, and the Gold Price Index. If the index you select rises, you receive an interest rate calculated on a predetermined formula. If it falls, you receive no interest at all, but your principal is returned. (Some financial institutions offer a bear market version which pays off if the market goes down.) It's a gimmick designed for people who want to play the stock market without risking their capital; I don't recommend it.

Flexible plans: A few companies offer GICs or term deposits which pay a slightly lower interest rate but allow you to withdraw your funds before maturity without penalty. Usually, you have to leave your money in for a minimum period — perhaps 45 days — or you won't receive any interest if you cash in early.

Discounted GICs: A few GICs are sold at a discounted price, in the same way as stripped bonds. At maturity, you cash them in for full face value. The difference represents your yield. Obviously, the longer the term, the deeper the discount. Buying GICs in this way permits you to invest less cash up-front.

"Used" GICs: Most people aren't aware of it, but there is a secondary market in GICs. Typically, these used GICs have been purchased by brokers at a discount from investors needing to get out early. You may be able to obtain a slightly higher yield by buying your GICs in this way.

Finally, before we leave GICs, a word about buying them. Because they are so convenient to purchase, many people don't shop the market. They go to the financial institution they normally deal with and take whatever is offered.

That's not such a hot idea. The interest rate paid on GICs can vary significantly; if you check around you may find a better deal.

On September 5, 1988, for instance, a check of the interest rates table in the *Report on Business* would have told you that the return on a five-year GIC ranged from a low of 9.75% to a high of 11.13%, depending on which financial institution you chose. That's a big difference: a $10,000 investment at the lowest rate, compounded annually, would be worth $15,923 at maturity. At the highest rate, it would be worth $16,949 — over $1,000 more.

Most major newspapers publish current interest rates at least once a week. Alternatively, you can use the service of a broker to shop the interest rate market for you. Many stockbrokers provide this service to clients. Or you can deal with a deposit broker. These are people who keep tabs on the interest rates being offered by all deposit-taking institutions in the country. They'll advise you of the best rate available and place your order. There are companies which specialize in providing this service or you may find a financial planner who offers it. Just be sure the financial institution issuing your certificate is covered by deposit insurance. Both stockbrokers and deposit brokers are paid a commission by the financial institution that issues the GIC; you don't pay anything for the service.

So much for the most popular income investment. Now let's look at some of the others you can select from.

Mortgage-backed securities. Whenever I mention mortgage-backed securities (MBS) on a radio hotline show, calls immediately start pouring in from people seeking more information. They're one of Canada's best-kept investing secrets, although they've been around in the States for years, where they're known as "Ginnie Maes".

What makes mortgage-backed securities attractive to many people is a combination of cash flow, government guarantees and competitive interest rates. However, they suffer from many of the same drawbacks as GICs. Here's how they work:

When you buy a mortgage-backed security, you're investing in a pool of high-quality residential mortgages put together by a financial institution. Each MBS pool is self-contained, and carries its own coupon rate and payment schedule. For example, a Metropolitan Trust issue maturing September 1, 1992, pays interest at the rate of 10% while a Royal Trust issue maturing in March of the same year pays only 8-3/8%.

Most MBS issues are for five-year terms, although there are a few available for 10 years. The minimum investment is $5,000 and they're eligible for RRSPs, RRIFs, and DPSPs.

They appeal to conservative investors because of their safety. Residential first mortgages have always been considered a low-risk investment. In addition, these securities are backed by guarantees of both principal and interest from Canada Mortgage and Housing Corporation. CMHC is, of course, a Crown Corporation, which means it's really the Government of Canada backing your investment. And — key point — there are no limits. Unlike deposit insurance, which has a $60,000 ceiling on any one investment, the protection on mortgage-backed securities is open-ended. So you don't have to worry about the financial health of the company putting the pool together or the quality of the individual mortgages within it. The government protects your investment right down the line.

The second feature investors like is the cash flow. Mortgage-backed securities are specifically designed for people looking for regular income — retirees, for example. There are very few securities around offering monthly payments, but MBS shares fill that bill. However, you should be aware that the monthly payment you receive is a blend of principal and interest. And it can sometimes vary significantly, since most MBS pools are made up of mortgages with prepayment clauses. Early prepayments will increase your monthly cheque, since they amount to repayment of principal. You'll then be faced with the problem of reinvesting that money elsewhere.

This also means that when your MBS matures, you'll receive back something less than your original investment. That's because part of your monthly income has consisted of repayment of principal. CMHC estimates that, on average, you'll receive about 94% of the original face value at maturity. So for every $5,000 you invest, expect to get back about $4,700 five years down the road. Unless you've reinvested part of your monthly income, this means a gradual erosion of your capital over time.

While prepayments can upset your income calculations, they aren't all bad. Prepayments often generate penalty interest charges, which are divided up among the investors in the pool. That money is a bonus you weren't counting on when you made the original investment.

The third factor that makes these securities appealing is the competitive yield. The coupon rate in any MBS pool is calculated on the interest rate being charged to the mortgage holders and must be at least half a point below the lowest mortgage rate in the pool. So in late 1988, when five-year mortgage rates were in the 12-1/4% range, mortgage-backed securities could theoretically yield up to 11-3/4%. In practice, the differential is usually more than that, with the rate usually settling about 15 to 20 basis points over the yield on five-year Government of Canada bonds.

There's an active secondary market for mortgage-backed securities, which means you can sell them if you need the cash. You aren't locked in until maturity. However, if interest rates have risen since you purchased your securities, you'll take a loss on the investment if you have to sell early.

As I mentioned earlier, mortgage-backed securities have many of the same drawbacks as GICs. Inflation will erode the value of your capital and your interest will be taxed at the highest rate. However, there are some ways to make a capital gain on an MBS. You can buy when interest rates are high and then resell at a profit when they decline. Or you can find resale securities which, because of a low coupon, are trading below par and hold on to them until maturity. The difference in the price you pay and the amount you receive at maturity will be a capital gain, which you may be able to shelter under your lifetime $100,000 exemption.

Revenue Canada may also treat any windfall profits you receive from prepayment penalties as capital gains; check with a tax advisor when you file your return.

These wrinkles give mortgage-backed securities a small advantage over GICs in terms of Tax Risk. If the rates being offered are about the same, the MBS is the better deal.

The best place to buy these securities is through a stockbroker, although some banks also make them available from time to time.

Mortgages. If you want to get the best possible return from a low-risk interest investment, cut out the intermediaries and invest directly in mortgages yourself. The returns can be lucrative (usually 1 to 1-1/2 percentage points higher than a GIC) and, if you stick to residential first mortgages, your investment should be quite safe. The drawbacks are that you need a lot of cash to play banker and your investment is very concentrated — if the bottom should fall out of the real estate market, you might have to deal with a default.

If this option interests you, there are mortgage brokers who will find you a borrower. Some lawyers also can point you in the right direction. You shouldn't have to pay any fee for this service; it will be charged to the homeowner. You can also find people looking for mortgage money through the classified ads. But be careful. Mortgage lending can be risky if you don't take steps to ensure the property is properly appraised, that all taxes are paid, that fire insurance is up to date, and that there are no other outstanding mortgages or other financial encumbrances involved.

Mortgage investment companies. An alternative to doing it yourself is to put your money into a mortgage investment firm. These usually offer a somewhat better rate of return than mortgage-backed securities, although you won't get monthly payments. There aren't many of these companies around, so you should ask your broker for current information.

Just remember that any income from mortgages, no matter how derived, is treated as interest for tax purposes. That means Revenue Canada will sock it to you. If you want an income investment that offers some tax relief, consider the next alternative.

Preferred shares. If you're investing for income outside a tax shelter, you should look very closely at preferred shares. They pay dividends rather than interest — and the tax treatment of dividends is much more favourable, as I pointed out in Chapter Nine.

Although they're called "shares", preferreds are really a hybrid of bonds and stocks. As with bond interest, the dividend is usually fixed. However, payment is made quarterly rather than semi-annually. Preferreds rank ahead of common stocks in the financial pecking order, which means that a company must pay all its preferred dividends first, including any which are overdue, before owners of common stock get a cent. In the event a firm is wound up, preferred shareholders rank ahead of common stock owners but behind bond holders in terms of asset distribution.

Although the price of preferreds will normally not vary as greatly as the common stock of the same company, these shares do carry the potential for a capital gain if interest rates decline. So you'll not only benefit from the favourable dividend tax credit; you'll also have the potential for tax-free capital gains as well, if you haven't used up your exemption.

The following table was prepared by the brokerage firm of Scotia

McLeod to illustrate the tax advantages of preferred shares. It shows, according to province of residence, the before-tax interest rate you would have to obtain to match various dividend rates. Figures are based on the 1988 tax year.

Province	Dividend Rate		
	7%	8%	9%
	Corresponding Interest Rate		
Nova Scotia	8.9%	10.2%	11.5%
New Brunswick	9.0	10.3	11.5
Newfoundland	9.0	10.3	11.6
P.E.I.	8.9	10.2	11.5
Ontario	8.8	10.1	11.3
Manitoba	9.0	10.2	11.5
Saskatchewan	8.9	10.2	11.5
Alberta	8.8	10.1	11.3
B.C.	8.8	10.1	11.4
Quebec	8.6	9.8	11.0

Floating rate securities. In an effort to make fixed-income securities more attractive, some companies have taken to issuing floating rate securities. These pay a rate of interest which fluctuates according to market conditions. For example, the Bank of Nova Scotia has an issue of floating rate preferreds which pays a dividend equivalent to 70% of the prime rate.

These floating rate securities come in several forms. Preferred shares and debentures (bond issues not backed by any specific asset) are the most common, but you can also find fixed-term notes around. This type of security offers built-in protection against rising interest rates and should be considered during periods when the economy appears to be overheating. Generally, they are not suitable when interest rates are declining; in those circumstances it's better to lock in high yields for as long as possible.

Fixed-income mutual funds. In Chapter Fifteen I mentioned certain types of fixed-income funds suitable for income investing. These are good alternatives when you want someone else to handle the decision-making and the management for you.

As with all other investing, diversification is required among the various types of fixed-income investments you hold. Your objective is twofold — to maximize the return on your money while minimizing the impact of taxes. There is no formula that is right for all times; your mix will depend on your situation.

If you're investing inside an RRSP, RRIF or DPSP, I suggest you consider a combination of quality mutual funds, GICs, stripped bonds, high-quality corporate bonds, and convertibles. Since income tax is not a consideration, your objective should be to generate the maximum possible return.

Outside an RRSP, a mix of good mutual funds, government and corporate bonds, convertibles and high-yielding preferreds will provide good yield with some tax relief.

If you need to generate a steady cash flow, look at a combination of mutual funds (you'll find some with monthly payment plans), high-yielding, top-grade corporate bonds, mortgage-backed securities and preferreds.

Understanding the Stock Market

CHAPTER 18

It will fluctuate.

— J.P. Morgan, when
asked for his outlook
on the stock market

L ET'S NOT PULL any punches. Investing in the stock market is tough. Consistently making a profit from it is even tougher. You must have discipline, patience, commitment, sound advice and a measure of luck if you are going to be a successful market player.

That's why many low-risk investors prefer to use equity funds for the growth component of their portfolio. It is much, much easier to select a few good equity funds than it is to put together a high-performance stock portfolio.

It is not, however, as much fun. There's nothing in the investment world that matches the rush of adrenalin you get when you pick up the business pages and discover that the stock you bought last week has doubled in value overnight because of a takeover bid. I've even heard some people say it's better than sex; I'll leave it to you to decide that.

That excitement is what keeps bringing many people back to the stock market, even when their track record is lousy. They remember the winners and put the losers out of their mind. It's similar to what they say about good and bad golfers: good golfers only remember the bad shots; bad golfers remember the good ones.

But hold on a minute, you may be saying. Isn't it true that studies on investment returns consistently show that common stocks are the best performers over the long haul? Yes, you're correct. It's also true that stocks offer two great tax advantages. Your dividends are taxed at a reduced rate because of the dividend tax credit, and your capital gains may be entirely tax-free if you haven't used up your $100,000 lifetime capital gains exemption. Those are pretty powerful arguments for having a stock portfolio.

I can make several arguments against a stock portfolio, however. First, it's difficult to consistently pick winning stocks. The choice is immense: you not only have to consider the Canadian market but U.S. and international markets as well. Second, it takes a great deal of hands-on management. Third, unless you have a lot of money to invest you'll have trouble getting adequate diversification. Fourth, you can get the tax breaks I mentioned from a Canadian equity fund. Fifth, your risks will be higher than by going the mutual fund route.

If, after reading this far, you've decided that equity funds are really preferable for your growth assets, you don't have to go any further into this chapter. And, as a bonus, you can skip the next three as well.

But if you're still determined to try it yourself, read on.

First, some history. Everyone is aware the stock market goes up and down. There was a period in the mid-1980s when people temporarily forgot the down part, but Black Monday jolted them back to reality.

Down is a word stock market investors hate, but can never afford to forget. No matter what stock you buy, it will eventually drop in price. The decline may be only temporary, but it will happen, and when it does you may become miserable, angry, frightened, or any combination of the three. If you can't live comfortably with that, you shouldn't be in the stock market.

It is true, however, that the long-term trend of the stock market is up. If you look at stock charts dating back to the early 19th century, you'll see a clear upward progression in prices. There are some pretty dramatic spikes along the way, of course — Toronto stock prices fell over 70% between 1929 and 1932. But history is clearly on the side of the stock market investor — if you can afford to wait.

That brings me to my first principle of market investing: *Make sure time is on your side.* Unless you're extremely knowledgeable, I do not recommend a large stock portfolio for people over 60. The time element is too short. If you run into a major, prolonged bear market, such as prevailed in the 1930s, you may be forced to sell out at a huge loss or face going into retirement with a large portion of your assets tied up in unproductive holdings. A younger person will be able to wait out the down cycle and benefit when the inevitable upturn occurs.

My second principle is: *Diversify*. Make sure your portfolio is properly balanced; don't put everything in one or two stocks. The greater your degree of diversification, the more you spread your risk. It's the same principle that mutual funds use.

The third principle is: *Never speculate*. This may seem like a contradiction since many people believe any stock is, by definition, a speculation. Well, there are speculations and speculations. A penny mining stock trading on the Vancouver Exchange carries a lot more risk than, say, a Bell Canada or a Royal Bank. The blue-chip stock may drop in value, but it's unlikely the company will go out of business and leave you with worthless share certificates. The penny mining company, on the other hand, might go belly-up at any time.

If you want to limit the degree of risk in your stock portfolio, you'll stick with shares of well-established companies that have been around for a long time and have a consistent record of profitability and dividend payments. Even these won't be immune to a general fall in the market. But they will eventually bounce back when economic conditions improve.

Principle four: *Never buy and hold cyclical stocks*. I told you in Chapter Eleven about the broker acquaintance of mine who cannot believe how many investors hold cyclical stocks in their portfolio for years. Even his aunt is guilty; she bought Inco (International Nickel Company of Canada) back in the 1960s and stubbornly refuses to let it go despite his pleas. Cyclical stocks, like the economy itself, go through boom and bust periods. When they're hot, they're terrific. When they're in an off period, they're dogs.

Many cyclical stocks are resource-based, which means we have a lot of them in Canada. Mining companies, forestry firms, and oil and gas conglomerates all qualify.

If you insist on buying them, do so when they're off-cycle (and therefore cheap) and sell them when they're approaching their cyclical high. In other words, these are trading stocks, not holders.

Principle five: *Ride the upward trends*. It was pretty hard to lose money in the stock market between August 1982 and August 1987. Some people did, of course, through a combination of poor selection and poor timing. But they were the unlucky ones. Most investors who held a diversified portfolio of quality stocks profited greatly during this period.

And well they should have. After all, the mid-1980s gave us the greatest bull market of this generation. If you couldn't make money in that market, you never will.

But what made it relatively easy was the fact you could ride a steadily upward trend. Some stocks performed better than others, of course. But as long as you didn't pick a bunch of dogs, the wave carried your portfolio along and you made money.

That's why it's important to have some stocks in your portfolio, whether you hold them directly or through equity funds. When the market starts to move up, you must be there if you are going to achieve the target returns I outlined at the start of this book. If you don't participate in market booms, you can't expect anything better than mediocre results.

The flip side of the coin is not to be around when the wave goes back out and the market drops. It won't do much for your total return if you ride the market up and then go back down with it. That's why the concept of Asset Mix is so important. The growth component of your portfolio should be at its peak when the market is moving up; it should be at its nadir when the market is declining.

Oh sure, easy enough to say. Making it work in the real world is something else.

Well, in fact, it isn't as hard as it may seem. When the market began to turn around in mid-1982, there was a possibility it could have been nothing more than a bear market rally. But by 1983 it was clear the economy had turned the corner and conditions were improving. Interest rates were dropping, the rate of inflation was slowing, business failures were declining and consumer spending was starting to recover. With clear signs like those, committing a larger portion of assets to stocks at that point was a reasonable risk to take.

The telltale signs of the bull market's end were also there for anyone who cared to read them. Renewed inflationary concerns in mid-1987 led to higher interest rates. The business recovery was getting long in the tooth by historical standards. There were sectorial depressions in the farming sector and the oil and gas industry. Bank failures in the U.S.

were increasing at an alarming rate. The world debt pyramid was continuing to grow. Analysts were warning that the end of the upward run was in sight — no one could be sure when, but it was coming.

The low-risk investor pays close attention to portents such as these, and acts on them. It's always better to leave the party six months too early than one day too late — as those who remained fully invested in the market on Black Monday found out.

Principle six: *Be patient*. There is always a right time and a wrong time to buy a stock. One of the things I've observed is that when a broker gives you a recommendation, seven times out of ten the stock will drop in price before it goes up again. That's because you aren't the only one hearing about it; in fact if it's a hot issue there will be a lot of action in the market. So don't be too quick to plunge in. If you like the sound of the stock, ask your broker to send you some information on it — the analyst's research, the latest annual report and anything else that's relevant. Look over the material carefully and see if the company fits your investment objectives. Also, take a look at how it will fit into your portfolio; would it overweight you in bank stocks, for example? Check the dividend record to see what kind of return it's paying and the prospects for higher dividends in future. If on close scrutiny it seems like a stock you should own, then set a realistic target purchase level and monitor its price movements over a period of time. When it comes within buying range — and more often than not it will — make the commitment.

The patient approach is a good general strategy to use for stock purchases. But it won't work when the market is in an explosive upward move. If the stock is a good one, it may not come back to your target buy level. In that situation, you have to decide whether the prospects are good enough to pay what may be an inflated price. My general inclination is not to chase a stock except in very special circumstances. The stock market has infinite variety; there's always another bargain coming along. Wait for it.

Principle seven: *Set target points*. In Chapter Eleven I explained why I regard all stocks as Traders. Even though the market may move up over the long haul, there are times when it's prudent to sell even your most cherished stocks with the idea of buying back in when the price drops. To do this, you need to set targets — points at which you'll sell, both on the profit side and the loss side. Your upside targets will depend on the state of the market and your personal objectives. If the market is strong and shows no signs of weakening, a profit gain of 50% to 100% over your purchase price is not unrealistic. If the market is moving sideways and you're looking for a fast trade, you may target a profit as low as 10% to 15%. Just be sure when you set a low selling target that there will be enough profit left after commissions to make the whole transaction worthwhile.

While you can be flexible on the high side, you should be quite rigid about taking losses. If the stock drops 25% from your purchase price, I'd get rid of it unless there are very unusual circumstances involved. I've seen too many cases of people holding on to a losing stock in the vain hope that it will turn around and at least come back to their purchase price. I've been guilty of it myself. What generally happens is that the stock just keeps on sliding, and a 25% loss turns into a 50% or 75% decline. When you guess wrong, take your lumps and move on. Don't compound your misery by hanging on, hoping for a miracle.

As with everything else in the stock market, there are some exceptions to this general rule. You may want to keep a core holding in a solid company even though it's fallen 25% because the drop is mainly due to a general market weakness. The company itself remains solid and will undoubtedly recover when the market rallies. This is appropriate action if you've decided to maintain a portion of your growth assets in long-term holdings and deliberately selected the stock for that purpose. In this case, you may decide to acquire additional shares at the lower price, to reduce the average per-share cost of your investment. This is called averaging down.

Another exception may arise if you've purchased a volatile low-priced stock despite my admonition not to speculate. If the prospects for the company remain good, you may decide to hold for longer. But if the price drops 50%, I'd be inclined to get out; something's badly wrong.

Principle eight: *Remember that the market is fickle*. Sometimes there is no clear reason why a particular stock performs as it does. All the fundamentals may suggest it is woefully underpriced. Yet it continues to languish while other stocks of lesser pedigree flourish. At any given time, there are hundreds of these "undiscovered" stocks around. The problem is, they may never be discovered, at least not while you're holding them. That means you should be doubly cautious when it comes to buying obscure stocks with a small float (the total value of its publicly traded shares outside any control block). It may look good on paper. But if it doesn't get discovered, the price may remain low.

What's true of individual stocks is also true of stock groups. At certain periods, almost every company in a particular group may be out of favour. In mid-1988, oil and gas stocks were on everyone's hate list. In that climate, even the most carefully selected stock may go nowhere. But every group will come back into favour at some point — something which is not necessarily true of individual stocks. So buying the top-quality stocks in out-of-favour groups can be a smart strategy — provided you have the patience to wait for the turnaround.

Principle nine: *Buy Canadian first.* The dividend tax credit is an important incentive in your stock purchase decisions — and the greater the importance you attach to dividends, the more important it is. As we saw in Chapter Nine, dividend income is taxed at a much lower rate than interest income. But that tax break only applies on dividends paid by taxable Canadian corporations. If your portfolio is full of U.S. stocks, you won't get it. In fact, you'll be subjected to a 15% withholding tax on all dividends from U.S. stocks, although you can recover that as a foreign tax credit at tax time as long as the stocks are not held in your RRSP.

If you live in Quebec, you'll get an additional tax break under the Quebec Stock Savings Plan if you buy shares in Quebec-based companies. Some other provinces have similar incentives.

So the tax benefits of buying Canadian can be significant. The drawback is that the Canadian stock market is tiny compared to the American market. It's much easier to build a fully diversified portfolio of U.S. stocks at reasonable prices than it is to construct a comparable Canadian portfolio. Once you get past Northern Telecom, for example, it's hard to find Canadian high-tech stocks that compare in size and performance with U.S. giants like IBM, Apple and Hewlett-Packard.

That's why I suggest starting with a core of Canadian stocks — you'll have no problem finding plenty of resource companies, utilities, financial firms, and communications companies to fill your needs in those areas. But you may not find the variety or quality you want in other areas: merchandising, entertainment, transportation, and major industrials are some. In that case, round out your portfolio with U.S. stocks (or, if you have an international bent, look farther afield to countries like West Germany and Japan). Just remember the tax consequences of your decisions.

Principle ten: *Keep your eye on the business cycle*. Some stocks perform better at certain stages of the business cycle. If you want to maximize your stock market profits, you should purchase these stocks when their prices are low and sell them as they reach their cyclical peak.

In the early phase of a new business cycle, when the economy is starting to pull out of a recession or a prolonged slowdown, merchandising stocks do well. Increased consumer confidence and low interest rates lead to an upsurge in buying activity, which helps merchandisers reduce inventories and improves their profits. Financial institutions and utilities also do well at this point. Lower interest rates mean reduced costs for utilities, which generally have a high debt load because of their expensive plant and equipment needs. Financial institutions do well because lower rates lead to increased business activity.

As the business cycle matures, profits of manufacturers start to rise. Usually, these companies have cut costs during the slowdown and are now benefiting from those savings. As well, increased business is pushing up revenues, thereby adding to profits. As quarterly earnings reports continue to improve, share prices for these companies are pushed up. Shares in brokerage houses are also strong at this point, as activity in the stock market picks up and earnings rise.

The late stages of the business cycle are good for resource stocks and real estate companies. By now, inflation is starting to creep back in. High commodity prices bolster the profits of mining, forestry and petroleum companies, and rising property values make real estate companies look good.

If you're an active trader and you want to maximize your profits, pay close attention to what the business cycle is doing at any given point in time. The buy and sell messages it generates can be extremely valuable.

Those are my ten basic stock market principles. Now let's move on to picking individual stocks. There's no sure-fire technique — but there are ways of tilting the odds in your favour.

Some Stock Basics

Buy when everyone else is selling and hold until everyone else is buying. This is not merely a catchy slogan. It is the very essence of successful investment.

— J. Paul Getty

J. PAUL GETTY was a contrarian. He made his millions by swimming against the tide, buying things no one else wanted and selling them when it looked like prices would go up forever. Had he lived a few hundred years ago, he would have made a fortune in tulip bulbs.

There's a lot to be said for contrarian investing. But it takes nerves of steel. You have to be prepared to go against the popular flow and not second-guess yourself. If you don't think you have the mental toughness to do that, you'd better try another approach.

In Chapter Twenty, I'll give you my suggestions for a successful stock selection strategy. But first, there are a number of basics you have to know before you venture into the stock picking minefield. You may be aware of some of these; others may be new to you. Make sure you understand them thoroughly before you proceed.

Stock exchanges: There are five stock exchanges in Canada, but only three that really matter: Toronto, Montreal and Vancouver. The Toronto Stock Exchange (TSE) is far and away the most important; the majority of your Canadian transactions will take place there. All the major public companies in Canada trade on the TSE, and the TSE 300 index is the most widely used measure of daily stock market activity in the country.

The Montreal Exchange (ME) has staged a comeback in recent years, helped in part by the success of the Quebec Stock Savings Plan in encouraging equity investment in the province. It is still very much a regional exchange, specializing in Quebec-based companies. But many national firms are listed on both the TSE and the ME.

The Vancouver Stock Exchange is a good place for low-risk investors to avoid. Many (but not all) of its listings are junior companies that are highly speculative in nature. It's a great place for taking a flyer on a penny mining stock, but very few blue-chip companies have VSE listings. Typically, when a firm really "makes it", it applies for a TSE listing for the built-in respectability that carries. If a company in which you're interested is listed only on Vancouver, ask a lot of questions before you invest.

There is also a small market for publicly traded stocks that haven't yet received an exchange listing. This is known as the over-the-counter market. In most cases, these will be junior companies with low capitalization.

If you're buying U.S. stocks, your broker will deal mainly with the New York Stock Exchange, although some U.S. companies, such as IBM, are interlisted on the TSE. There's also the American Stock Exchange and a number of regional exchanges. The over-the-counter market in the U.S. is huge compared to Canada's, with stocks traded through (how's this for a mouthful?) the National Association of Securities Dealers Automated Quotations System, or NASDAQ for short.

If a stock isn't listed on an exchange or traded through one of the over-the-counter systems, don't touch it. You may have a difficult time getting your money out. Investors sometimes get unsolicited calls from brokerage houses they've never heard of, touting some junior resource stock. Typically, the pitch is that the selling broker will "make the market" for these shares, buying them back from you when you wish to sell.

I've talked to people who have been hooked by these deals and gotten badly hurt. In one case, the broker who sold the stock wouldn't pay more than forty cents on the dollar to repurchase it. So if you get a call from any of these so-called "boiler shops", hang up. If the stock isn't publicly traded, you're not interested.

Fundamental analysis: There are two common techniques used to analyze a stock. One is called fundamental analysis. Essentially, it amounts to taking a detailed look at the strengths and weaknesses of the company whose stock you're considering and using that information as the basis for your decision. The rationale is that if the company is solid and the stock is properly priced, sooner or later the market will reflect that.

There have been entire books written on fundamental analysis, so I'm not going to try to explain the procedure to you in a few paragraphs. If you want to learn how to do it yourself, I suggest you take one of the *Canadian Securities Course*, Hume Publishing's *Successful Investing and Money Management* course, or the *Stock Study Course* offered by the Windsor, Ontario-based Canadian Shareowners Association.

Most investors will be content to read the analyses prepared by the research department of their brokerage firm. These usually cover all the key points, but the five I pay closest attention to are these:

1. Earnings record: As with mutual funds, I like to see a company with a long and consistent record of earnings growth. If profits seem highly volatile or the company has had several years of losses, be cautious.

2. Dividend record: Low-risk investors should concentrate on stocks with a solid track record of dividend payments, a history of dividend increases, and an acceptable rate of return. More on this in the next chapter.

3. Debt level: In principle, I worry about companies that are heavily leveraged. In times of recession or periods of high interest rates they are highly vulnerable — as investors in Dome Petroleum discovered. When you're reading a research report, see what it says about the debt level.

4. Price/earnings ratio: The p/e ratio, as it's called, is one of the key indicators in determining if a particular stock is cheap or expensive. It is calculated by dividing the price of the stock by the most recent annual earnings per share. So if a company had earnings of $2 a share last year and the stock is trading at $8, the p/e ratio is 4 (8 divided by 2). That would be considered a low p/e. If, on the other hand, the company had earnings of only 25 cents a share, the p/e ratio would be 32 (8 divided by .25). That would be considered quite high. You may find companies with even higher p/e ratios. These are generally new firms with a great concept or product but few sales to date. The share price has been bid up, not on the basis of results, but in anticipation of a promising future.

Such stocks, by their nature, will be highly speculative. A good general rule to remember is that the lower the p/e ratio, the less the risk.

Good research reports will contain estimates of future corporate earnings and projected p/e ratios based on these earnings. Just remember that unexpected developments — a recession, a change in company management, higher interest rates, higher metal prices or whatever — could knock these estimates for a loop. I always take future p/e projections with a grain of salt. Historical and current numbers tell the real story.

5. Book value: The last key item to look for is the company's book value per share. Book value is the net worth of a company's assets, based on the balance sheet. You can find these numbers in the company's annual report. The book value and the market value are usually quite different. For example, the company may have real estate holdings valued at the purchase price for book purposes. But the real value of the properties may actually be much higher today. So, in a case like this, the book value of a company may greatly understate its real worth. However, you may also run into a situation where the book value overstates the true worth of a firm — assets which have declined in value may still be shown at acquisition price. When you look at a balance sheet, try to determine how the major assets are valued to see if this is in fact the situation with the firm you're studying.

The book value per share is simply the stated book value of the company divided by the number of shares outstanding. Proponents of the Value Investing approach of Benjamin Graham, which I outlined in Chapter Fifteen, regard this as the most important measure in determining whether a stock is inexpensive or overpriced. A stock trading below book value is often regarded as a buy if the accounting methods used accurately reflect or understate the current market value of the company's assets. In such cases, you'd be acquiring the company's assets at a discount to their true value. The higher the stock is trading above book value, the more speculative it is felt to be.

Even if you don't slavishly follow the principles of Value Investing, it's worth looking at the current price of the stock in relation to the book value per share. A stock trading well above book value may be more vulnerable in a market correction, especially if the company's earnings don't support the high price. Conversely, a stock trading below book value in a down market may be a good candidate to move up when share prices recover.

Fundamental analysts study many other factors besides these in assessing a company. But as far as I'm concerned, these five points tell the story. If they all look positive, the stock is probably a buy.

Technical analysis: This is the other method used for evaluating stocks. I'm oversimplifying a bit, but essentially technical analysts ignore all the fundamental factors and concentrate instead on trend patterns. The theory is that the price of any given stock will follow defined patterns, and buy/sell decisions should be made on that basis. Every stock has an identifiable support level, the downside price at which new buyers will move in. And each stock has an upside resistance level, the price at which buyers are reluctant to make purchases and sellers may take profits. Any breakthrough at either level is regarded as a significant development and generates a flood of buy or sell signals, depending on what's happening.

Technical analysis is immensely complex and, unless you enjoy endless reading of charts, I don't recommend getting deeply involved with it. It's useful to know in general what the technical analysts are saying. But I guess I'm the old-fashioned type. I'm much more impressed by the underlying soundness of a company than with what its stock price looks like on a graph.

Betas: I hate betas, perhaps because math was never one of my strengths. In fact, for several years I tried to pretend they didn't exist. But you do need to know what a beta is if you're going to be able to evaluate stocks properly.

The beta is simply a measurement of a stock's volatility compared to other stocks. A stock whose performance exactly coincides with the market average, or the average of its particular industry group, will have a beta of one. A beta over one is high; under one is low.

The higher the beta, the more volatile a stock's performance has been. So a stock with a high beta can be expected to outpace the market, either up or down. When the market is strong, a high-beta stock may produce better-than-average profits. When the market drops, it will be subject to greater losses.

A low-beta stock, on the other hand, will tend to be more stable.

It will not swing as sharply in one direction or the other as the market moves.

The low-risk investor, therefore, will prefer to concentrate on stocks with a low beta. These stocks are unlikely to produce spectacular returns, but they will also carry less risk than those with a higher beta rating.

You can't calculate beta yourself, but the research reports on any stock in which you're interested should provide it. If not, ask your broker to find the beta for you.

Stock groups: If you look at the TSE listings in the business pages of your paper, you'll see a number of industry groups shown: gold and silver, oil and gas, transportation, pipelines, and so on. Often, stocks within an industry group will move in concert; the announcement of the failure of an OPEC meeting may send the entire oil and gas group down. A rise in interest rates may hit the utilities. A tax on advertising would have a negative impact on stock prices in the communications sector.

That's why it's important to diversify your holdings across several groups. By doing this, you make yourself less vulnerable to bad news affecting any one particular industry.

Cash balances: Your brokerage account will usually have a cash balance. This may be quite large or only a few dollars, depending on whether you're fully invested. Make sure you know what interest your cash balance is earning, especially if it's a large amount. Many brokerage houses pay low interest on cash balances; if that's the case instruct your broker to hold your cash balances in T-bills, banker's acceptances, or something similar.

Margin: Buying stocks on margin simply means borrowing part of the money from your broker. It's not a practice I encourage, and the true low-risk investor won't do it. If you must try it, compare the interest rate being charged by your broker with rates being charged at financial institutions. You may find cheaper ways to borrow the funds, such as a personal line of credit.

Buying stocks: Purchasing a stock isn't quite as simple as picking up the phone and telling your broker to buy. There are different types of orders you can use, depending on the situation.

The most commonly used is the "market order". This is simply an instruction to your broker to buy (or sell) a stock at whatever price the market is offering. The danger with market orders is that if a stock is moving quickly, you may end up paying a great deal more than you anticipated by the time your order is filled.

I much prefer "limit orders". Here you give the broker a maximum price you're prepared to pay. If the trade can't be made at that level or better, it won't be completed and your broker will advise you accordingly. Limit orders ensure that you don't end up paying more for a stock than you planned. The disadvantage is that you could miss out on a stock you really want for a price difference of an eighth of a point.

When you're buying a large quantity of inexpensive stocks, consider using an "all-or-nothing" order. If you don't, you risk paying commissions on several small transactions rather than one large one as the broker picks up small blocks at different prices. That's an expensive way to accumulate stock, so try to avoid it.

The "stop-loss" order, which I described in Chapter Seven, is a useful way of protecting profits or minimizing losses. But avoid setting your stop too close to the current market price, otherwise you may lose your stock as a result of a temporary downward swing. That's called being "stopped out".

Normally, a stock order stands until it's filled. If you want to limit the time, however, ask your broker to place a "day order" for the shares you want. If it isn't filled by the time the market closes, it will expire automatically.

Another limiting order is the "fill or kill". This is normally used when you're trying to execute two connected trades, perhaps the purchase of a stock at a certain price plus the sale of a call option (which I'll explain later). Fill or kill is an instruction to the floor trader to complete both ends of the trade quickly or cancel the entire order.

When purchasing stocks, you should try to buy "board lots" or multiples thereof only. A board lot is normally 100 shares; however, stocks trading for less than $1 may have board lots of 500 or 1,000 shares. Any other stock purchase is considered an "odd lot" and you'll have to pay a slightly higher commission to acquire it. Odd lots are also harder to sell later.

Brokers' reports: You'll receive monthly reports from your broker on your security holdings and your cash position. Check them carefully! I've had several experiences with incorrect brokerage reports. In some cases, stock holdings have vanished into computer limbo; in others, dividend or interest payments have been incorrectly attributed to me or have been credited to someone else. Take nothing for granted; make sure the report is correct.

Stock registration: There are two ways to hold stock. You may either register it in your own name or hold it in what's known as "street form", which means the certificate remains with your broker and is not registered personally to you.

The disadvantage of personal registration is the nuisance it creates when it comes time to sell. You have to sign the share certificate, have the signature witnessed, and transmit it to your broker. If you want to move quickly on a sale, this can be a hassle.

Holding your shares in street form makes trading much easier. But until recently, it meant that you were cut off from the normal flow of company information. While registered shareholders received annual and quarterly reports, dividend notices, proxy cards, and other data, those holding the stock in street form got nothing.

In 1988, the various provincial securities commissions across Canada decided this practice was unfair and imposed new procedures which require certain basic company information to be sent to street form stockholders. The brokerage industry wasn't thrilled with this move because of the extra costs involved and was slow to implement it in some cases. Now the policy has taken hold and you can expect to receive financial information about a company and a proxy card to support management at the annual meeting, even if you don't formally register your shares.

Dealing with brokers: There are a number of questionable practices in the brokerage industry, but two especially concern me. The first is "churning", a practice by which a broker encourages frequent trading in your account in order to generate more commissions. If you suspect your broker is guilty of this, switch your account elsewhere.

The second is pushing new stock issues the brokerage house has underwritten. There's a real conflict of interest here: on one side the brokerage firm has a commitment to do everything possible to ensure the successful placement of a new issue; on the other, the individual broker has a responsibility to make recommendations which are in a client's best interest. These two objectives may not always coincide; I've had brokers try to sell me new issues their firm was underwriting that were obvious losers. In the best of all possible worlds, an underwriting broker would be prohibited from selling the stock to its retail clients, but that isn't likely to happen. So all you can do is be skeptical. If your broker tries to put you into a new issue, ask if his or her firm is involved in the underwriting. If it is, try to find an unbiased opinion on the worth of the stock before committing yourself.

Stock trading can be extremely complex, but these basics will help you get started. The next chapter provides a plan for building a stock portfolio in such a way as to minimize risks. Before you start reading it, let me caution you that stocks, by their nature, are far more risk-prone than the cash or fixed-income investments in your portfolio. Keep that in mind as you proceed.

Building a Stock Portfolio

If you don't know who you are, the stock market is an expensive place to find out.

— George Goodman

I F I HAD TO pick one single virtue that a stock market investor must have, it would be self-discipline. Without it, you haven't a hope of success.

You need discipline in constructing your portfolio. It must be as diversified as possible, so as to spread your risk across a number of companies and industry groups. But it mustn't become so unwieldy you can't easily keep track of the companies you own and how they're performing. A well-constructed portfolio of 10 to 15 stocks is probably about right.

You need discipline in your stock selection. You'll be bombarded with advice from all sides, some of which will be difficult to ignore. Even though you carefully lay out your investment philosophy to your broker, he or she will almost certainly be on the phone to you with recommendations that don't fit. You'll hear hot tips at cocktail parties. You'll read articles in the financial press about stocks that sound good. You'll receive glowing research reports about attractive issues. You'll quickly discover that your major problem will be ignoring most of these tips and sticking with your game plan.

You'll need discipline in selling. Buying stocks is easy. Selling is always a wrench. If the stock has moved up, you'll be reluctant to let it go because it may move still higher. If it has dropped in value, you'll be reluctant to sell because it means locking in a loss. There never seems to be a right time to sell. Sooner or later, however, if you want to secure your profits, you have to sell. In Chapter Eighteen, I stressed the importance of establishing target points for selling every stock you buy. I said that, while you can be flexible on the high side, you should be prepared to dump out losers when they reach your pre-set level. This is probably the toughest investment decision you'll ever have to make. It's the one that will really stretch your self-discipline to the limit.

Selling when a stock has moved up is psychologically much easier, because you have the satisfaction of a profit. There are also ways to hedge your bets if you think it may go higher still. One technique is trailing stops, which I described in Chapter Seven. Another is the "half-profits" approach. This involves selling half your holdings to lock in that portion of your profits, while holding on to the rest of the shares. You can also use the "zero-cost" approach, one of the favourite techniques of noted investor Dr. Morton Shulman. This means selling enough shares to recover your entire original investment. The stock remaining is, in effect, free and represents clear profit.

For example, suppose you bought 1,000 shares of a stock at $5. Your cost, not including commission, is therefore $5,000. The stock price rises to $8.50. At this point you sell 600 shares, for a return of $5,100 before commission. You've now recovered your investment and are left with 400 shares of "free" stock with which to continue riding the upward trend.

Back to my original point — self-discipline. Never lose sight of it as you build and manage your stock portfolio. Write down your objectives at the outset and make the time to review them periodically. Ask yourself whether the portfolio you've put together meets your goals and, if not, where and how you got off track. And make sure your objectives are still valid — all things human change. If you decide to switch direction, fine. Just be sure you know why you're doing so and how you plan to proceed.

That said, let me outline my seven rules for successful stock selection. These are designed to help you build a conservative portfolio with relatively low risk, good yield, and moderate growth potential. These criteria should be applied in conjunction with the general principles I outlined in Chapter Eighteen and with my comments on stock analysis in Chapter Nineteen.

BUILDING A STOCK PORTFOLIO

1. Buy quality. As with anything else — cars, paintings, clothes — true quality will eventually show its value. You're not going to hold shares in hundreds of companies, so every stock you purchase should be selected with quality in mind. That means the company should be a proven leader in its field, should have a reputation for excellent management, should consistently show good earnings, should be innovative, and should have a good public image. If a company doesn't fit the bill, don't buy it, no matter how good a story someone tells you.

2. Buy stocks in the lower end of their recent trading range. You're not only looking for quality; you're looking for quality at bargain prices. Many people who would haggle endlessly over a car price or negotiate tenaciously on a house deal will go out and pay top dollar for their stocks. Don't be one of them. The stock market has sales, just like any other business. That's when you do your shopping.

Let me give you an example. Laidlaw Transportation has been one of the great Canadian corporate success stories in recent years. The firm's owner, Michael DeGroote, took a small company and within a decade turned it into a North American leader in the trucking, school bus and waste disposal industries. Investors who bought the stock made huge profits as the company grew; I bought stock in 1985 at an average price of $5.77 a share including commissions and sold in 1987 at an average of $17.97 a share after all commissions were paid.

In early 1988, DeGroote announced his intention to sell controlling interest in the company. Investors, expecting to ride on the coattails of a takeover bid, pushed the price of Laidlaw "A" shares to a high of $24-3/8. Then DeGroote dropped his bombshell. In mid-May he revealed he was selling his controlling interest in the company to Canadian Pacific for almost $500 million. But the deal was structured in such a way that no offer was made for the other outstanding shares. The minority shareholders were left out in the cold.

The stock plummeted, dropping all the way to $14-1/4 — a huge decline for a company as big and profitable as Laidlaw. It was clearly an overreaction to the bad news, and canny stock buyers knew it. The bargain hunters moved in and began accumulating stock at the super

191

sale prices. It didn't take long for them to be rewarded; by mid-September the share price had recovered to the $18 range. For those who bought at the low, that represented a 26% gain in about four months — and this at a time when the stock market generally was going nowhere.

A stock may be trading in the low end of its range because of specific bad news, such as in the Laidlaw case. Or it may be down because of a general market slump. After the Black Monday crash, a lot of quality, blue-chip issues could be had for bargain prices.

So be patient and wait for the sales. They'll come along eventually.

3. Buy stocks that pay dividends. There are two ways to make money from your stocks: dividends and capital gains. So with all the stocks that are available, why limit yourself by selecting only those with capital gains potential? A steady dividend flow will ensure a continuing return on your investment and, if your stocks are Canadian and held outside a retirement plan, will entitle you to claim the dividend tax credit.

You'll hear a lot of conflicting arguments on this point. Many investment counsellors will advise you to forget about dividends, especially if you're younger, and concentrate on stocks with the greatest growth potential. High dividends and strong growth potential usually don't come together in the same package, they'll point out.

They're absolutely correct. They don't. Stocks with high dividend yields will usually be those of large, well-established companies with a low beta, such as banks and utilities. Their share prices will appreciate in value as the market rises, but not as much as some of the more volatile high-flyers. So if maximum growth is your objective, then forget about dividends. But also recognize the fact your stocks will carry a higher degree of risk.

My criteria are designed to build a stock portfolio that will be as low-risk as possible. After all, that's what this book is all about. So I'm prepared to sacrifice some growth potential for greater safety and a steady dividend flow.

Dividend yields on common stocks will vary depending on the company and the current state of the market. But in September 1988, Bank of Montreal shares were paying a healthy 7%, Bell Canada and Trans-Alberta Utilities shares were yielding 6.6%, TransCanada Pipelines was paying 5.2% and Power Corporation 4.8%. These are all very attractive returns on quality common stocks.

Be wary if the dividend yield seems *unrealistically* high. On the same day as the yields I've just mentioned were available, you could also have found some common stocks paying ridiculously high returns — in one case, almost 66%. That's a sure sign the company is in some sort of difficulty, which has knocked down the price of the stock. Avoid such situations.

By making respectable dividend yields a condition for stock purchase, you'll ensure your portfolio will generate some revenue for you, regardless of what the market does. Remember, two streams of income are better than one.

4. Buy stocks of companies with low debt. As I said in the last chapter, I don't like companies with a lot of debt. Many stock experts would dispute this particular bias, pointing out that some companies have used debt successfully to increase their asset base many times over. Robert Campeau is one of the most successful practitioners of this approach; he's skillfully managed debt to become one of North America's retailing giants.

But I have a conservative's fundamental aversion to debt. I've made it one of my priorities to reduce my family's debt to zero. I don't like chronic deficits in government. And I don't like owning shares in companies that owe other people a great deal of money. For every firm that has managed debt successfully, I can point to one that has been devastated by it. Dome Petroleum, which was finally taken over in 1988 by U.S.-owned Amoco, is the classic example, but there are plenty of others. I once lost money on shares of a real estate high-flyer called Nu-West, which overextended itself and then took a battering when western real estate values collapsed in the early 1980s.

There are some blue-chip companies which, by their nature, will carry a high debt load. The utilities, such as Bell Canada and TransAlta, fall into this group. I'm prepared to make an exception in these cases because the companies are conservatively managed and government-regulated. The chances of them going under because of an overextended debt load are remote, to say the least.

Nevertheless, as a general rule, I prefer to avoid high debt. How do you know when a company's debt is out of line? A standard measure is a company's debt/equity ratio. This is arrived at by dividing the total long-term debt by the current market value of the company's common stock (calculated by multiplying the number of outstanding shares by the market price). A good research report will contain this information; otherwise, ask your broker for it. A debt/equity ratio of less than one is good; under 0.5 is excellent.

5. Buy stocks that are trading near book value. As I explained in the last chapter, the relationship of a stock's market price to its book value can be an excellent guide for bargain-hunting — as long as the book value accurately reflects or understates the true value of a firm's assets. Always take a look at the relationship between the two values before making a final decision.

6. Buy stocks that are widely traded. Every once in a while you'll come across a stock that looks good but has only a limited number of shares outstanding. It may trade only a few hundred shares a day, and may go for days at a time with no action at all. These are called "thinly traded" stocks and they can be dangerous. They're subject to sharp price movements, up and down. And you may have difficulty getting your price when you want to sell because of a lack of buyers. Low-risk portfolios should avoid these thin issues and concentrate on stocks that are widely held and traded.

7. Buy in the secondary market. Every so often your broker will call with the offer of a hot new issue. (New issues are always "hot"; can you imagine a broker telling you it's a loser but you should buy anyway?) The problem with new issues, as I pointed out in the last chapter, is the conflict of interest involved. That makes them a crap shoot. Some do very well; others will die once they start trading in the over-the-counter market or on a stock exchange.

I've had experience with both kinds. Early in 1988, I purchased 1,000 shares in a new company being launched by Dr. Morton Shulman called Deprenyl Research Limited. There's a fascinating story behind it. Dr. Shulman, who I'd met through my affiliation with Hume Publishing and *The MoneyLetter*, had been suffering for some time from Parkinson's disease, a neurological disorder that affects the body's motor functions. His condition was gradually deteriorating when he heard about Eldepryl. This was a drug widely used in Europe for the treatment of Parkinson's that had been developed by the renowned Chinoin Pharmaceutical and

Chemical Works in Hungary. He made arrangements to obtain a sample and was astonished at the results. Within a short time, he was moving normally and felt like a new man.

Shulman immediately saw the potential for other Parkinson's sufferers and set up a company to market the drug in Canada, after obtaining the rights to do so from a U.S. firm that held North American distribution rights. Shares in the company, Deprenyl Research, were issued in early 1988 at $3 each. They immediately started trading on the Ontario over-the-counter market in the $5 range.

It was a classic case of a concept stock taking off. The company had not at that time received permission from the Health Protection Branch of Health & Welfare Canada to market the drug here, nor had the United States Food and Drug Administration given the go-ahead in that country. So Deprenyl had no earnings and no guarantee that it ever would have. But the apparent effectiveness of the drug and its successful use in other countries convinced many investors it was for real. The stock climbed though $8, $10, and approached the $15 range within a few months. By mid-November it was trading in the $10 to $11 range. Those who had bought at issue tripled or quadrupled their money in a very short time. And this was during a period when the stock market generally was weak and most companies were holding back on new underwritings.

If all new issues did as well, I'd be advising you to buy every one that came along. Unfortunately, that's not the way it works. In Chapter Seven I told you about my unhappy experience with the Canada Development Corporation. At least in that case I could have eventually made money, had I held on long enough. Another new issue I bought several years ago at the urging of my broker never went anywhere. The company was called Biotech Electronics, a Montreal-based firm that produced ion generators, humidifiers and the like. The stock came out at $5 and if it ever traded above that, it wasn't for very long. It gradually declined in price and I finally dumped it at about $3.50. The last time I looked it was trading in the $1.50 range.

A new issue with which most people are familiar is the highly touted partial sale of Air Canada to the public. Tens of thousands of Canadians signed up to buy when Ottawa announced it was selling off 45% of the company. The price was set at $8 per share at the end of September

1988. When the stock started trading in the over-the-counter market, it got as high as $8-7/8. Those who sold then realized a small profit for their effort. But by the time Air Canada started trading on the stock exchanges in October, the price was already weakening. There were reports that RBC Dominion Securities, the lead underwriting firm, was trying to support the stock to keep it from falling below issue price prior to the November 21 general election. If that was true, it didn't work; by mid-November Air Canada was trading in the $7 range and the investors who had bought a small piece of Canada's national airline were out of pocket. What the future may have in store is an open question, but, at the outset at least, Air Canada became another example of why most new issues should be avoided.

So for every new issue winner, there's at least one loser — maybe more, depending on what the market is doing generally.

That's why I advise waiting until the stock starts to trade in the secondary market before considering it. At least that way you get an idea of what the pros think of its chances.

That's it. Stick with stocks that meet most or all of these criteria, and you'll be able to construct a portfolio that will provide you with income, moderate growth and tax benefits while allowing you to sleep comfortably at night. And if you'd like to squeeze a little more out of your stocks, you'll find two strategies for doing so in the next chapter.

Squeezing a Little More

Capital is saved from profits.

— David Ricardo

THE TRULY SUCCESSFUL investor is always looking for that extra edge
— something that will generate the additional return that transforms
an average investment into a terrific one.

There are dozens of ways to achieve this within the stock section
of your portfolio. Unfortunately, most of these techniques are quite complicated and some add a degree of danger unacceptable to a low-risk investor. But there are two strategies anyone can employ to squeeze a higher
return out of stocks. Both are low risk, but require some careful advance
planning in setting up your stock portfolio.

The first is to concentrate on shares of companies with good Dividend Reinvestment Plans (the unglamorous acronym for which is DRIPs).
These are programs that reinvest any dividends due you in additional
shares of the company's common stock, instead of paying them out in
cash. When you become a shareholder, you complete a form indicating
you want to participate in the plan; it doesn't happen automatically. These
programs are becoming increasingly popular with investors and, if you
don't need the cash flow from your dividends, you should seek them out.

They offer two advantages which may seem small, but which are part
of the "edge" I mentioned. First, they allow you to acquire additional
shares without paying brokerage fees. Since brokerage costs on small orders
can be high in percentage terms (most full-service brokers charge a minimum commission of $50 on any trade), this is a valuable saving.

Second, many companies with these plans will sell you shares at a slight discount to current market price. The saving is usually 5%, which represents an immediate capital gain for the shareholder. That gain is tax-free if you haven't used up your lifetime exemption. According to a survey done by *The Financial Post* in August 1988, companies offering this discount in their dividend reinvestment plans included AGF Management, Alberta Energy, Bank of Montreal, Bank of Nova Scotia, B.C. Sugar, Dofasco, Dominion Textile, Inland Natural Gas, Maritime T&T, Moore Corporation, National Bank, Northern Telecom, Oshawa Group, Royal Bank, Selkirk Communications, Southam Inc., Standard Trustco, and Westcoast Energy. That's a pretty good selection and, given the increasing popularity of these plans, there may be more by the time you read this. Check with your broker.

Let's take a look at how such a plan can add to the return on a stock. I mentioned in the previous chapter that Bank of Montreal shares were paying a 7% dividend in September 1988. That was calculated by taking the quarterly dividend of fifty cents a share, multiplying by four to get the annual dividend of $2, and dividing by the market price for the shares at that time, which was $28-5/8.

Let's assume you bought 500 shares of Bank of Montreal stock at that time. Your initial investment would have been $14,312. The table below illustrates your before-tax return under three different scenarios in the year following, assuming no change in the dividend (and Bank of Montreal has an excellent dividend track record). I've left out the effect of commissions to keep the example simple.

Stock Performance
(One Year)

	Up 10%	Flat	Down 10%
Dividends	$1,000	$1,000	$1,000
Capital Gain/(Loss)	1,431	0	(1,431)
Profit/(Loss) for year	2,431	1,000	(431)
% Profit/(Loss)	17%	7%	(3%)

Now let's assume that, instead of taking your dividends in cash, you had joined the Bank of Montreal's DRIP and received stock at 95% of the market price.

The actual formula used by the Bank of Montreal for calculating the price of shares under their dividend reinvestment plan is complicated. They work out the average price of the closing board lot on the Toronto and Montreal exchanges during the five business days before the last business day of the month in which a dividend is credited. That price is the one that applies for the dividend reinvestment plan that particular quarter. The actual stock purchase is made on the last business day of that month.

For this example, I'll again use $28-5/8 as the going-in price of the stock. I'll assume a 2.4% gain in the price per quarter in the 10% increase scenario and a 2.6% quarterly loss in the 10% loss example. Compounded quarterly, these will work out to almost exactly 10% over a year. The bank will credit your account with fractional shares so they're shown as well.

Assuming a quarterly dividend of fifty cents, your extra shares acquired would be as follows:

	Stock Performance (One Year)		
	Up 10%	Flat	Down 10%
First quarter			
Shares held	500	500	500
Dividend	$250	$250	$250
Price per share	$ 27.85	$ 27.19	$ 26.49
Shares acquired	8.98	9.19	9.44
Second quarter			
Shares held	508.98	509.19	509.44
Dividend	$254.49	$254.60	$254.72
Price per share	$ 28.51	$ 27.19	$ 25.80
Shares acquired	8.93	9.36	9.87

(cont'd)

Third quarter

Shares held	517.91	518.55	519.31
Dividend	$258.96	$259.28	$259.66
Price per share	$ 29.90	$ 27.19	$ 25.13
Shares acquired	8.87	9.54	10.33

Fourth quarter

Shares held	526.78	528.09	529.64
Dividend	$263.39	$264.05	$264.82
Price per share	$ 29.90	$ 27.19	$ 24.47
Shares acquired	8.81	9.71	10.82
Total new shares	35.59	37.80	40.46

Now let's look in the difference in the one-year return using the dividend reinvestment plan.

	Stock Performance (One Year)		
	Up 10%	Flat	Down 10%
Original investment	$14,312	$14,312	$14,312
Total shares held	535.59	537.80	540.46
Current market price	$ 31.47	$ 28.63	$ 25.76
Current value	$16,855.02	$15,397.21	$13,922.25
One-year profit/(loss)	$ 2,543.02	$ 1,085.21	($ 389.75)
% profit/(loss)	17.8%	7.6%	(2.7%)

As you can see, in all cases your performance is better with the dividend reinvestment plan. Your profit improved almost a full percentage point in the best case scenario. In the worst case, your loss is reduced by better than a quarter of a percent.

These may not seem like big numbers. But multiply them by your entire stock portfolio and they'll add up. And remember, you don't have to do any work to achieve this modest improvement in your returns. It all happens because you fill out a form when you originally acquire your shares. The Bank of Montreal (or whichever company you're investing in) looks after all the details for you. If you can put a few more dollars in your pocket that way, why not?

There are a couple of other advantages to DRIPs. They're one of the few effective ways to apply dollar-cost averaging to stock purchases. And many companies allow you to purchase additional shares at the special price to round up odd lot holdings.

The major disadvantage of these plans is that you must register the shares in your own name — they cannot be held in street form. But if you're going into a plan like this, it should be with a fairly long-range perspective. Don't bother if you expect to turn over the stock quickly.

For tax purposes, the dividends are treated as if they'd been paid in cash. But, as I mentioned earlier, you do benefit from an immediate 5% capital gain on shares bought at a discount.

The other method of squeezing a bit more out of your stock portfolio is to get involved with writing covered call options. This is a bit more complicated than a dividend reinvestment plan, but the rewards can be greater. And, though it may seem complicated at the outset, once you get the hang of it, it's quite easy.

Before I get into the strategy, an explanation of options and how they work is in order.

An option is simply the right to buy or sell stock at a specific price within a certain time. There are two basic types: call options allow you to purchase stock at a set price; put options allow you to sell. The price at which you can buy or sell the stock is called the *strike price*.

Options are valued in two ways. The *intrinsic value* is the difference between the strike price and the current market price of the stock. For example, if you're holding a call option on Toronto Dominion Bank stock with a strike price of $35 and the current market price is $37, your option has an intrinsic value of $2 ($37–$35 = $2). In that case, your option is said to be *in the money*. If the stock were trading at $34, your option would have no intrinsic value and would be *out of the money*. If T-D Bank were trading at $35, your option would still have no intrinsic value but would be described as *at the money*. (Sorry for all these technical terms, but bear with me. It'll be worth it, believe me.)

The other value an option has is *time value*. The longer it has to run before the expiry date, the greater the chance the stock will reach the strike price and the higher the time value of the option. As the option approaches expiry date, the time value decreases — technically, it's said to "decay". On the eve of the expiration date, the time value is virtually nil.

Put options are purchased if you think stock prices are going to fall. If the price of Inco Ltd. is currently at $32-1/2 and you think it will decline, you could buy a put option to sell the stock at, say, $32. If the price dropped below that level by the expiry date, you'd make money because you could sell the stock at higher than the current market value.

Put options can be useful but they don't figure in the strategy I'll be describing in this chapter. Call options do, however, and you have to understand how they work.

You would typically buy call options if you expect the price of the stock to rise. For example, on September 19, 1988, shares of Canadian Pacific closed at $20-5/8. If you expected the price to increase in the coming months, you could buy the stock itself. Or you could buy options. November 21 options closed that day at sixty cents. That means that for sixty dollars plus commission you could acquire the right to buy 100 shares of Canadian Pacific at $21 until the expiry of the option on the third Friday in November. If the price of the stock doesn't reach $21, you lose your investment. But if it increases significantly, you win.

Here's a comparison of the profit you'd make by buying the stock itself or the option, if the price reached $25 a share. I've assumed the purchase of one option, giving the right to purchase 100 shares of CP Ltd., although in reality an options trader would buy more. The market value shown for the option is simply the intrinsic value on the expiry date, calculated by subtracting the strike price ($21) from the market price ($25). This gives an intrinsic value of $4 per share. I've left out the effect of commissions for simplicity.

	Total Investment	Market Value	Profit	Percentage
Stock				
(100 shares @ $20-5/8)	$2,063	$2,500	$437	21.2%
Options				
(1 option @ 60¢)	60	400	340	566.7%

As you can see, the return on the options is far greater than from the stock itself. If you'd invested about the same amount of money in options as in the stock, you'd have purchased 34 options at a cost of $2,040 (34 x $60), which would have given you the right to 3,400 shares of CP Ltd. stock at $21 a share. The profit on your investment would have been $13,600 (3,400 x $4). Compare that with the $437 profit you made by holding the stock itself!

Of course, your risk is far greater too. Look what happens if the price of the stock only rises to $20-7/8 while you're holding the option:

	Total Investment	Market Value	Profit (Loss)	Percentage
Stock				
(100 shares @ $20-5/8)	$2,063	$2,088	$25	1.2%
Options				
(1 option @ 60¢)	60	0	(60)	(100%)

In this case, you've lost your entire investment! So while the potential rewards are great, so are the risks. This is speculator country; a true low-risk investor will never trade options in this way.

However, there is a way of turning other people's speculation to your own profit, and that's what this strategy is all about. It's known as *covered call writing*, and it's a low-risk way to substantially increase the return from stocks in your portfolio.

Suppose, for example, you own 500 shares of Canadian Tire "A" stock and you want to generate additional income from it. The stock is currently trading at $16-1/2. You decide to sell, or "write" to use the technical term, five call options at $18. These give the buyer the right to purchase your 500 shares at $18 by the expiry date, no matter what happens to the market price. For this privilege, the purchaser pays sixty cents a share.

By writing the call options, you've earned $300 (500 x 60¢) less commissions. If the stock price doesn't hit $18 by the expiry date, you've pocketed the option premium and can write new call options. If it has, you're obliged to sell your Canadian Tire shares at the agreed $18 price.

But you've made a total of $2.10 a share on the deal — 60¢ from the option premium and $1.50 on the stock price.

Covered call writing is low risk because you already own the stock. If it's called away from you, there's no problem. If you wrote the options and didn't own the stock, however, your risk would be tremendous. Suppose there were a takeover bid and the price rose to $35 a share. You'd still be obligated to sell at $18, which would mean you'd have to go into the market and buy the stock at $35 to meet your requirements. You'd lose $17 a share ($35–$18). That's known as "naked" call writing, and it's a tactic low-risk investors avoid.

Covered calls are a different matter. Given the right stock holdings, it's an excellent way to improve the yield on the stock portion of your portfolio. But not all stocks are good candidates for this strategy. Here's what to look for:

An active options market: Look for the Trans Canada Options quotes in the financial pages of your newspaper. There you'll find a listing of the Canadian stocks that have an active options market. You'll see at a glance which ones are most popular; they'll include Alcan, Bank of Montreal, Campeau Corporation, Canadian Pacific, Cineplex Odeon, Echo Bay Mines, Inco Ltd., Lac Minerals, Laidlaw "B", Nova, Placer Dome, and Royal Bank.

A typical listing will look like this:

Series	Bid	Ask	Last	Vol	Op Int
Campeau	C	19-3/4	Opt Vol		175
Ja $20	165	175	165	3	104
$20 P	145	165	145	5	98
Ap $20	210	230	210	20	108

The options quoted here are on Campeau Corporation shares which closed the day at $19-3/4 — you'll see that closing price in boldface opposite the company name. The total option volume that day was 175 contracts, which also shows on the same line in boldface.

In the series column on the left, you'll see three option contracts shown: a January call with a $20 strike price, a January put (identified by the letter P) with a $20 strike price, and an April $20 call. The "bid" column shows the price in cents which buyers were offering to pay for the option; the "ask" column shows the price sellers were requesting; the "last" column gives you the price of the last trade. So you can see that the last trade on the January $20 calls was at 165, or $1.65.

The "vol" column shows the trading volume in that contract during the day — in this case, only three contracts were traded, very little activity. The "op int" column shows "open interest" — the total number of outstanding contracts in existence for that particular option. For the January $20 call, 104 option contracts currently exist.

In looking through the quotes, watch especially for those companies with a number of different contracts and a relatively high trading volume. They're the ones buyers will be most interested in — and since you plan to be a seller, that's important to you.

Relatively high beta: The more volatile a stock, the more attractive its options. That's because options traders make money from big price swings. Stable stocks that trade within a narrow range don't have much appeal to these high rollers. But they'll pay a higher premium for an option on a stock that can move up or down quickly.

Since part of your strategy is to get the highest possible price for the options you sell, high-beta stocks will work better for you than low-beta ones. Low-risk investors generally prefer lower-beta stocks. But if you're going to make effective use of this strategy, you'll have to add some higher betas to your portfolio.

Dividend payments: One of my rules for stock selection is to choose those with dividends, and I'll reinforce it here. You'll get maximum yield from a stock if you combine dividends with option premiums. That way, you're generating two income streams.

Relatively inexpensive: All other things being equal, choose a stock with a lower price. That way you can acquire more shares for the same amount of money. This enables you to write a greater number of covered call options, thus increasing your revenue and spreading the commission over more contracts.

Now let's see how all this works in the real world. One of my favourite stocks for covered call writing is Alcan Aluminum. It's widely traded, quite volatile, and pays a modest dividend. Its only disadvantage is that it's not as cheap as I would like. But when I looked at it as a candidate for this strategy, I decided the potential rewards offset that concern.

In January 1988 I purchased 300 shares of Alcan at $33-5/8. At the time, the stock paid a quarterly dividend of US22¢ a share, or about 27.5¢ Canadian. This was later increased. The total cost of my investment, including commission, was $10,258.73. On the same day, I wrote three March 37-1/2 covered call options at $1 per share. That produced revenue of $300 (remember, each option covers 100 shares). Commission was $30, leaving $270 in my pocket.

On March 18, the expiry date of those options, Alcan stock was trading in the $37 range. I didn't want to lose the stock in a quick, last-minute price run-up, so I bought back those options I had sold for $1 at 10¢ each. That cost me $33. This is a tactic that is always open to you if you don't want the stock to be called away. But in most situations, don't buy back your option until the very last minute. That way there's virtually no time value left, so you're basically paying for intrinsic value.

Once I had bought back my old options, I wrote new covered calls for May at $40 a share. I sold these for 95¢ each, which produced $256.50 after commissions.

May came along and the price was well below $40. The option expired worthless and I was free to write yet another covered call. This time I sold August $35 calls at $1.35 each, which generated $364.50 after commissions.

The price of aluminum soared during the summer and so did the price of Alcan shares. When August came, the stock was trading above the $35 strike price. I could either let it go, or buy back my options again.

I decided to keep the stock. That meant I had to pay 95¢ each to buy back the options I had sold in May for $1.35. Not great, but there was at least a small profit in the deal. Plus I was able to immediately turn around and write November $35 options at a whopping $2.85. That deal was worth just over $800 after commissions.

On November 3, with Alcan stock trading at $36-5/8, the holder of my calls exercised the options. I was obliged to sell my shares for the $35 strike price.

The options were exercised two weeks before expiry so that the buyer could claim the quarterly dividend, which was to be paid to shareholders registered as of November 4. Had he waited, the dividend would have been credited to me. So dividend dates are important if you're writing covered calls. If the market price of the stock is above the option strike price when a dividend rate approaches, you may want to buy back the option early. That's one of the rare occasions when you wouldn't wait until just before the expiry date to buy back an option.

In this case, I decided to let the stock go with the idea of buying back in again later at a lower price. So let's see how I made out on this particular deal. All the figures below include commissions, so these are real-world numbers.

Date	Transaction	Investment	Revenues
Jan. 26	Buy 300 Alcan @ 33-5/8	$10,258.73)	
	Sell 3 March 37-1/2 calls		$270.00
Mar. 4	Dividend		67.71
Mar. 18	Buy back 3 March 37-1/2 calls		(33.00)
	Sell 3 May 40 calls		256.50
May 27	Sell 3 Aug. 35 calls		364.50
June 10	Dividend		65.86
Aug. 18	Buy back 3 Aug. 35 calls		(313.50)
	Sell 3 Nov. 35 calls		802.53
Sep. 10	Dividend		81.83
Nov. 4	Sell 300 Alcan @ $35	10,324.77	
	Total Profit	$1,628.47	
	Return on Investment	15.9%	
	Annualized Return	20.5%	

The real return I made on this transaction was 15.9%. That was from holding the stock about 9-1/2 months, so on an annualized basis my return was 20.5%. If I hadn't written the call options but had simply sold the stock at the market price on November 4, my return would have been much less. After commissions, I would have realized a capital gain of about $550 plus dividends of $215 for a total return of $765 — less than half what I actually received by going the covered call route, even though I had to sell the stock at a lower price.

I don't know about you, but when I can realize an annualized yield of 20.5% on a quality stock, I feel quite content. On top of that, this is a very tax-effective way of generating income. The dividends qualify for the dividend tax credit, which reduces the tax rate. Revenue from the option premiums is more complicated, but essentially Revenue Canada takes the position that it can be treated in the same way as the underlying stock for tax purposes. If you show your stock profits as capital gains, your option premiums may be treated in the same way. That means you can shelter them under the lifetime capital gains exemption, if it hasn't been used up. Even if you have to pay tax on them, it will be at a lower rate than any interest income.

You'll find some investment experts who argue against covered call writing as a strategy. There are two common objections. "If the stock drops in price, you can't get out." Nonsense. If the stock declines and you want to sell, you simply buy back your call options and get out. You'll pay less for your options than your selling price because the stock price will be down and the time value less.

"If the stock goes up, you won't benefit." True, to an extent — but you aren't helpless in this situation. If the stock rises above the strike price, you'll have to let it go at less than market value or buy back your options. If you decide to buy them back, as I did in March and August, you can immediately write new call options for a later date and pocket more profit. Or you can let them go, as I did in November, and wait for a new opportunity to buy back in.

The main problem with a covered call strategy is that only a few Canadian stocks lend themselves well to it. There are many more in the U.S. and you may want to ask your broker to investigate the possibilities there. But remember, you'll lose the benefit of the dividend tax credit if you deal in U.S. stocks.

Don't expect to be able to do this with every stock in your portfolio. It simply won't be practical. However, when this strategy can be used, it's an excellent way to squeeze a little bit more out of your stocks and give yourself that extra, low-risk edge.

Gold:
Fairy Tales
and Profits

I HAVE TO ADMIT that gold fascinates me. There's a mystique about it that far transcends its actual value. It's the stuff of fairy tale and legend; we're told wondrous tales of gold from the moment mom or dad first tucks us in at night and reads us a bedtime story. Remember Jason and the Golden Fleece, King Midas and his golden touch, the goose that laid golden eggs, Cleopatra's golden barge, the Seven Cities of Gold, sunken treasure ships laden with gold, the lost gold of Napoleon, the Oak Island treasure pit? They all conjure up images of romance, intrigue and high adventure. Little wonder gold retains its almost magical position as a universally accepted medium of exchange; it's been bred in us from the time we were babies. Sometimes I think international gold producers have secretly conspired to create the most effective public relations campaign in history.

There is something about gold that drives sane people mad. Think of the Klondike and California gold rushes — people from around the world leaving their jobs and homes in hopes of striking it rich in the wilderness. Consider the modern version of the gold rush that we witnessed in the late 1970s, which culminated with people actually lining up in the street to buy bullion at ridiculous prices. Had Charles Mackay been writing his book on the madness of crowds in this century, he would have had a field day.

The reality is that gold is really a soft, rather useless metal that has very few functional purposes apart from the manufacture of jewellery — and that only because of the arbitrary value we've attached to it. There are many metals that are rarer — platinum, for example. And there are others, such as silver, which have greater commercial use. Despite this, gold has become the standard by which wealth is measured.

So what does all this mean to you, as a low-risk investor? It means you ignore gold at your peril. This quote, attributed to Janos Fekete, says it all: "There are about three hundred economists in the world who are against gold. They think that gold is a barbarous relic — and they may be right. Unfortunately, there are three billion inhabitants of the world who believe in gold."

Let me say it categorically: every investor should hold some gold in his or her portfolio. I hope that doesn't make me a raving goldbug — and there are a lot of them around. Every time I attend an investing conference, I watch half-a-dozen experts use their elaborate charts to convince attentive audiences that $1,000-an-ounce gold is just around the corner. Strangely, though, it hasn't happened yet. I'm sure it will eventually, but timing doesn't seem to be a particular strength of these people.

So I'm not suggesting you buy gold with a view to making a quick buck. On the contrary, it could actually end up costing you money, depending on which form of gold you buy. I regard gold as a type of disaster insurance. No one likes to consider the possibility of a major war, or an economic collapse, or runaway inflation that devalues paper money hourly. But all these things have happened before, and it's not inconceivable they'll happen again. If they do, you'll get down on your knees and thank whichever deity you worship that you had the foresight to include a little gold in your holdings.

That's not to say you won't be able to profit from your gold trades, and part of this chapter will be devoted to ways of doing so — setting up your own dividend-paying insurance policy, as it were. But your first priority is to disaster-proof at least part of your holdings. If you can do that and make some money in the process, so much the better.

How does gold function as disaster insurance? It goes back to the universal acceptance of the metal as a medium of exchange. If, heaven forbid, civilization were devastated by atomic war, gold would still be

valued by the unhappy survivors, once their basic needs for food, water
and shelter had been met. Even in less dramatic circumstances, gold takes
on disproportionate value; the global energy crisis and the rise to power
of the Ayatollah Khomeini in Iran helped fuel the international rise in
gold prices in the late 1970s.

Refugees from countries torn by war, revolution or political coups
traditionally bring out their assets in gold — a phenomenon we've seen
repeatedly in this century, from eastern Europe to Vietnam.

In hard economic times, gold is king. If the purchasing power of paper
currency is destroyed by hyperinflation, as occurred in Germany in the
1920s, gold becomes one of the few acceptable forms of money. In times
of depression, gold is used to stabilize and reflate the economy, as Franklin
Roosevelt did in 1934 when he arbitrarily increased the then-controlled
price of gold from $20.67 U.S. an ounce to $35 U.S., effectively inflat-
ing the value of the depressed U.S. dollar in one quick move. So even
though the world was in the midst of a terrible deflation, holders of gold
saw the value of their investment almost double overnight. Unfortunately,
Americans weren't able to take advantage of this windfall since Roosevelt
made private ownership of gold by U.S. citizens illegal — a ban which
remained in force until December 31, 1974.

I hope you're convinced by now of the value of owning some gold.
Now the questions are when to buy, how much to own, and what form
to hold it in.

The first question is the easiest. To return to J. Paul Getty's philosophy,
buy when gold is cheap. Gold moves in and out of favour with investors; the time to add to your holdings is when it's temporarily in an
"out" phase.

International crises, real or perceived, will often touch off a buying
wave for gold. Inflationary signs, such as rising oil prices, will also put
gold into an "in" phase.

Conversely, disinflation (a falling inflation rate) will depress gold prices.
So will high interest rates, which usually help move gold into an "out"
mode. There are two reasons for this. First, high interest rates are generally a signal that governments are moving aggressively to contain inflationary trends. That's bad news for gold investors, who know that price
inflation tends to boost gold values. Second, high interest rates make

gold, which pays no interest, more expensive to hold. It's difficult to convince yourself to keep several thousand dollars in gold-based assets when that money could be earning 11% in Treasury bills.

During the early 1980s, global disinflation knocked gold prices down — at one stage they actually dropped below $300 an ounce for a brief period. Many gold mines reduced production and some closed down entirely. By early 1985, economists were speculating on how low the gold price might **go** and such highly respected publications as the *Bank Credit Analyst* were advising against taking positions in gold and warning that it might be years before gold again became a buy.

Of course, J. Paul Getty, on reading this advice, would have immediately picked up a phone and told his broker to buy. And he would have been right. As this is written, in late 1988, gold has never again been that low. It flirted briefly with $500 an ounce in early 1988 amidst speculation a new wave of inflation was about to hit — a time to sell, in retrospect — only to settle back to the $400 range by autumn when it became apparent central banks around the world were determined to nip inflation in the bud by jacking up interest rates.

So add to your gold holdings when you can get the metal on sale. Look for buying opportunities when the gold price has been declining steadily for several months, when inflation seems to be well contained, and when the business pages are full of speculation on how low the price can go. If you want an unmistakable buy signal, watch the cover of *Business Week* magazine. Some U.S. financial commentators have a great deal of fun by claiming that whenever *Business Week* runs a cover story on an economic or financial trend, everything immediately turns around. So if a *Business Week* cover promotes an article titled "The Lost Lustre of Gold", buy.

On the other hand, reduce your gold holdings when the price of the metal moves up sharply as a result of disturbing international news, an increase in oil prices, or new inflation speculation. Don't sell off everything — you should always keep some gold in reserve just in case the rumoured disaster really happens. But it probably won't, gold prices will fall back, and you can use your profits to buy additional gold more cheaply on the downswing.

This isn't theory. It really does happen this way; just look at a history of gold prices over the past decade. But you must have the nerve to buy more when the "out" phase is dominant and to sell when the "in" phase inevitably re-emerges. That's the key to making profits from your disaster insurance.

The second question you must deal with is how much gold to own. You'll hear all manner of theories on this; I've seen recommendations that as much as 30% of an investment portfolio should be in gold.

If you're a dyed-in-the-wool goldbug, you might consider such a disproportionate holding. But this is a book about low-risk investing and no low-risk portfolio would ever contain that much gold.

My suggestion is that you vary your gold holdings in a range of 5% to 10% of your total portfolio assets. Add to the proportion when gold prices are low and you can acquire the metal cheaply; reduce it to the minimum when you can sell at a substantial profit. So for a $100,000 portfolio, I suggest you always hold a minimum of $5,000 in gold, rising to a maximum of $10,000 in the right circumstances. This is a conservative range, but a low-risk investor shouldn't be speculating in gold in a big way. Remember, your main objective is to have a dividend-paying insurance policy; don't succumb to gold fever.

Finally, what type of gold should you buy? There's a wide range of choices, depending on your inclination and objectives. Here are the main alternatives:

Bars and wafers: This is the purest way to hold gold — buying the actual bullion, either in bar or wafer form, and storing it in a bank vault or safety deposit box. Wafers and bars come in a variety of shapes and sizes, depending on the refiner. Some dealers will sell you a wafer as tiny as five grams (.161 ounces) if that's what you want. But you really shouldn't consider anything smaller than a one-ounce bar because of the premium attached to buying bullion in smaller quantities. The so-called "standard" gold bar — the one you see in all those movies about gold heists — weighs 400 ounces and represents a pretty hefty cash commitment — $160,000 if gold is selling at $400 an ounce. But most retail dealers don't sell bars that large — 100 ounces is usually the biggest. Even those aren't cheap; with gold at $400 an ounce, one of those bars fetches $40,000.

By the way, there doesn't seem to be any clear definition as to when a "wafer" becomes a "bar". So if your friends are more likely to be impressed if you tell them you've just bought some gold bars, feel free — even if they're only the five-gram size.

Your bar or wafer should be stamped with its purity, weight and identification number, as well as the hallmark of the refiner. If it's not, don't buy it. You have no guarantee as to the quality of the gold you're getting, and you'll have to pay an assay fee if you want to sell it later.

When you purchase bars or wafers, you'll pay a premium in the form of a manufacturing charge, or *bar charge* as it's called in the precious metals trade. The smaller the amount of gold you buy, the higher this charge will be in proportionate terms. For example, Deak International, one of the leading gold dealers in Canada, has a bar charge of $5.50 for a five-gram bar. But you'll pay exactly the same bar charge for a one-ounce bar. So the larger the bar, the lower the premium; on a twenty-ounce bar it drops to $1.25 per ounce.

The bar charge is gold's equivalent of the brokerage commission; it's money you'll never see again. So if you do decide to hold gold in this form, be prepared to pay a premium of a few dollars an ounce. Incidentally, bar charges will vary from one dealer to another, so do some comparative shopping first.

On top of the premium, you'll have to pay provincial sales taxes in many provinces. They can be steep, ranging from 7% to 12%. Check with your dealer before you buy to determine whether sales taxes apply where you live.

That's still not the end of your costs. Your precious bars or wafers have to be stored somewhere secure, unless you intend to bury them. That isn't a joke — lots of Canadians, especially those who have come here from unstable countries, do exactly that. Gold dealers will tell you stories of people tucking newly-purchased bars into shopping bags and carrying them off to be buried in a hole in the backyard or hidden under the floorboards.

Assuming that's not your intention, though, you'll need a secure storage place. If your holdings are small, a safety deposit box will do the trick. But if they're substantial — a few 100-ounce bars, for instance — you'll have to pay an annual charge to keep them in someone's vault.

All of this makes bars an unattractive way to hold gold unless you have a fetish for the metal itself or you fear a genuine social calamity and want to have quick access to your treasure trove. Otherwise, I suggest you buy your gold in some other form.

Coins: Several countries have gotten into the gold coin business, minting special bullion coins. The best-known are Canada's own Maple Leaf coins and the South African Krugerrands. But you'll also find gold coins from such countries as the U.S. (the Eagle), China (the Panda), Australia (the Nugget), Britain (the Britannia), Mexico (the gold Peso), New Zealand (the Kiwi), and Austria (the Corona).

For years the Krugerrand was the staple of the industry. But the racial unrest in South Africa and international campaigns against apartheid have virtually destroyed its North American market. No Canadian gold dealers offer it for sale any more.

Although you'll usually see gold coins referred to in the singular ("the Maple Leaf"), they're often a family of different sizes. The Maple Leaf, for example, is struck in three sizes: one ounce, one-quarter ounce, and one-tenth ounce.

Promotions for these gold coins often stress their beauty and classic design as reasons for buying them. But the qualities you should be primarily concerned with are purity (technically known as "fineness") and price. The Maple Leaf coin is .9999 pure, or 24-karat, which is as good as you'll find.

Gold coins are sold at a premium over the actual gold value. This will vary depending on which coin you buy and which dealer you buy from, so it's a good idea to check around before you make a commitment. In late 1988, Deak International was charging a premium of about 4% on the Maple Leaf and the American Eagle. However, if you resell the coin later, you'll get part of that premium back.

Premiums on coins are generally higher than on bars and wafers and will be proportionately higher on small coins. Sales taxes also apply.

Gold coins have the same advantage as bars and wafers if you think the world may be coming to an end and you want to own real bullion. In addition, some first edition coins may have an enhanced numismatic value, although you shouldn't purchase them on that basis alone. But, like bars and wafers, they have to be stored somewhere and that can add an annual cost to holding them. If you're a coin collector, you may not mind that. If not, buying coins isn't the route to go either.

Certificates and storage accounts: The best way to own bullion or gold coins directly is through a certificate or a storage account. You get a piece of paper recording your holdings instead of the actual gold, so it's not quite as satisfying, but it's quick, cheap and easy.

A storage account operates in much the same way as a stockbroker's account. Once you've opened a storage account, you simply call the dealer and place your order for wafers, bars, or coins — whichever you prefer. The dealer makes the purchase for you and places your gold in insured storage in a bank or trust company. You receive twice-yearly statements, showing exactly what you own.

If you want to sell part or all of your holdings, you advise the dealer accordingly and it's taken care of — much the same as a stock transaction. You can also take delivery of the gold itself at any point if you wish, although there will be additional charges for doing that.

By buying gold this way, you get around the sales tax in provinces where it's applicable. You may also not have to pay any bar charge, depending on your dealer. Deak, for example, will not hit you for any bar charges or commissions on your purchases. But you will be assessed a 1% fee if you liquidate any portion of your holdings.

A gold certificate is the equivalent to a share certificate. It confirms ownership of a specific quantity of the metal.

Although you're receiving paper instead of gold, most dealers will also charge a fee for storing and insuring your holdings. Typically, this will run to 1/2% per year of the market value of your gold. The fee is calculated semi-annually, based on the value of your holdings at the time.

Most dealers require a minimum initial purchase to open a gold storage account. This may be a cash amount, typically $1,000. Deak uses this policy, but allows subsequent purchases of as little as $100.

Storage accounts and certificates are clearly the easiest way to own bullion, as long as you don't insist on having the physical gold in your possession. But they're not my personal choice for my gold holdings.

Stocks: Shares in gold mining companies are a more indirect way of owning gold, but they have distinct advantages over the bullion itself. There are no sales taxes or storage charges involved, you can buy and sell them easily, and, if you choose carefully, you can even find some that pay a modest dividend.

For several years, North American gold stocks were greatly overpriced. However, the October 1987 stock market crash and the slide in bullion prices in the second half of 1988 brought most of these issues back to more attractive ranges. American Barrick, one of the new gold glamour stocks, was trading in the $40 range in early 1987; by the fall of 1988 you could buy it for less than half that price. Hemlo Gold, one of Canada's most cost-efficient gold producers, also saw its share price drop by more than 50% in the same period. The story was repeated right across the industry.

Gold bullion also declined in value during this time — but not by anything like the same amount in percentage terms. In retrospect, it's clear North American share prices had been bid up to unrealistic levels, partly because of expectations of higher gold prices, partly because of the continuing racial problems in South Africa, one of the world's leading gold producers.

Obviously, buying gold stocks at those high levels would have been highly speculative and therefore inappropriate for low-risk investors. But adding quality gold issues when prices are down is a different matter. Since gold stocks tend to move disproportionately to changes in bullion prices, the profit potential in owning good stocks bought cheaply is greater than in owning the gold itself.

Granted, your insurance policy may not be quite as solid, in the sense you won't be able to trade a share in a gold mining company for food in the event of a nuclear holocaust. But the inflation hedge is even better with stocks, since they can be expected to rise more quickly in price than bullion itself if inflationary concerns take hold. And that, after all, is a much more immediate danger than The Bomb.

Two other advantages: first, you can hold shares in gold mining companies in an RRSP or RRIF. Gold itself is not eligible. Second, you can generate some additional income from your gold holdings by using a covered call writing strategy. Since gold stocks are quite volatile, there's an active options market for several of the major companies, including International Corona, American Barrick, Echo Bay, Hemlo, Lac Minerals and Placer Dome.

But if you plan to write covered calls on gold, I suggest you set a higher selling price, choose expiry dates that are no more than three months out, and take a correspondingly lower premium. Remember, the main purpose of holding gold in your portfolio is as an insurance policy against such unexpected events as high inflation, not to generate a large income. A well-planned covered call strategy can be consistent with that objective, while producing some extra cash flow at the same time.

Mutual funds: There are a number of mutual funds, both closed- and open-end, which specialize in gold and precious metals investing. As you might expect, their performance is spotty, rising and falling with the fortunes of gold itself. But results will vary from one fund to another, depending on the mix of bullion, stock, and cash they hold.

The open-end fund with the longest track record is CSA Management's Goldfund Ltd. It's been around since 1967, and had a 10-year average annual compound rate of return of 17.1% for the period ending August 31, 1988, according to figures published by *The Financial Post.*

Because Goldfund invests internationally, it is not RRSP/RRIF eligible. But another CSA Management fund, Goldtrust, does qualify for retirement plans. Its average annual compound rate of return for the same period was 11.9%. The Dynamic Precious Metals Fund is another major entry, but it was only started in 1986 so has no long-term track record, although its performance for the first three years of operation was very good.

Among the closed-end funds, three dominate: Central Fund, Goldcorp, and BGR Precious Metals. All trade on the Toronto Stock Exchange (Central Fund also trades on the American Stock Exchange in New York). What gives these funds a touch of added appeal to the bargain hunter is the fact they trade at a discount to their true net asset value (NAV) — in other words, you can buy $1 worth of gold for 85¢ or 90¢. For example, in October 1988 BGR Precious Metals was trading on the TSE for $10-7/8 but the actual value of the fund's holdings was $12.41 per share. So you could buy them at a discount of 12.4% to their true value.

Low-risk investors who like to do a little safe speculating will buy these funds when the share price is low and the discounts are highest (you'll find the week-end net asset value in Saturday's *Report on Business* under Closed-End Fund Asset Values; compare it with the current market price to determine the discount). Many closed-end funds have converted to open-end status in recent years; when this happens the share price rises to the true net asset value. That's because open-end funds will redeem their units at the NAV at any time. If it happens to a fund you own, you'll make a nice capital gain.

Some of these funds also pay dividends; BGR holders received quarterly payments of 25¢ per share during 1987-88. Check with your broker.

There are other ways of investing in gold besides those described here. You can trade gold futures or options if you like, but this sort of speculation is not appropriate for a low-risk portfolio. Some people hold their gold in the form of jewellery, but this isn't a good way to invest unless you're an expert in the field. You'll pay too big a premium for the esthetic value of your pieces.

My preference is to own gold through shares in dividend-paying Canadian gold producers and units in mutual funds, both closed- and open-end. In late 1988, my holdings included Hemlo Gold (stock), Dynamic Precious Metals (open-end fund), and BGR Precious Metals (closed-end fund). I was gradually adding to them as the price of gold declined. At that point, some experts were predicting the price could fall to $300 an ounce. If that happens — and you'll know by the time you read this — I'll increase my holdings to the 10% ceiling I've set. Gold will come back sooner or later. It always has.

After all, how much romance is there in a sunken ship with a cargo of lead?

Investing
for
Retirement

*Young people, nowadays, imagine that money is
everything, and when they grow older they know it.*
— Oscar Wilde

I DON'T EVER plan to retire, in the sense that I stop work completely.
Frankly, I enjoy work too much. Call me a workaholic if you like
(don't be shy, my wife does it all the time). But the fact is I think I'd
go crazy if I didn't have a book to write or an investment decision to
make or a radio script to prepare.

But I *do* intend to slow down at some stage. My eventual goal is to
have a place by the water where I can work when I want, fish when
I'm in the mood, walk on the beach or just sit and watch waves roll
in. I'm not sure when that will come about. But I don't intend to wait
until I'm too old to enjoy it.

We all have our personal dream about how we want to live in later
years, and a lot of people are trying to make money by fulfilling that
dream for us. One major insurance company has been running a televi-
sion ad campaign for the past few years, telling young people they can
have the good life in the sun by their mid-fifties if they buy the right
policy now.

Well, maybe. But I think it takes more than that to make it all happen. It requires careful planning and skillful financial management on
your part. That's what this chapter is all about.

Back in Chapter Two, I introduced the concept of Tax Risk and
explained how it can erode your investment profits. In Chapter Nine

we looked at taxes in more detail and I mentioned the tremendous advantages in being able to shelter your money in various retirement plans, the most common being RRSPs. Before this book ends, I want to return to that theme because it's central to a low-risk investment strategy for retirement.

If you read *Building Wealth* you'll know that I am a diehard, unrepentant believer in RRSPs. I am convinced that, properly managed, there is no better way to create personal wealth in this country. That's because the investment decisions you make for an RRSP portfolio can be determined entirely on the basis of maximizing profits. They aren't clouded by the tax considerations that must be taken into account outside a retirement plan.

As a result, a low-risk investment strategy inside an RRSP can be somewhat different than for an ordinary portfolio.

The first step in establishing an RRSP portfolio strategy is to set up the right plan. That means if you don't have a self-directed RRSP at the moment, get one. There are two routes to go. One is to set up a plan through a stockbroker. There are a number of advantages to doing it this way. The annual maintenance fee will be extremely low (some brokers are even offering free self-administered plans to attract your business). You'll receive regular monthly reports — a major plus. And you'll be able to get up-to-the-minute information on the status of your account quickly and easily.

The major disadvantage of a brokerage house account is that it locks you in. You can't transact any trades in the plan except through your broker. That means you can't shop the market for the best T-bill rates and bond offerings or take advantage on occasion of the lower commissions charged by discount brokers.

You can get around this by opening an independent self-administered plan at a bank or trust company. You can then designate any number of brokers you want to conduct trades in the account. This enables you to do business with whomever is most appropriate for a particular transaction.

These RRSPs have their own built-in disadvantages, however. They often cost slightly more than a broker's plan, but the difference isn't usually significant. What is important, however, is the reporting. Most of these RRSPs provide you with written reports only twice a year; some only once. If you want more frequent written updates on your holdings, you may have to pay extra. Also, I can report from experience that some trust companies are extremely disorganized when it comes to keeping you informed about the assets in your RRSP and their current value. It can be immensely frustrating when you want to make a few trades and you can't easily find out what your cash balance is.

So if you want to set up an independent plan, spend some time checking out the programs offered by various financial institutions. In particular, ask to see a sample of the report they'll be sending you and find out how frequently it goes out. Also ask whether they update your portfolio valuation to current market prices — I've seen reports based on book value, which are, of course, worthless.

Whichever company you deal with, make sure you review their reports thoroughly when they come in. Look especially at the cash transactions — the record of your purchases, sales, interest and dividend payments received, and the like. I am constantly appalled at the number of errors I find in these statements. Just recently, I was looking over a semi-annual cash transaction statement for my wife's self-directed RRSP from a major trust company. There were two mistakes. In one case, a dividend of 18¢ a share on 500 shares was credited as $74.95, even though 18¢ times 500 is $90. When I called to inquire, there was no explanation for this strange error, just an acknowledgement that I was right and they were wrong. In another case, a dividend credit of $38 had been reversed with the notation it was a duplication of a dividend paid on June 30, 1987. When I checked back in my records, I found no dividend had been credited on that date.

In these two cases, the total amount of money involved wasn't large, although my wife would have been out $53 if I hadn't discovered the mistakes. But I've had other situations in which hundreds of dollars were involved — dividends mistakenly credited to me or which I should have received but didn't. And once a trust company (not the same one) actually managed to lose 200 shares of stock in its computer, worth about $5,000.

So take nothing for granted when you receive your reports. Make sure they're absolutely correct.

Once you've set up a self-administered plan, the next step is to have a clear understanding of what you can, and cannot, invest in. RRSPs are reasonably flexible, and the government has expanded the range of eligible investments in recent years. But there are still limitations you'll have to keep in mind.

As I mentioned in the last chapter, you can't hold gold directly in an RRSP. So if you want to include some gold in your plan, it will have to be in the form of stocks or mutual funds. Any foreign property, such as U.S. stocks, cannot exceed 10% of the book value of the fund (not the market value; many people get this confused). And only foreign stocks listed on certain specified exchanges are eligible; your broker should be able to get you an up-to-date list. U.S. stocks traded over-the-counter through NASDAQ are not eligible investments, a major exclusion that has caught many people by surprise and that Ottawa should reconsider.

You may not hold foreign currency in your RRSP. Bonds and debentures issued by foreign governments, states or companies are also ineligible. You can get around this limitation, however, by buying bonds denominated in foreign currencies which are issued periodically by the Government of Canada and some provinces and large companies. At one time or another, I've held yen and deutsche mark bonds in my RRSP in this way.

You may not trade commodities or futures contracts in an RRSP. However, you can write covered call options, at least theoretically. The problem here is that, while Revenue Canada allows covered calls, many self-directed plans do not permit them because of the paperwork involved. If you set up your plan through a brokerage house you'll probably have no difficulty. But if you do it independently through a bank or trust company, find out their policy if you plan to incorporate a covered call strategy into your RRSP.

Direct real estate holdings are another RRSP no-no. But you can get around that by using an RRSP-eligible real estate mutual fund. Most of these are still quite new, the oldest being First City RealFund, which started selling units in March 1983. Its five-year average annual compound rate of return to the end of September 1988 was 12.7%, according to the *Financial Times Mutual Fund Sourcebook*.

You can also hold mortgages in your RRSP, including the mortgage on your own home if you're so inclined.

Step three is to determine your objectives. I said in Chapter Eleven that, as a low-risk investor, safety should rank high on your priority scale.

This is especially true with RRSPs. This is, after all, the money you're earmarking for your retirement years (or whatever it is you intend to do when you get older). This is not money with which you should be speculating.

But (there's always a "but") don't be so cautious that you build an RRSP with no growth potential. Even though taxes won't be eating away at your returns, inflation will. An 11% GIC in times of 5% inflation produces a real return of only 6%. That's not enough in my book.

In Chapter Eight, I suggested an Asset Mix range for your portfolio in good and bad economic times. For your RRSP, I'd suggest some modifications to that formula, based on age, as follows:

	Under Fifty	
	Good Times	Bad/Uncertain Times
Cash	5%-15%	15%-30%
Fixed Income	25%-50%	30%-60%
Growth	20%-50%	10%-20%
	Over Fifty	
Cash	10%-20%	25%-50%
Fixed Income	40%-75%	50%-80%
Growth	10%-25%	5%-10%

Let me explain the rationale I've used here. First, I'm assuming you don't necessarily want to wait until age 65 or later to begin easing off a bit. These age targets are therefore based on a workload reduction starting around age 60. If you intend to keep at it full tilt until 65, change the cut-off age to 55 instead of 50. If, on the other hand, you'd like to retire at age 55, then drop the cut-off to 45. In other words, there should be a ten-year difference between the age you expect to start making use of your RRSP funds and the age at which you switch your Asset Mix approach.

The above ranges are more conservative in all cases than those I set out in Chapter Eight. That's because of my belief that RRSP money should be managed very carefully. That's especially true if you don't have a company pension plan; in that case your RRSP funds will be the foundation of your retirement income.

Nonetheless, I've allowed for a substantial investment in growth assets in the Under Fifty stage — up to 50% of the total portfolio in good economic times. In troubled or uncertain times I suggest pulling in your horns, cutting back growth assets to 20% maximum.

When you pass age fifty, the situation changes. Now you're into that zone where stock market reversals can hurt you more severely because of the lack of time to recover. That's why I suggest increasing your fixed-income assets and reducing your growth component to a maximum of 25%. When times are bad, don't be afraid to drop the growth assets right down and hold most of your assets in cash and fixed-income securities. In this situation, follow the two cardinal rules of Warren Buffett, one of the world's most successful investors: "Rule number one: never lose money. Rule number two: never forget rule number one".

One other factor should be taken into account as you determine your RRSP objectives — whether or not you're running parallel portfolios.

If you have an investment portfolio of any size outside your RRSP, that will change the picture. In this case, concentrate your growth assets there and keep cash and fixed-income securities inside your RRSP. This enables you to claim the benefits of the dividend tax credit and the life-time capital gains exemption, while shielding all your high-tax interest income inside the RRSP. But make sure you have adequate assets outside your retirement plan to give you the growth component you need, especially during your younger years.

Now let's take a look at some model RRSP portfolios. Before we do, though, let me make one point absolutely clear. I am *not* suggesting you immediately rush out and attempt to duplicate the portfolios I'm about to show you. By the time you read this book, many months will have passed since I sat down to write it and economic conditions may have changed dramatically. So might the performance record or the prospects for the assets I'll be mentioning.

These portfolios are designed *for illustration only*, to give you an idea of how you might build your own RRSP. So with that caveat firmly in mind, here are some suggestions. Interest rates are based on those prevailing in the fall of 1988. Mutual fund returns are based on the average annual compound rate of return for the three-year period ending June 30, 1988. I have not included any individual stocks for purposes of sim-plicity.

Let's start with a younger person, a woman age 35 named Anne, who has built up RRSP assets of $40,000 in the ten years since she began to contribute to her plan. And let's assume that times are reasonably good so she can expand her growth holdings. Here's what her plan might look like.

Security	Amount	Return	Annual Revenue/ Growth
Cash			
Trust Savings Certificates	$ 2,000	10%	$ 200
Cash total	2,000	10%	200
Fixed Income			
Prov. of Quebec Stripped Coupons, maturing 2004	5,000	11%	550
Royal Bank bonds, maturing 1999	4,000	10.9%	436
Mackenzie Mortgage & Income Fund	5,000	13%	650
Universal Savings Income Fund	4,000	12.1%	484
Fixed-income total	18,000	11.8%	2,120
Growth			
Industrial Growth Fund	6,000	15.8%	948
Industrial Income Fund	6,000	14.7%	882
Dynamic Precious Metals Fund	4,000	14%	560
Cundill Value Fund (foreign property)	4,000	16.4%	656
Growth total	20,000	15.2%	3,046
Portfolio total	$40,000	13.4%	$5,366

Some comments: yields on Treasury bills were higher than 10% in late 1988. However, since this portfolio is holding only $2,000 cash, T-bills would not be an option. The Counsel Trust Savings Certificates require only a $1,000 minimum investment. Since they're protected by deposit insurance, they are quite suitable here.

The Quebec stripped bonds were providing an excellent yield at that point in time, and are a good RRSP holding because their return is guaranteed to maturity. Since the owner of this RRSP is only 35, a maturity date in the year 2004, when she would be 51, is acceptable.

The other bond holding could have been a Government of Canada issue. But these Royal Bank bonds were paying half a percentage point more and are almost as safe.

The balance of the fixed-income assets are held in top-quality mutual funds.

The growth portion is divided between four excellent mutual funds. This is because with only $20,000 to invest, it would be impossible for Anne to get proper diversification in a common stock portfolio. Note that she has invested the maximum possible amount (10% of her RRSP's book value) in the high-performing Cundill Value Fund, which is classified as foreign property. She has also put money into a precious metals fund, since gold at that time had fallen below $400.

Nit-pickers might point out that the mutual funds I've selected are among the top performers in recent years. That's correct, they are — and I don't apologize for it. If you follow the criteria for selecting mutual funds I outlined in Chapter Fourteen, you should be able to select top-quality funds for your portfolio. This RRSP simply reflects that.

The projected annual return on this portfolio is 13.4%. However, it could perform much more strongly if interest rates decline, producing a capital gain in the bond values, and/or the stock market strengthens.

This RRSP is well-protected on the downside. The selected mutual funds all have good track records in weak markets, with the Cundill Value Fund especially good in such situations. A rise in interest rates would hurt the market value of the bond holdings, but the yields, based on the original amount invested, would remain intact.

The portfolio is reasonably diversified, with nine different securities. But, by its nature, it can be managed with a minimum amount of attention and effort.

Now let's look at a larger portfolio, again for someone under 50. This time our subject is Ed, a 46-year-old business person with $150,000 in his RRSP. In this case, we'll assume he's operating in an uncertain economic climate with rising interest rates, such as that which prevailed in mid-1988. As a result, he wants to retain flexibility, take advantage of rising rates, and put greater emphasis on safety than he might otherwise.

Security	Amount	Return	Annual Revenue/ Growth
Cash			
90-day Banker's Acceptances	$ 20,000	10.4%	$ 2,080
182-day Treasury bills	15,000	10.4%	1,560
364-day Treasury bills	10,000	10.6%	1,060
Cash total	45,000	10.4%	4,700
Fixed Income			
Prov. of Quebec Stripped Coupons, maturing 1996	15,000	10.85%	1,628
Ontario Hydro bonds, maturing 1998	10,000	10.5%	1,050
Royal Bank bonds maturing 1991	10,000	10.9%	1,090
Stelco convertible bonds, maturing 1998	5,000	8.5%	425
Mackenzie Mortgage & Income Fund	15,000	14.3%	2,145
Universal Savings Income Fund	10,000	11.5%	1,150
PH&N Bond Fund	10,000	12.4%	1,240
Fixed-income total	75,000	11.6%	8,728
Growth			
Industrial Dividend Fund	10,000	16.3%	1,630
Dynamic Precious Metals Fund	7,500	14 %	1,050
Cundill Value Fund (foreign property)	12,500	16.4%	2,050
Growth total	30,000	15.8%	4,730
Portfolio total	$150,000	12.1%	$18,158

Comments: In this case, Ed has sacrificed some of his growth potential and accepted a lower return on his portfolio in return for a higher degree of safety. Given the uncertain economic times in which he finds himself, he has built his cash balances to the maximum suggested amount for his age group, 30%. His fixed-income assets make up 50% of the portfolio, while his growth assets amount to 20%.

His cash assets have staggered maturities, enabling him to take advantage of increasing interest rates or to switch some funds into other types of assets if the situation warrants.

His fixed-income securities are more diversified than Anne's were. He has invested a small amount in a Steel Company of Canada convertible bond, accepting a lower yield because he thinks the prospects are good for a comeback in the steel industry that would drive up share prices and increase the bond's value. He has also added another mutual fund to the mix, the Vancouver-based Phillips, Hager and North Bond Fund, which has been among the top performers in its group in recent years.

His growth assets are at the maximum level suggested for this situation because he thinks the stock market may begin to show a move soon. He has divided the $30,000 between two mutual funds with excellent track records in bear markets, Cundill Value and Industrial Dividend. He is also holding a small amount of gold through the Dynamic Precious Metals Fund.

Once the economic situation begins to clarify, Ed will have to shift some of his cash into other areas, otherwise the total return on his portfolio will be below my targeted levels. But, given the circumstances, he has a solid portfolio with a high degree of safety. His downside risk is relatively low, his main exposure being a prolonged and continued increase in interest rates which would erode the market value of his fixed-income assets. But given the fragile nature of the economy, he doesn't see that as a likely occurrence. On the contrary, he expects interest rates may soon begin to decline, thus driving up the value of his bonds.

For our final portfolio, let's look at Bill. He's 63 years old and has his own small printing business. He's not ready to retire yet but he's slowing down and handing over more of the work to his son and daughter, who will be taking over from him. Over the years, he's carefully nurtured his RRSP assets to the point where they are now worth $500,000. He knows he'll start drawing on that money fairly soon. Economic conditions are pretty good, with interest rates declining and the stock market appearing healthy. Here's what his portfolio might look like:

Security	Amount	Return	Annual Revenue/ Growth
Cash			
Savings certificates	$ 50,000	10 %	$ 5,000
364-day Treasury bills	50,000	10.6 %	5,300
Cash total	100,000	10.3 %	10,300
Fixed Income			
Government of Canada bonds, maturing 1995	100,000	10.1 %	10,100
Ontario Hydro bonds, maturing 1998	50,000	10.5 %	5,250
Royal Bank bonds, maturing 1991	30,000	10.9 %	3,270
Province of Quebec stripped coupons, maturing 1996	30,000	10.85%	3,255
Mackenzie Mortgage & Income Fund	50,000	14.3 %	7,150
Universal Savings Income Fund	20,000	11.5 %	2,300
PH&N Bond Fund	20,000	12.4 %	2,480
Fixed- income total	300,000	11.3 %	33,805
Growth			
Industrial Income Fund	25,000	14.7 %	3,675
Cambridge Balanced Fund	25,000	15.1 %	3,775
Dynamic Precious Metals Fund	20,000	14 %	2,800
Cundill Value Fund (foreign property)	30,000	16.4 %	4,920
Growth total	100,000	15.2 %	15,170
Portfolio total	$500,000	11.9 %	$59,275

Bill has constructed a portfolio that generates a healthy cash flow, which is important since he'll need to begin drawing on that money before too long. He is heavily weighted in fixed-income securities (60%). He also has a higher growth component (20%) than you might expect at his age; that's because the stock market is strong and he wants to take advantage of that situation to provide some inflation protection. But notice that he's done so by selecting conservatively managed mutual funds: Industrial Income, Cambridge Balanced and the Cundill fund. All put a high degree of emphasis on safety. He's also holding a small amount of gold, as an inflation hedge.

His cash assets are equally divided between savings certificates and 364-day T-bills. That's because, with interest rates declining, he wants to lock in the higher rate levels for as long as possible while retaining some flexibility. The savings certificates, which can be cashed any time, enable him to do that. The T-bills can be sold before maturity if he wants the money, at a profit if rates continue down.

The fixed-income assets are well diversified, with the single largest investment being in Government of Canada bonds because of their security. His stripped coupons don't mature until 1996, but he's decided that's okay because he'll have cash flow from other sources in the meantime. And if interest rates continue to decline, he'll be able to sell them sooner for a capital gain.

The Mackenzie and Universal funds both have systematic withdrawal plans available which will allow him to obtain monthly income payments if he needs them. The PH&N plan doesn't offer such a scheme, but makes quarterly income distributions, which he feels will be satisfactory.

Although at 11.9% Bill's rate of return is lower than the other portfolios we've looked at, he feels he's constructed an RRSP that is quite safe, generates good cash flow, and has continued growth potential, especially if interest rates keep going down.

As I explained, these are only sample portfolios. I haven't attempted to make them overly complicated, for example by creating a diversified stock portfolio for Ed or Bill. You can do that if you enjoy it, but mutual funds can provide that component quite nicely if you don't want to work at it.

Just remember, no two people are the same when it comes to money. Your own needs and objectives may be quite different from those of Anne, Ed or Bill. So don't try to imitate any of these approaches; rather, use the information in this book to create a unique retirement portfolio perfectly suited to you.

Some Final Thoughts

Not having to worry about money is almost like not having to worry about dying.

— Mario Puzo

WITHOUT DOUBT, the most dramatic financial event in recent years was the Great Stock Market Crash of October 19, 1987. If you had any money invested in shares that day, you'll remember vividly the wrench in your stomach when you first heard the news that the market was collapsing.

The degree of discomfort you felt was in direct relation to the amount of money you had tied up in stocks. If you had only a few hundred shares, you probably kicked yourself for not heeding the warnings and getting out sooner; if you were in over your head, perhaps with borrowed money, you may have felt the world was coming to an end.

Our reaction to disaster in any form is proportionate to the degree to which we're touched by it. When Hurricane Gilbert swept across Jamaica in September 1988, people in Europe and Asia were barely aware of it. North Americans with no ties to the Caribbean island were fascinated by the story for a day or two, then mentally moved on. Those who have vacationed there in the past idly wondered how people and places they had known had fared. Those planning vacations within the next few months were concerned about whether their holiday would be ruined. Those with close friends or relatives on the island worried through the long hours of communications silence, waiting for news.

Those visiting Jamaica when Gilbert hit suffered through several days of discomfort and inconvenience. Residents of the island, with nowhere else to go, saw their homes and livelihood damaged or destroyed, and found themselves facing a bleak future. Those who lost parents or children to the storm experienced the acute anguish known only to the survivors of sudden and capricious death.

The more you're involved in the event, the greater the impact it has on you.

There's a message here for low-risk investors: stay out of financial hurricanes. Unlike natural disasters, most financial calamities send out warning signals long before they occur. The prudent investor recognizes them and acts before it's too late.

Take the October 19 market meltdown, for example. Anyone who was paying attention knew stocks were heading for a fall. The markets had been moving up steadily since 1982, with a brief pause for breath in 1984. It couldn't go on forever.

The X-factor, as usual, was when the fall would come. Beginning in 1986, a few isolated voices started to express concern that stock prices were too high. By mid-1987, predictions of trouble ahead were becoming a chorus. But most of the experts figured the demise of the bull was still six months to a year away. The general message was: there's still money to be made but don't hang around too much longer.

For low-risk investors, that was a clear signal to cut and run. As Roy Hardaker advised in his "Conservative Investor" column in *The Money-Letter* in mid-April 1987: "Sell banks, financial holding companies, forest products, major oils, and special situations that are vulnerable because of one product or one market; take profits in mutual fund shares; reduce the number of common share issues held to the shares of only five companies and cut the percentage of common shares to 25% of your total investment portfolio."

Hardaker was about four months early with his call — the market decline which culminated in Black Monday actually started in late August. But the true low-risk investor would rather be out four months early than one day late.

That's because to be a low-risk investor, you have to be driven more by fear than by greed. You have to be more concerned with the safety and preservation of your capital than in squeezing out every last cent of profit. That means you have to be prepared to collect your chips and walk away when it becomes apparent there's trouble brewing.

This mindset is central to my whole philosophy of low-risk investing. Without a healthy dose of fear to guide you, sooner or later you'll run into trouble. If you're one of those people who regards fear as being somehow weak and unmacho, you'll never succeed as a low-risk investor. That's not to say you won't get rich; great gambles sometimes pay off. But you won't do it by following the approach outlined in this book.

Even a dedicated low-risk investor can be tempted to stray at times. You may be in a situation where you've done quite well over several years by using a low-risk approach. In fact, your success may make you a bit cocky; after all, if you don't suffer an occasional loss the fear instinct may deteriorate through disuse. I call this the "I can't lose" syndrome; it's a belief in their own infallibility which many successful investors develop over time. If you sense it's happening to you at any point, fight it. The less effective your fear mechanism, the more chances you're liable to take. And, sooner or later, those risks will hurt you.

Please don't misunderstand me. I'm not using the term "fear" in the sense of a dread or terror that will leave you paralyzed and unable to act. The Funk and Wagnalls dictionary contains a definition that says what I mean precisely: "An uneasy feeling that something may happen contrary to one's desires". When you start getting those uneasy feelings about your investment portfolio, that's the signal to make some changes.

So watch for warning signs. Pay close attention to developments which can impact negatively on your investments. And when you see them appearing, take action.

That's another thought I'd like to leave with you: once you've made up your mind, don't procrastinate. If you do, the opportunity may be lost.

Delaying action is incredibly easy. All it takes is a little inertia. And every investor is guilty of it at one time or another, including me. I don't know how many times I've said to my wife, "I must buy some shares in such and such, because . . . ." From there I've gone on to give her a detailed explanation as to why this particular investment looks good. But I haven't followed up, usually because I've been too busy to pick up the phone. Almost invariably, the stock went up.

Once you've looked at a situation carefully and thought it through, act. Don't wait. That doesn't mean you should plunge in up to your neck, however. It means you should begin a carefully planned investing process.

Suppose, for example, you've identified the shares of a particular company as a good acquisition for your portfolio. Your next step should be to identify the minimum and maximum percentage of your portfolio that you're prepared to devote to that stock, and to put a dollar value on that. You then give your broker instructions to purchase the minimum amount. Watch the stock, see how it performs. If it heads straight up, great — you have a position in the stock and you're making money. If, on the other hand, it declines a bit, you have the opportunity to bring your holdings up to your target maximum at a cheaper price.

Now let's go back to Black Monday again. When the market crashed, those who were still invested in stocks did one of four things:

A) They got on the phone and screamed at their broker to sell everything at any price.

B) They got on the phone and screamed at their broker to buy as prices collapsed.

C) They ignored the whole thing and played golf.

D) They took a couple of hours to assess the damage and to work out a new investing strategy.

Which group would you have fallen into?

Group A — No one admits now they were in this group, but somebody was flooding the stock markets with sell orders. Within months, they regretted it — they were the ones who took the biggest losses on that historic day. Acting promptly on news is great — but, of course, you have to take the *right* action.

Group B — It takes a lot of guts to buy when the market is collapsing, but those who picked up stocks on Black Monday and the day following got some great bargains. This isn't low-risk investing, though. The risks in such action are clearly high.

Group C — It's nice to be in a position where sinking a putt is more important than a market collapse. It probably means you're either very rich, very stupid or very drunk.

Group D — Here's where most low-risk investors would be found, carefully assessing their losses and determining how to mitigate damages. In my own case, I decided on Tuesday that if the market continued to drop the next day, I'd move in and start some selective buying. But when Wednesday morning produced a major rally, I changed my approach and sold some of my marginal stocks into that strength. A year later, most of the shares I sold that day were trading at a lower price than I received.

The lesson in all this is: Never Panic. If you are caught in a financial hurricane, keep your head, consider the alternatives, and prepare a new approach.

I've talked a lot about low-risk investing techniques in this book. But low-risk investing is more than a strategy. It's a whole philosophical approach to managing your money, based on security before profits. A true low-risk investor will accept a lower rate of return in exchange for a higher measure of safety; will emphasize proven quality over uncertain potential; and will never allow greed to override common sense. In exchange, the low-risk investor expects a reasonable but not spectacular return on his or her money and a minimum amount of worry.

If you've never thought about investing in this way before, that means you may have to shift your mental gears. The fact you've completed this book indicates your desire to do that. But good intentions aren't enough. You have to make things happen.

So here's a basic plan of action to get you started:

This week: Sit down and review your current investment position. List any securities that would form the basis of a portfolio, and your available cash. Determine what your current Asset Mix is, and decide what it ideally should be. Identify which securities meet the criteria for a low-risk portfolio, and which do not. If you have securities both inside and outside an RRSP, determine which should go where. If you don't have any securities at present, evaluate how much money you have available to invest.

Next week: Develop a strategy for disposing of those securities which don't fit your new criteria. That doesn't mean you have to rush right out and sell them; market conditions may not be right. But you should know what you're going to do with them and begin to take action.

Before month-end: Identify at least two new investments that should be included in your portfolio. Concentrate on the area that your Asset Mix evaluation suggests is weakest. As cash becomes available, begin your new investment process.

Within six months: Complete the restructuring of your portfolio (or the building of a new one if you're just starting).

Monthly thereafter: Evaluate each security you own to determine if it is still worth holding or should be sold. Keep a current list of alternative investment possibilities to be considered.

Quarterly thereafter: Review your Asset Mix to see if it is still suitable, given existing economic conditions and your own needs. If it isn't, decide what securities should be disposed of and what should be acquired instead.

Do these things, combine the advice in this book with your own good sense, stick with investments you know and understand, and I will make you two promises.

First, your wealth will increase, perhaps more than you ever thought possible.

Second, you will never lose a night's sleep worrying about your money.

You may not attain great riches.

But you *will* attain security and a comfortable peace of mind.

There are worse ways to live.

INDEX